T0332862

HOW BUSINESS WORKS

HOW BUSINESS WORKS

The FACTS visually explained

Penguin Random House

Produced for DK by Dynamo Limited
1 Cathedral Court, Southernhay East, Exeter, EX1 1AF

Senior editor	Georgina Palffy
Project art editor	Saffron Stocker
Editors	Anna Fischel, Alison Sturgeon, Suhel Ahmed, Hannah Bowen, Joanna Edwards, Alex Beeden, Sam Kennedy
Designers	Natalie Clay, Stephen Bere, Phil Gamble, Vanessa Hamilton, Jemma Westing
Managing editors	Stephanie Farrow, Gareth Jones
Senior managing art editor	Lee Griffiths
Publisher	Liz Wheeler
Deputy art director	Karen Self
Publishing director	Jonathan Metcalf
Art director	Phil Ormerod
Senior jacket designer	Mark Cavanagh
Jacket assistant	Claire Gell
Jacket design development manager	Sophia MTT
Pre-production producers	Ben Marcus, Nikoleta Parasaki
Producer	Christine Ni

First published in Great Britain in 2015.
This edition in 2022 by
Dorling Kindersley Limited,
DK, One Embassy Gardens, 8 Viaduct Gardens,
London, SW11 7BW

Imported into the EEA by Dorling Kindersley Verlag GmbH.
Arnulfstr. 124, 80636 Munich, Germany

Copyright © 2015, 2022 Dorling Kindersley Limited
A Penguin Random House Company
10 9 8 7 6
011 - 325014 - Mar/22

All rights reserved.
No part of this publication may be reproduced,
stored in or introduced into a retrieval system, or transmitted,
in any form, or by any means (electronic, mechanical,
photocopying, recording, or otherwise), without the prior
written permission of the copyright owner.

A CIP catalogue record for this book is
available from the British Library.

ISBN: 978-0-2415-1565-5

Printed in China

For the curious
www.dk.com

MIX
Paper | Supporting
responsible forestry
FSC™ C018179

This book was made with Forest
Stewardship Council ™ certified
paper – one small step in DK's
commitment to a sustainable future.
For more information go to
www.dk.com/our-green-pledge

Contents

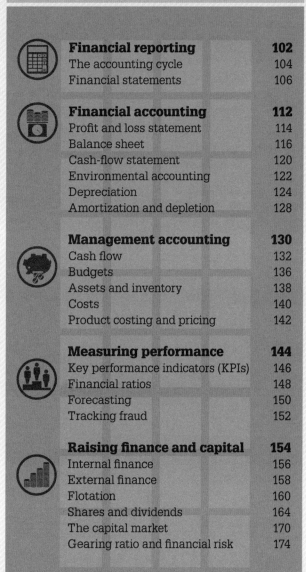

HOW SALES AND MARKETING WORK 176

HOW OPERATIONS AND PRODUCTION WORK 268

Contributors

Dr Julian Sims (consultant editor) entered academia after a successful career in industry in the US and UK. He is a lecturer in the Department of Management at Birkbeck, University of London, UK; a Chartered Accountant (CPA Aus); and a Chartered Information Technology Practitioner (CITP). His work is widely published in academic journals.

Philippa Anderson is a business writer and communications consultant, who has advised multinationals including 3M, Anglo American, and Coca-Cola. She collaborated with Lord Browne, former CEO of BP, on his memoir, *Beyond Business*, and was a contributor to DK's *The Business Book*.

Alexandra Black studied business communications before writing for financial newspaper group Nikkei Inc. in Japan. While in Tokyo, she was an editor at the Risk Analysis division of investment bank JP Morgan. Now based in Cambridge, UK, she covers subjects as varied as business, technology, and fashion. She was a contributor DK's *The Business Book*.

Joe Stanley-Smith is a reporter at the *International Tax Review* in London, UK, where he specializes in indirect tax and tax disputes. He graduated in journalism with a business specialism from Kingston University, UK and has previously worked in social media and local news.

Introduction

The term "business" refers to an organization or commercial enterprise engaged in producing and trading goods and services for money. We can trace the origins of business to the very foundations of human society. When *Homo sapiens* evolved, mankind left behind the nomadic hunter-gatherer lifestyle to become farmers. This allowed for specialization of work, where individuals would become skilled at specific tasks to serve a particular community need. Over time, this enabled more complex goods and services to be produced and traded, in order to provide for all members of society. Thus, human society has been engaging in "business" for thousands of years.

Today the world of business is inescapable – businesses are no longer confined to local service- and goods-providers, but extend to vast corporate enterprises operating on a global scale. At the same time, technological advances have made it easier than ever for entrepreneurs to start their own companies, and propel internet-based businesses to the heart of the global economy. But whether businesses are small or large, public or private, for-profit or not-for-profit, they each play a key role in allowing governments to function and economies to flourish, and in combination form the backbone of the modern world. Business underpins every aspect of the world we live in today, and understanding how it works is the key to understanding modern society.

This book explains the complex world of business in a simple and graphic way. It examines every aspect of how a business works, including forming a company, raising capital, product development and marketing, management strategies, tracking revenue, financial reporting, and legal, social, and environmental responsibilities. Through visual explanations as well as real-life examples to make even the most complex concept immediately accessible, *How Business Works* offers a clear understanding of what business is all about and how business, in its many forms, shapes modern society.

HOW **COMPANIES** WORK

Business ownership ❯ Start-ups
Buying & selling businesses ❯ Who's who
Corporate structure ❯ Human resources

Business ownership

Every type of business has to choose an ownership structure. Although there are global variations, most countries offer analogous legal entities, from a single-person private enterprise to a massive organization trading on a stock exchange. There are three key considerations: how big the venture is expected to grow; the complexity of financial recording, management, and reporting that the proprietor is willing to take on; and the amount of liability the owner is willing to accept.

Small and simple

> Basic structures, such as a sole trader or partnership are simple to set up and require little capital.

> One or more people own the business – usually a small enterprise – and trade as a legal entity.

> Owners are personally liable for business debts. *See pp.14-15.*

Private companies

> More complex to set up and run, private companies are legal entities that are separate from their owners. They may have some financial reporting obligations.

> Owners are not usually personally liable for business debts.

> Owned by shareholders, who are often the company's managers. *See pp.16–19.*

Public companies

> Companies that go public are large businesses, and they have many legal and financial reporting obligations.

> The general public and other institutions can buy shares in public companies.

> The public company structure is good for a major capital injection, allowing the business to expand. *See pp.16–19.*

7%
of global economic activity is accounted for by the world's 100 largest companies

NAMING A COMPANY

Do	*Don't*
❯ **Use a domain suggestion tool** to search for available internet domain names and work back from there.	❯ **Include your name**, as if the venture fails your name will be associated with it.
❯ **Be descriptive** so potential customers instantly grasp the nature of the business.	❯ **Ape competition**, because if your name is unique, you have a much better chance of topping search-engine results. If your name is similar to that of competitors, customers can't distinguish.
❯ **Say the name out loud** as it may come across differently. The aim is that people can find it just from hearing it.	❯ **Spend time** thinking of a name until your product and brand is finalized. Get the product right first and the name will naturally follow.
❯ **Check what the name means** in other languages.	
❯ **Keep it short** and simple and avoid puns.	

Multinationals

❯ Multinationals have operations in various countries, enabling growth and flexibility.

❯ Multinationals can save money by setting up operations in countries where costs are cheaper.

❯ Foreign branches can adapt to the local market and also find new markets. *See pp.20–21.*

Franchises

❯ In this model, a business (the franchisor) authorizes an individual (the franchisee) to set up a branch, in return for a fee.

❯ The franchisor needs less capital than it otherwise would to develop the business.

❯ The franchisee takes on a known, successful business model and name, so minimizing risk. *See pp.22–23.*

Not-for-profit sector

❯ Common not-for-profit organizations include charities, mutuals, and cooperatives.

❯ Their organizational structure is similar to that of a company.

❯ NPOs may generate substantial sums of money, but reinvest it in beneficial causes rather than distributing profit. *See pp.24–25.*

Sole traders and partnerships

The simplest business structures are those formed by one person as a sole trader, or by two or more people as a partnership, for commercial activity. Many cost little to set up and some are easy to run.

How it works

Many businesses start out as the most basic unit – either a sole trader (sometimes called a sole proprietor) or a partnership. A sole trader is an individual who is the only owner of the business. This structure is easy to set up and there are no extra taxes to pay, unlike with a company. Instead, the sole trader files a personal tax return. There is risk attached, however. A sole trader has unlimited liability, so if the business fails, the owner must personally pay its debts. Partnerships have more than one owner, and each can be held liable for the whole debt of the business.

Pros and cons

Both sole trader and partnership structures are excellent for anyone starting out or running a small business – as long as partners have a good working relationship and the business stays out of debt: owners are personally liable for business debts.

Unlimited liability: business debts paid personally

Tax-efficient way to be self-employed

Simple registration process

Little capital needed

Easy to move from sole trader to company status

No annual business accounts to file

Trade under own name or chosen business name

Keep all business profits after paying tax on them

Sole trader

Working alone requires only simple administration and relatively few start-up costs.

FROM INDIVIDUAL TO MULTINATIONAL

Many sole traders and partnerships have grown into global names:

❯ **Sir Richard Branson** Sole trader that expanded into Virgin empire

❯ **Steve Jobs and Steve Wozniak** Partnership that created Apple brand

❯ **Bill Hewlett and David Packard** Partners who founded HP technology

❯ **Fusajiro Yamauchi** Sole trader whose playing card shop became the Nintendo video-game company

66% of EU private-sector jobs **are in** small **or** medium-sized enterprises

WHEN TO MOVE TO COMPANY STATUS

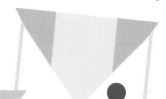

If the need for capital increases (and potential debts grow), forming a company may be beneficial. *See pp.16–17.*

Profit and control of the business shared

Allows for specialization by each partner

Option to set up a limited liability partnership

No annual business accounts to file

More partners mean more capital and expansion

New partners bring new business skills

If partner leaves, new partnership needed

Each partner pays tax on their portion of profit

Partnership

Like a sole trader, partners file only personal tax returns and are liable for business debts.

Limited companies

By setting up an organization that is legally and financially independent – a limited company – business owners can limit their level of risk, as personal assets are largely protected.

How it works

A limited company is more complex than the simpler business entities of sole trader and partnership, as a limited company is a self-contained legal entity. Its owners have to formally register, or incorporate, the company. They typically invest their own money to set the company up; they are issued with shares in it and take on legal responsibility for running the business. The company retains any profit and distributes part of it to the owners – the shareholders – as dividend payments. Company regulations place restrictions on the number of shareholders and the sale of shares. Legally, the shareholders cannot be held fully liable for company debts.

Types of limited company

Limited companies can be privately owned or go public (*see pp.18–19*), usually to attract more investment. Most limited companies are private ones limited by shares. It is possible, but rare, to own a private *unlimited* company, in which directors or shareholders are liable for all debts if the business does not stay in profit. In the UK, private limited companies must by law have the abbreviation "Ltd" after their name, while public limited company names have to end in "PLC/plc".

Public company

A public limited company (plc) is typically a large business, such as a supermarket chain or manufacturer of a well-known brand. Its shares are traded on a stock exchange.

✓ NEED TO KNOW

> **Members** People or institutions (such as pension funds and insurance firms) that own shares in a company; directors may own shares but are not compelled to do so; also known as subscribers

> **Doing business as (DBA)** Operational rather than registered company name

> **Professional corporation (PC)** Corporate form used in the US and suitable for doctors, lawyers, and similar professional service providers

Limited by shares

> Most common form of public limited company

> Must have at least one shareholder; no maximum

> Shares issued to shareholders, who are owners and have certain rights

> Profits distributed to shareholders as dividends

> Liability limited to value of shares

> Used by profit-making organizations

Limited company

Limited companies come in various forms, but all operate as entities that are legally and financially independent from their owners.

LIMITED COMPANIES IN THE US

The names given to limited business entities differ from country to country. In the US, a limited company ends with Corp. or Inc. (short for Corporation or Incorporated), the US equivalent of Ltd in the UK. There are variations from state to state, and a company name is only protected in the state where it is registered.

LTD VS PLC

Most businesses are limited companies and become public limited companies if they grow and need to raise more finance by selling shares in the business. Public limited companies are subject to more complex accounting and legal requirements. They also carry a risk of takeover as they cannot control who owns their shares.

Private company

❯ **Single-member company (SMC)** Small company owned by one person

❯ **Company with employees** Larger company that employs one or more people

53.4%
of UK limited companies have employees; the remaining 46.6% are single-member companies (SMCs)

Limited by shares

❯ Most common form of private limited company; operates in a similar way to public limited company

Limited by guarantee

❯ No shares issued; has members not shareholders

❯ Members guarantee debt up to a nominal fixed amount; no profits distributed

❯ Used by clubs, charities, and community enterprises; may be known as a Community Interest Company

Private and public companies

While the owner-shareholders of a private company may buy and sell their shares privately (usually with director approval), any investor in the financial market can trade the shares of a public company.

How it works

Although most of the world's companies are set up as private, public companies are seen as more prestigious and profitable. For business ventures requiring large amounts of capital, a public company offers greater opportunity for raising funds, since shares can be sold to public investors to generate cash. Private companies must rely on private investors or use the capital investment of their owners. Public companies are subject to more stringent legal controls than private ones, and are expected to disclose financial details.

27 million
the number of companies in the US, fewer than 1% of which are public

FAMOUS PRIVATE COMPANIES

> **Mars** Confectionery and pet food; third-largest private US company

> **Aldi** German supermarket chain comprising two private firms, Aldi Süd and Aldi Nord, trading under one name

> **The LEGO Group** Danish company producing household-name toy bricks

> **Hearst Corporation** Mass-media multinational based in New York City

> **IKEA** Swedish retailer registered in Netherlands selling flatpack furniture

> **PwC** Professional services network

Differences between private and public companies

Private company directors have to weigh up the potential capital increase of floating on the stock exchange against the legal red tape aimed at protecting public shareholders.

Private

Directors
Usually control all of the shares.

Reporting
In the UK, it is mandatory to file accounts at Companies House; no disclosure is required outside the company in the US.

Shareholders and management
Shareholders are often actively involved in management so decisions can be made quickly.

Financing
Company must rely on private investment, which is often harder to attract because there are fewer financial details available.

Valuation
Value of the company is more likely to fluctuate; it is more difficult to assess because there are fewer available financial details.

Size
Number of shareholders is limited, usually to fewer than 2,000.

3,800
companies **are** listed **on** the Tokyo Stock Exchange

Public

Directors
Not necessarily shareholders.

Reporting
Company has legal obligation to disclose accounts and submit regular financial reports.

Shareholders and management
Clear boundary is drawn between the role of shareholders and management; there may be conflicts of interest between them. Freely transferable shares mean original owners could lose control if major shareholders launch hostile takeover bid.

Financing
Company can tap financial markets to raise capital by selling stock or bonds.

Valuation
Value of the company is easier to assess, from the trading price of shares and financial statements.

Size
Number of shareholders is unlimited.

GOING PUBLIC

There are legal requirements at each stage of converting a company from private to public, not least voting in the board of directors and deciding on a new name.

Choose board members
Usually at least three directors to allow future board decisions to be made with only two members present (representing a majority)

Inform staff
Must notify in writing anyone with an interest (including employees and proposed board members) that company intends to go public

Vote for conversion
Board meeting held to vote in favour of changing company's Articles of Association (specifying private or public company)

Register company
Documents setting out board resolutions sent to company registry, which issues certificate declaring the company is public

Make public announcement
Press releases issued, events for business held, and emails sent to inform contacts of change

✓ NEED TO KNOW

▶ **Unquoted/unlisted company** Another term for a private company

▶ **Initial public offering (IPO)** Stock-market launch

▶ **Secondary stock offering** Second-round sale of shares to raise more capital

▶ **Ticker symbols** Unique codes assigned to publicly traded companies and used by stock exchanges

Multinationals

A multinational corporation has business operations in more than one country. It usually starts as a national company and sets up subsidiary (branch) companies abroad for production, sales, and marketing.

How it works

Multinationals have several aims: to increase revenue by finding new markets; to streamline operations and production by taking advantage of global locations with lower labour and/or transport costs; and to adapt to local cultural/market differences. A company may achieve such goals by outsourcing (using external suppliers) or offshoring (relocating functions). Companies may also insource (move operations in-house) to rightsource (find a good balance).

Case study: mapping a multinational

Sportswear company Nike has successfully spread around the globe from its corporate base in the US. It has manufacturing functions where technical expertise maximizes efficiency and keeps costs down; distribution hubs in strategic locations; and marketing and retail departments in countries where it is establishing local markets.

United Kingdom
London

One of many country HQs in major European cities, the London office serves the UK market.

 Regional HQ Management and core admin functions

 Marketing UK campaigns and merchandising

GLOBAL VS MULTINATIONAL

A global company has facilities in different countries but they operate as a single corporate culture with common processes. A multinational has facilities in different countries but each functions as its own entity, adapting locally, with little communication between geographic divisions.

Global

Apple is an example of a global company – the product is the same apart from a language change.

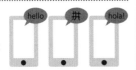

Multinational

McDonald's is a multinational – the product changes to suit the market. For example, it serves shrimp burgers in Japan and chicken rice porridge in Malaysia.

United States
Beaverton, Oregon

Senior management are located at the company's corporate base, or "campus", its centre for decision-making on global strategy, design, and marketing, and core functions. Facilities of Nike subsidiary Air Manufacturing Innovation (AMI), which develops and supplies materials, are here, as well as in St Charles, Missouri.

 Regional HQ Operations for Americas, Asia-Pacific, and US

World HQ Management, finance, legal, IT, and admin

 R and D Sport research lab and design facilities

 Global marketing Branding and marketing

 Supplier Subsidiary AMI develops and supplies materials

Memphis, Tennessee

 Distribution Four hi-tech centres in location with good links. Other centres in Indianapolis, Indiana, and Dayton, Tennessee

The Netherlands
Hilversum

Based in a central location, a European hub supports operations across Europe, the Middle East, and Africa, and is close to the company's European distribution hub in Belgium.

 European HQ Management, finance, legal, IT, and admin

 Distribution European logistics centre based in Laakdal, Belgium

China
Shanghai

The company's fastest-growing market, China is also a manufacturing and distribution base due to local expertise and low production costs.

 Chinese HQ Operations and core support functions

 Marketing Campaigns for the Chinese market

 Manufacturing Sportswear factories and innovation hubs

 Distribution Centres in Taicang and Suzhou

Japan & South Korea
Tomisato & Incheon

Major company-owned distribution centres

 Distribution Hubs for retail stores across Asia

Vietnam
Dong Nai province

Home to facilities of Nike's AMI subsidiary, which supplies materials. Most manufacturing is carried out by contract factories in Vietnam and Cambodia, benefiting from expertise and lower wages.

 Supplier Subsidiary AMI supplies materials to factories

 Manufacturing Sites in several countries

Rest of the world
Multiple locations

Nike runs international branch offices and subsidiaries in around 50 countries, as well as 1,000 retail stores and 45 digital commerce platforms across the globe.

 Regional HQ Core operations and marketing

 Retail Online sales and stores around the world

Franchises

A franchise is a business model in which an independent entity – the franchisee – is entitled to set up a branch of an established brand. There are advantages for both parties.

How it works

Rather than developing an original business idea, the franchisee pays for the right to represent an existing, successful brand in a particular location. The size of a franchise can vary from a single unit – one outlet only – to an area development in which the franchisee takes on the option to represent the brand through several branches in a city or region. The franchisor can develop the business with modest capital outlay while the franchisee takes on a proven business model and brand name, so everyone reaps the benefits.

> ## "I put the hamburger on the assembly line."
>
> Ray Kroc, founder of McDonald's

Three types of franchise

The franchisor's level of control varies from managing the contracts for the entire supply chain to input on every detail down to the last French fry. In a product franchise, the franchisor lends its trademark and brand but not an entire business system.

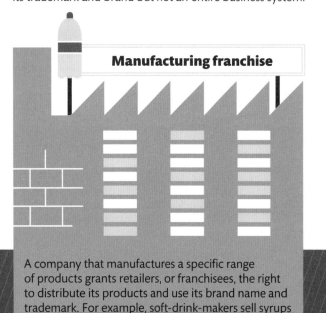

Manufacturing franchise

A company that manufactures a specific range of products grants retailers, or franchisees, the right to distribute its products and use its brand name and trademark. For example, soft-drink-makers sell syrups to the franchisee, who then bottles the drink.

Product franchise

This is a supplier-dealer relationship in which the franchisee sells the franchisor's products. Examples include tyres, cars, and fuel.

TOP 10

Fastest-growing franchises worldwide

1. **Century 21 Real Estate** property
2. **KFC** fast-food outlets
3. **Circle K** convenience stores
4. **Jan-Pro** commercial cleaning
5. **McDonald's** fast-food outlets
6. **Taco Bell** fast-food outlets
7. **7-Eleven** convenience stores
8. **F45 Training** fitness
9. **Stratus Building Solutions** commercial cleaning
10. **Anytime Fitness** gyms

CASE STUDY

Business-format franchise: fast-food outlets

The business-format franchise, in which a franchisee takes on a whole blueprint for running the business as well as the product itself, was pioneered in the US in the 1940s.

Fast-food outlets were a new concept at the time and were generating great demand. To increase the rate of expansion, these original fast-food entrepreneurs developed a franchise system under which the franchisee was contractually obliged to run the outlet according to strict guidelines.

A limited and uniform menu was the key to the success of these franchises. The consistency of the menu, service, and surroundings helped to establish a strong brand identity, since customers were assured that the product and experience would be the same anywhere in the country.

McDonald's is one of the most successful examples, collecting a 4 per cent service fee and rent from its 36,000 franchises worldwide.

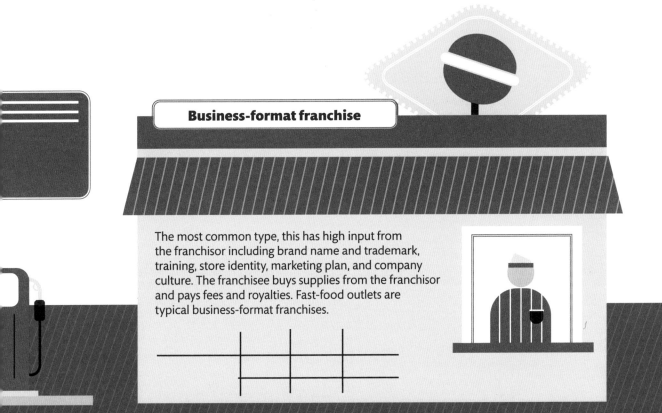

Business-format franchise

The most common type, this has high input from the franchisor including brand name and trademark, training, store identity, marketing plan, and company culture. The franchisee buys supplies from the franchisor and pays fees and royalties. Fast-food outlets are typical business-format franchises.

Not-for-profits

Some organizations are run not for the benefit of shareholders, but for the benefit of their members or an external community or charity. Unlike conventional businesses, profit is not the aim.

How it works

Organizations that do not intend to generate profit for their shareholders, are self-governing, and committed to a common cause come under the broad umbrella of not-primarily-for-profit, not-for-profit, and non-profit entities. On this spectrum, cooperatives may disburse profits to members, but charities are strictly non-profit. Although their goals differ, not-for-profits have a similar type of company status and structure to businesses.

8.6%
of all wages and salaries paid in the US come from the not-for-profit sector

The not-for-profit universe

There are many forms of not-for-profit organization (NPO). Joel L. Fleishman, Professor of Public Policy and Law at Duke University, US, has characterized the not-for-profit sector as a universe that embraces all NPOs, whatever their mission.

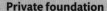

Cooperative
Owned by members; can benefit from profit; clear ethos of pursuing common economic, social, or cultural goals; one member, one vote

Private foundation
Similar to a charity but funded by one source, as opposed to the general public; generates revenue from investments; makes grants to other charitable bodies

Social organization
Based on common interests or beliefs, such as social or academic interest or a benevolent cause; civic clubs and college fraternities/sororities are examples

THRIVING SECTOR

Despite being NPOs, many cooperatives and mutuals have a sizeable annual turnover (gross revenue transacted).

❯ **France**   Crédit Agricole Group of cooperatives and mutuals: US$89 billion
❯ **Germany**   REWE Group: US$63 billion

❯ **Japan**   Zen-Noh cooperative: US$56 billion
❯ **US**   State Farm mutual: US$43 billion
❯ **Korea**   Nonghyup (NACF) : US$41 billion
❯ **UK**   Co-operative Group: US$14 billion
❯ **Spain**   Mondragón cooperative: US$14 billion

✓ NEED TO KNOW

❯ **Philanthropic sector** Alternative umbrella term for the not-for-profit sector or universe

❯ **Disbursement quota** Set percentage (usually around 80 per cent) of its income that a charity must devote to charitable activities, as distinct from income that pays administrative costs

❯ **Pemsel test** Classification system used to ascertain if an organization qualifies as a charity

❯ **Associated charity** Organization related to a main charity that takes on a particular aspect of the charity's work

NOT-FOR-PROFIT STRUCTURE

 Chair coordinates work of the directors.

 Board of directors is usually unpaid; may also be called the board of trustees.

 Committees formed by board members carry out specific tasks, such as fundraising.

 Administration staff often includes a proportion of voluntary workers.

Non-governmental organization (NGO)
Funded by government or by international donor agencies, such as the World Health Organization (WHO); operates independently

Mutual
Raises funds from its members (usually customers); often takes the form of financial institutions; profits reinvested in the mutual or to sustain or grow the organization

Chamber of commerce
Group of business people that gathers to promote trade, investment, and cooperation; usually funded by subscriptions from local businesses

Charity
Must be registered as charity status; tax exempt; all resources must be devoted to the charity's stated charitable activities; may be organized as a trust, corporation, or association

Social enterprise
May sell goods or services to fund community projects; any surplus revenue is reinvested in the enterprise for the community

Start-ups

A start-up is a new business in the early stages of development and operation, during which an entrepreneur or founding group comes up with an idea for a product or service, researches it, develops a business plan, raises funds, and launches. Registering intellectual property (IP) – a unique creation, not just an idea – in order to protect it is an important stage of the start-up process. Protection includes trademarks, patents, and copyright.

The early days

Before a company is fully developed, with a working business model, it is known as a start-up. The start-up evolves from an entrepreneur, or group of entrepreneurs, with a scheme or invention. It can take a few years to turn the initial concept or prototype into a viable, profitable venture, so the start-up founder tries to attract support and financial backing to achieve rapid growth. During this phase, which can take anything from a few months to several years, the business changes quickly.

4.35 million
new business applications were submitted in 2020 in the US

NEED TO KNOW

> **Internal start-ups** Start-ups that originate from inside a large organization
> **Patent trolls** Individuals or companies who buy up the patents of failed start-ups and attempt to collect licensing fees from potential infringers of the patent

INTELLECTUAL PROPERTY (IP) VALUE

The term "start-up" became commonplace during the dot.com boom of the late 1990s, when thousands of entrepreneurs with web-based products and services found funding, many on the strength of their intellectual property alone. Giants Google and Amazon both started up at this time. Since then, technology businesses have become one of the most talked-about start-up types. Their value is often based 100 per cent on intellectual property.

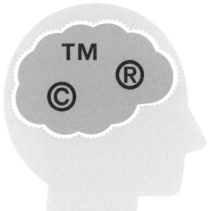

The big idea

Consider the IP
> Register IP.
> Find a name.
> Buy a domain.
> Research market.

Launch
> Win? Lose?
> Research indicates that, in most Western countries, 80–90 per cent of start-ups fail.

Choose a start-up type
> With a social conscience?
> Primed to grow big?
> To fit lifestyle?
See pp.30–31.

Prepare to launch
> Plan a marketing campaign.
> Run a test launch and refine message and offer.
See pp.196–197.

Make a business plan
> Explain how the business will make money.
> Describe the unique aspects of the business.
> Set out how much money the business will need and how much it will make.
See pp.32–33.

Find funding
> Invest savings.
> Ask friends and family.
> Take out a bank loan.
> Seek venture capital.
> Try crowdfunding.
See pp.34–37.

Seek help
> Join a business accelerator.

> Enter a business incubator.
> Go it alone.
> Find an investor.
See pp.38–39.

49.6%
of adults **in Angola**
are starting or
running **a new
business**

Start-ups from concept to launch

A new business can be described as a start-up in the early phases of its launch, when an entrepreneur comes up with the idea for a product or service, and develops the concept into something that will sell.

How it works

The idea is just the start. Next comes the process of expanding the concept into a viable business. Specialist help may be needed in some areas – hiring a digital marketing advisor, or an accountant to advise on the best structure and financial set-up, for example. What the business and product or service are called can make or break the start-up, so it is worth spending some time doing online research to check that no one else is using an intended name, especially in a negative context. Location is another consideration – it may be possible to create a virtual office and work from home. Finding premises is an extra stage, but the aim at start-up is to keep costs low.

START

Come up with a good idea
Develop a product, or an idea for a product or service.

Register IP
For an invention or innovation, register intellectual property (IP) with copyright, trademark, or patent.

Set up an online presence
Register the domain name and set up web hosting.

Decide on a name
Check to determine whether your proposed name is available; check that the domain name is available; search online for competitors with similar names.

Create a look
Design a logo and visual scheme for the business.

Make a website
Build a website. Research search engine optimization (SEO) words to use on it (see pp.230–231).

CASE STUDY

Om Engineering Works

Om Engineering Works was started in 1987 by Om Prakash Jaiswal. Operating from a shop in Uttar Pradesh, in northern India, he used to sell rubber containers and plates to battery companies, but in 2000 came up with the idea of producing the batteries himself, and later on, with the idea of smelting and recycling them.

Since then, the market for these batteries has grown, and breakthroughs in manufacturing technology have allowed the firm to go from making 20 to 300 batteries a day.

Now known as Highflow Industries and run by Om Prakash Jaiswal's son, Sumit Jaiswal, the company makes batteries for e-rickshaws, solar panels, inverters, cars, tractors, two-wheeled vehicles, and more.

"There is a huge market potential with the advent of solar and e-rickshaw segments," says Sumit Jaiswal. "This is because they help cut down air pollution and reduce overall carbon emissions. The batteries have always played a vital role in this."

8%
of start-ups go on to become successful businesses

Research market
Study your proposed target market and potential competitors, and evaluate the viability of the idea.

Decide structure
Choose a business structure that suits your initial needs, but also allows flexibility for growth.

Obtain backing funds
Consider a business incubator (pp.38–39) if the business requires large-scale support.

Devise a plan
Draw up a plan (see pp.32–33), including your goals, mission statement, and key financial information.

Set up finances
Include an accounting and cash-flow system, sales tax if applicable, and bank account.

Start marketing
Plan a marketing campaign. Run a test and make any refinements to the message or strategy.

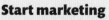

LAUNCH

Types of start-up

Entrepreneurs go into business for many reasons: some start-up decisions are based on personal ethos and conviction; some are founded on the desire to make money; others are a mix of the two.

How it works

Not all start-ups fit the same mould. Although they often follow a similar process in their initial evolution, they are as varied in type as the personalities behind them. Start-ups can broadly be divided into those that are intended from the outset to be large ventures within a corporate environment, and those intended to work on a more personal scale to suit the lives and passions of individuals.

Lifestyle

Motivation
Working is a passion

Example
Ex-athlete starts fitness-consulting business

Type of funding
Self, friends, peers, bank loan

Social start-ups

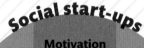

Motivation
Making a difference

Example
Malaria blood-test kit for smartphone

Type of funding
Community, charity, government, donation, crowdfunding

72%
growth in the number of fintech start-ups between 2018 and 2020

Initiative within a large corporation

Motivation
Innovating

Example
PC manufacturer starts
a separate business
providing cloud
data storage

Type of funding
Internal company
funding

Scalable start-up

Motivation
Readiness to grow

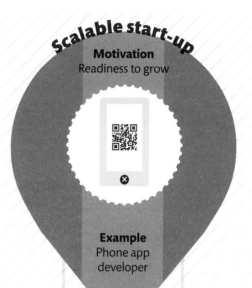

Example
Phone app
developer

Type of funding
Crowdfunding,
angel funding

Small business

Motivation
Feeding the family

Example
Neighbourhood
grocery shop

Type of funding
Self, family,
bank loan

Acquisition targets

Motivation
Looking to sell the business
on from the beginning

Example
Biotech
laboratory

Type of funding
Outside
investment

Business plans

Writing a business plan is one of the most important steps in developing a start-up. The plan sets out the new business's goals, market analysis, and projected income and profit.

How it works

Before a start-up entrepreneur can write a business plan, they need to have done enough research to identify a clear opportunity in the market for the product or service, and to define how the proposed new business will be uniquely positioned to capture that market, given the services or product on offer. An outline of existing finances and an accurate projection of sales and profit are essential components, especially if seeking external funding.

Key elements

Preparing a business plan can take several weeks, and it is worth doing thoroughly. It is a vital document for securing funding, so the financial forecast must be both realistic and accurate. If showing it to others, pare the executive summary down to two A4 pages, write it in plain language, and explain any technical terms.

69%
of current small business owners recommend writing a plan

Executive summary

Fill in this section last, bearing in mind that it may be the only part a busy person reads:

> **Business summary** Company structure, name, product or service, and customer profile

> **Business aims** Three objectives over one, three, and five years

> **Financial summary** Expected sales and costs, and funding

> **Elevator pitch** Two-minute talk to sell your idea to an investor

Business background

Provide details of each person in the business:

> **Experience** Relevant work carried out to date; achievements; contacts made

> **Qualifications** Credentials, such as diploma in horticulture for a gardening service

> **Training** Past and future, including business skills such as assertiveness

Products and services

Describe what the business is going to sell:

> **Product or service** With a picture if product is new

> **Range** If more than one, such as garden design and maintenance

> **How it is different** What makes the product or service stand out from the crowd?

The market

Set out specific details of your potential market:

> **Typical customer** Businesses or individuals and their profile; local, national, or international

> **Market research** What the local market is for similar products or services

Marketing strategy

Choose about three of these methods:

> Social media
> Website

> Word of mouth
> Advertising
> Business literature
> Direct marketing

TOP FIVE REASONS TO WRITE A PLAN

> **The process** Working through each element ensures nothing is forgotten.

> **Costing** The only way to find out whether the business is viable is to work out details of costs and sales.

> **Funding** A good business plan improves chances of getting a loan.

> **Areas of expertise** Making a business plan clarifies where outside help is needed – for instance, for book-keeping or marketing.

> **Getting to know the competition** Conducting market research is the best way to give a business an edge.

Competitor analysis

Show how the business idea compares with the competition:

> **Table of competitors** Who and where they are, what they sell and for how much, how good they are

> **SWOT analysis** Including how to remedy any weaknesses and combat known threats, such as a garden centre opening nearby

> **USP** Unique selling point of the product or service

See Need to Know panel, above.

Operations and logistics

Describe how the business will run day to day:

> **Supply and delivery** How the goods or service will get from A to B

> **Equipment** Details of transport, office items, and premises

> **Payment, legal, and insurance** How customers will pay and how that translates into salaries; compliance with the law

Costs and pricing strategy

Work out how much the product or service costs and its sale price:

> **Cost** How much each unit or batch costs to make and deliver

> **Price** How much each unit or batch will sell for

> **Profit margin** The difference between cost and price per unit

Financial forecasts

Predict sales and costs over the year, allowing for seasonal fluctuation, such as spring demand for garden services:

> **Sales calculations** For each month, the expected number of sales

> **Costs calculations** The costs of the predicted sales each month

> **Cash-flow forecast** The money coming in and out of the business

See How Finance Works, pp.98–175.

Back-up plan

Make a Plan B in case something goes unexpectedly wrong:

> **Short-term changes** Cutting costs or boosting sales immediately

> **Longer-term changes** Shifts, such as working online, not on premises

> **Closure** Lessons learned and skills acquired if the business closes

Raising money

Almost every new enterprise needs funding to get it going, and to keep afloat until it turns a profit. Financial help is at hand from a variety of sources, suitable at different stages of start-up growth.

How it works

Capital for new enterprises comes from two main sources – lenders and investors. Lenders, such as banks, provide debt capital in the form of a loan that is returned with interest. Investors, such as business angels and venture capitalists (VCs), provide equity capital in the form of a share in the business that includes a proportionate share of control and rewards. Both types of funding can be corporate – from a company – or come from other sources, such as crowdfunding.

Types of start-up funding

Corporate, traditional, and substantial funding comes largely from banks and VCs, while smaller sums come from more personal sources.

Lenders

Debt capital most often takes the form of loans paid back with interest.

Term loan Paid back regularly over a set period of time

- **Bank** Offers either personal or business loans
- **Building society** Offers loans to buy a property (a mortgage)
- **Government** Offers low-interest start-up loans
- **Credit union** Cooperative that offers members low-interest loans
- **Peer-to-peer (P2P) lending** Unsecured personal loans
- **Friends and family** May offer interest-free loans

Bank overdraft or credit card Interest charged monthly if balance not paid in full

- **Bank or credit company** Finance organization that makes loans to commercial ventures

Factoring/invoice discounting Unpaid invoices sold at a discount to a company that collects them for commission

- **Factor or discounter** Company that offers advance on unpaid invoices, for a profit

✓ NEED TO KNOW

- **P2P lending** Loans made between individuals over internet
- **Crowdfunding** Debt or equity raised via internet platforms

Start-up funding

36% of prospective small business owners say getting start-up funding is a priority

Investors
Equity capital is paid to the start-up in return for a share of the business.

Grants

Financial awards and prizes are provided by public bodies.

Founders, friends, family (FFF) May buy shares in the company rather than lending money

Local, national, global Funded by a local authority, government initiative, or international charity

Crowdfunding Large number of supporters, each contributing a small amount of money, usually online

Business angels Investors who give favourable terms as their focus is on the company's success rather than profit

Venture capitalists (VCs) Companies that provide capital for new businesses in the hope of reaping profit

TYPES OF CROWDFUNDING

Crowdfunding is becoming a more acceptable source of alternative funding. There are three main types:

❯ **Equity-based** Where the company sells shares to raise capital. In return, the investor gets to own part of the business.

❯ **Debt-based** Where individuals lend money to the company, and in return, the company agrees to pay it back at given intervals, either with or without interest.

❯ **Royalty-based** In this case, crowdfunders receive a percentage of the company's revenues once it starts to generate returns.

Alternative models

In the wake of the economic downturn that started in 2008, several innovative and more personal types of funding, such as crowdfunding and peer-to-peer (P2P) lending, have evolved and blossomed on the internet. All involve the principle of raising small amounts of money from large numbers of individuals, who pool their resources to provide the loan or equity needed.

CREDIT ANALYSIS CRITERIA FOR LENDING

Capacity
The borrower's ability to repay the loan is shown by the business plan.

Capital
Many lenders assess a borrower's net worth to check assets exceed debts.

Character
The borrower needs to show a good credit history and ability to succeed.

Collateral
The borrower is often expected to pledge an asset that can be sold to pay off the loan if funds are too low to pay the monthly interest or repay the capital at the end of the term.

Conditions
The lender is swayed by the current economic climate as well as by the sum requested.

Life cycle of investment

The key to successful funding is to choose the right type of finance at each stage of a company's early growth. Start-ups usually begin modestly, with self-funding and help from friends, family, and anyone else who is prepared to take a high risk. Crowdfunders are amateurs willing the entrepreneur to succeed, while business angels and venture capitalists will likely take more risks than other lenders, such as banks, if they believe injecting substantial funds will return them a healthy profit. As sales soar and success looks probable, public markets, such as stock exchanges, can provide an extra funding boost. At all stages, investors will conduct credit analysis to assess a firm's ability to repay its debt.

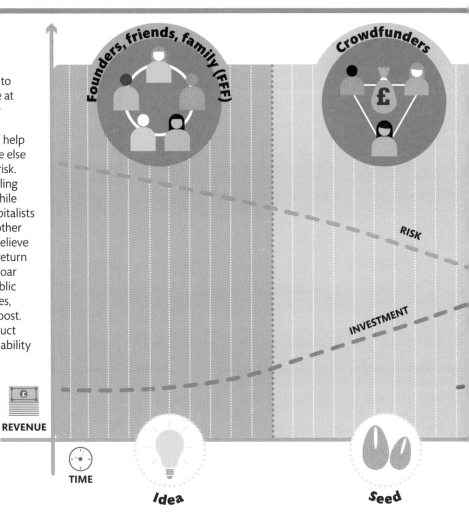

Founders, friends, family (FFF)

Crowdfunders

RISK

INVESTMENT

REVENUE

TIME

Idea

Seed

Start-up finance of small and medium-sized enterprises (SMEs)

The chart shows sources of start-up finance of new SMEs (established in the previous five years) from 2017 to 2019 in the UK, taken from a 2019 survey by the British Business Bank. By far the most funding comes from individual savings.

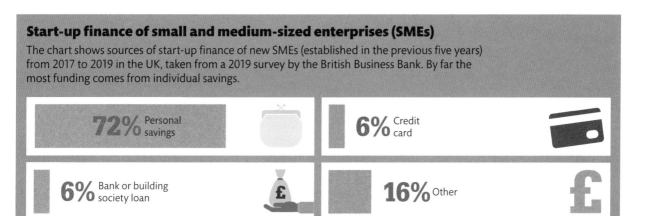

72% Personal savings

6% Credit card

6% Bank or building society loan

16% Other

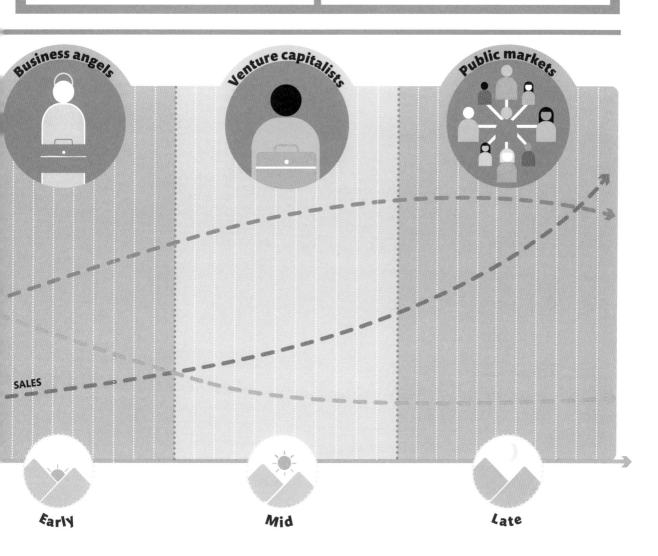

Business angels

Venture capitalists

Public markets

SALES

Early

Mid

Late

Business accelerators and incubators

Starting a new venture can be a long process. Business (also called venture) accelerators and incubators are specialist organizations devoted to developing and supporting start-ups.

How it works

Business accelerators and incubators provide expertise and connections in the formative stages of a business in return for a percentage of ownership. They are two separate types of service. Business accelerators are short-term programmes that offer wide-ranging support including mentorship, business advice, and connections to potential sources of finance. Business incubators, on the other hand, provide a supportive environment in which fledgling start-ups can develop, with technical assistance, working space, and networking opportunities.

Business accelerators

Suited to start-ups that have limited financing, accelerators offer short–term (one to three months) boot camps. Individual accelerators may specialize in a specific area, such as software development.

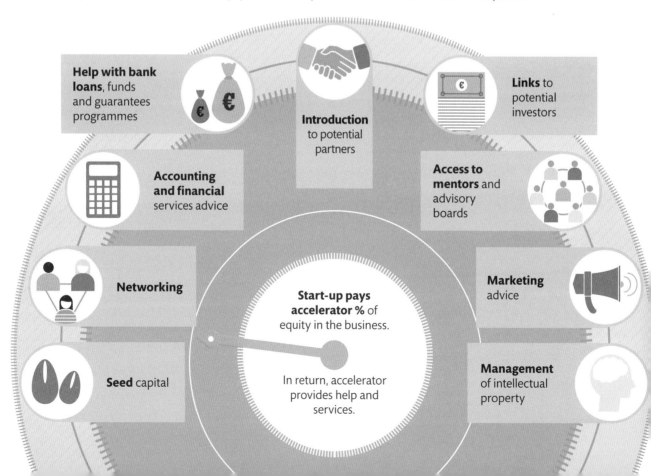

Help with bank **loans**, funds and guarantees programmes

Introduction to potential partners

Links to potential investors

Accounting and financial services advice

Access to mentors and advisory boards

Networking

Start-up pays accelerator % of equity in the business.

In return, accelerator provides help and services.

Marketing advice

Seed capital

Management of intellectual property

Business incubators

Often sponsored by non-profit organizations, incubators tend to be longer term (one to five years) and cater for a variety of clients, many science-based.

Start-up introduced to incubator

US$**107** million

invested globally by US and Canadian **accelerators** from 2012 to 2017

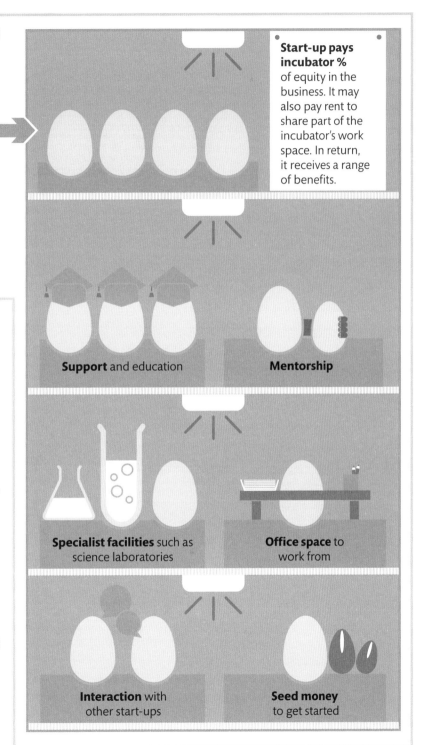

Start-up pays incubator % of equity in the business. It may also pay rent to share part of the incubator's work space. In return, it receives a range of benefits.

Support and education

Mentorship

Specialist facilities such as science laboratories

Office space to work from

Interaction with other start-ups

Seed money to get started

Buying & selling businesses

Both private and public companies regularly change hands – they are bought, sold, and restructured to reflect changing business conditions. These deals all come under the umbrella term of mergers and acquisitions (M and A). Acquisition financing is usually needed to pay for the purchase of another company, often in the form of a loan or venture capital.

How to acquire a company

A company is typically acquired in one of two ways – either by a management team or by another company. When a company is buying, the result can be a merger, in which two companies join forces, an acquisition (outright purchase), or a demerger, in which part of a company is hived off and may be sold. Management team purchases are often funded by private equity.

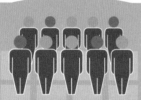

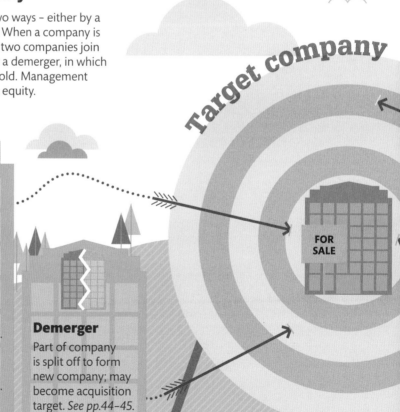

Target company

FOR SALE

Mangement team acquiring
Private equity firms look for companies to buy and then sell their shares when profits have maximized. They fund the management team. *See pp.48–49.*

Buy-out
The existing management team buys out the company they work for.

Buy-in
An external management team buys into the company.

Demerger
Part of company is split off to form new company; may become acquisition target. *See pp.44–45.*

45,652
the number of M and A deals, globally, in 2020

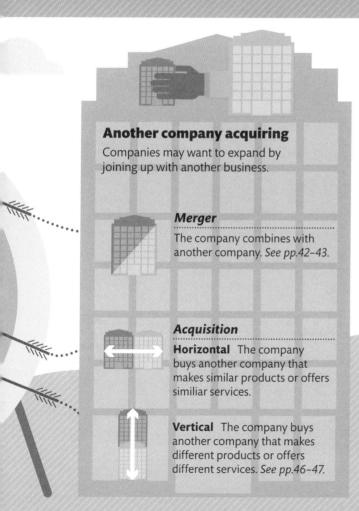

Another company acquiring

Companies may want to expand by joining up with another business.

Merger

The company combines with another company. *See pp.42–43.*

Acquisition

Horizontal The company buys another company that makes similar products or offers similiar services.

Vertical The company buys another company that makes different products or offers different services. *See pp.46–47.*

M AND A KNOW-HOW

Measuring a big deal

The corporate world categorizes acquisition deals according to the capitalization size (the value of the company's shares).

 Small Under US$500 million

 Mid-market US$500 million to US$2 billion

 Large US$2 billion to US$10 billion

 **Megadeal** Over US$10 billion

Due diligence

Before any company sale, the potential buyers see a detailed report prepared by lawyers, covering key aspects of the target business.

 ❯ **Financial** Identifies problem areas that could affect the future value of the company.

 ❯ **Legal** Gauges possible legal risks attached to corporate status, assets, securities, intellectual property, and employee restructuring.

 ❯ **Commercial** Includes industry trends, market environment, the company's capabilities, and the competition.

 ❯ **Environmental** Uncovers potential liabilities, such as land or water contamination and estimates remedial cost.

Mergers and acquisitions

Two of the quickest ways to accelerate expansion are for a business to buy out another – an acquisition – or to amalgamate with another business in a merger.

How it works

Mergers and acquisitions (M and A) is a general term used to describe the ways in which companies are bought, sold, and recombined. In the case of either a merger or an acquisition, two separate legal entities are unified into a single legal entity. While a merger combines two companies on a reasonably equal footing to create a new company, which will make both parties better off, an acquisition is usually a purchase of a smaller company by a larger one. This benefits the company making the purchase but may not necessarily benefit the target company. M and A can be friendly or hostile – agreed or imposed.

Merger

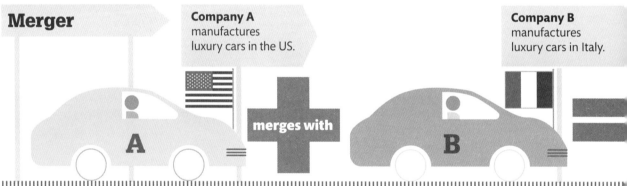

Company A manufactures luxury cars in the US.

merges with

Company B manufactures luxury cars in Italy.

Acquisition

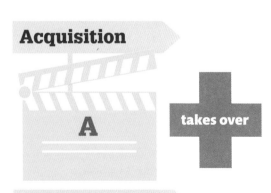

takes over

Company A produces films.

Company B creates animations.

FRIENDLY VS HOSTILE

> The target company's board of directors and management agree to be bought out.

> The acquiring company makes an offer of cash or stock to the target company's board and management.

> The stock or cash offer is set at a premium level.

> Because the offer is above actual market level, shareholders usually agree to it.

> The acquiring company bypasses management and goes straight to the target company's shareholders.

> The target company's management fight the deal.

> The buying company convinces shareholders to vote out the management (a proxy fight) *or* it makes an offer to shareholders to buy shares at an above-market price (a tender offer).

✓ NEED TO KNOW

> **Pacman strategy** The target company tries to take over the very company attempting the hostile buyout

> **Swap ratio** An exchange rate between the value of the shares of two companies when merging

> **Defensive merger** Undertaken to anticipate a merger or takeover attempt that threatens a company

> **Economies of scale** Benefit to a company of M and A expansion

New company A + B now has an expanded market spanning Europe and North America.

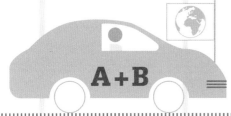

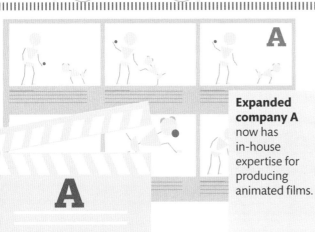

Expanded company A now has in-house expertise for producing animated films.

US$734 billion

the value of all mergers and acquisitions in the Asia-Pacific region in 2020

Demergers

While a merger results in a bigger company, a demerger reduces the size of a business by breaking it down into smaller components or divisions, which are then sold off or dissolved.

How it works

The typical scenario for a demerger is a company that is struggling to pay off debt it has taken on to expand into new areas of business that are not yet profitable. To save the rest of the company from the burden of debt, management decides to start a demerger. Generally, the aim is to shed the least profitable areas of operation, or from the potential buyer's point of view, those which have promise but are not yet profitable. The process of restructuring by demerger is designed to free the company of divisions with low return, to reduce debt and financing requirements, and to give the shareholders a stronger return. The market price of the parent company's shares often bounces back strongly and its spin-off companies may thrive too.

Demerger in practice

An industrial paint conglomerate, Power Paints Ltd, has grown rapidly over the past five years, due to an increase in profits from its expanding sales in China. The company diversified into agricultural chemicals, textiles, and biotechnology, and set up a separate division for each. Share prices fell in response to poor financial performance.

Making a decision

Faced with a downturn in business, the company demerges the newer business areas that have not yet shown strong returns despite positive signs of growth.

INDUSTRIAL PAINT

TEXTILES

Power Paints Ltd

AGRICULTURAL CHEMICALS

BIOTECHNOLOGY

Announcing the sale

Power Paints Ltd now announces the sale of its three remaining divisions: agricultural chemicals, textiles, and biotechnology.

INDUSTRIAL PAINT

Power Paints Ltd

FOR SALE *FOR SALE* *FOR SALE*

AGRICULTURAL CHEMICALS

TEXTILES

BIOTECHNOLOGY

✔ NEED TO KNOW

> **Spin-off** New company formed as the result of a demerger; also called a hive-off

> **Tracking stock** Special type of shares issued by a parent company for the division or subsidiary they will sell; tracking stock is tied to the performance of the specific division rather than the company as a whole; also known as targeted stock

> **Letter of intent** Letter stating serious intention to do business, often concerning M and A

> **Reverse merger** Not to be confused with a demerger, a quick and cheap method for a private company to go public by buying a shell stock – a public company that is no longer operating because it went bankrupt or was simply closed

> **Divestiture** Term commonly used in the US for demerger

3.3%
the average rise in a company's share price following a demerger announcement

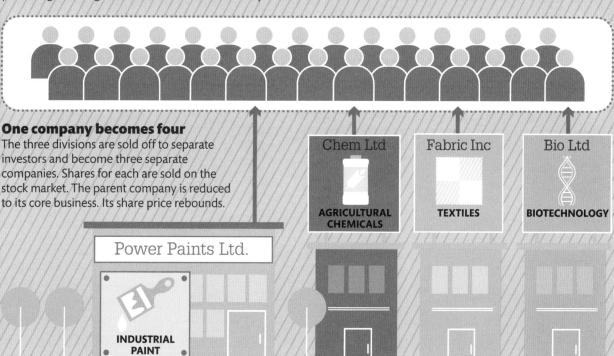

The shareholders benefit
Shareholders in the original company also receive the same percentage holding in shares of the three new companies.

One company becomes four
The three divisions are sold off to separate investors and become three separate companies. Shares for each are sold on the stock market. The parent company is reduced to its core business. Its share price rebounds.

Chem Ltd

AGRICULTURAL CHEMICALS

Fabric Inc

TEXTILES

Bio Ltd

BIOTECHNOLOGY

Power Paints Ltd.

INDUSTRIAL PAINT

Vertical vs horizontal integration

Companies that want to expand through a merger or acquisition may decide on a strategy of either horizontal or vertical integration, combining businesses involved in similar or dissimilar activities.

How it works

Companies can choose from several strategies when they merge or are part of an acquisition. Two of the most common are horizontal and vertical integration.

Horizontal deals are done between competitors that produce similar types of products, such as cars or mobile phones, and often share – or compete for – the same suppliers and clients. As a result of

merger or acquisition, the newly formed company can make cost savings in production, distribution, sales, and marketing. Vertical deals are usually between businesses involved in the same industry but at different stages – for example, a computer and a component manufacturer. These deals can be upstream (towards the market) or downstream (in the direction of operations and production).

Integration models in practice

In these hypothetical examples, a cluster of printers, publishers, and bookshops merge or acquire each other in horizontal or vertical deals that aim to strengthen their market position, take advantage of economies of scale, and exploit synergy.

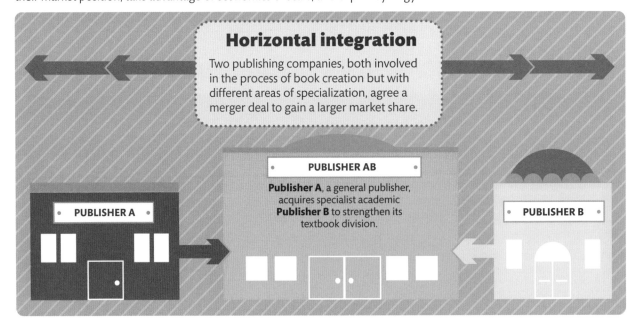

Horizontal integration

Two publishing companies, both involved in the process of book creation but with different areas of specialization, agree a merger deal to gain a larger market share.

PUBLISHER AB

Publisher A, a general publisher, acquires specialist academic **Publisher B** to strengthen its textbook division.

PUBLISHER A

PUBLISHER B

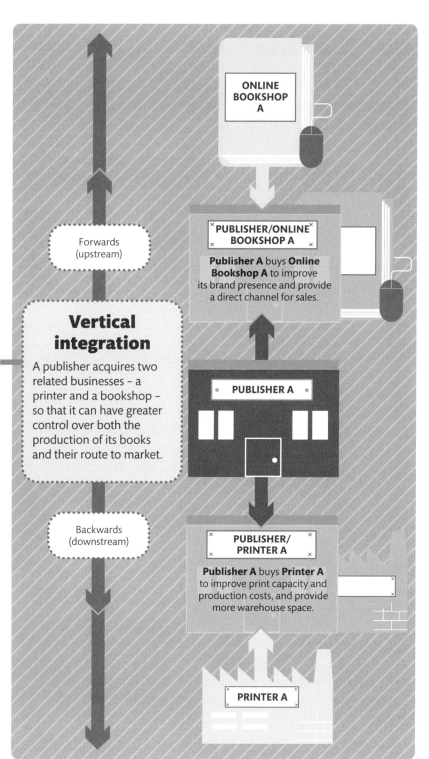

ONLINE
BOOKSHOP
A

× PUBLISHER/ONLINE ×
× BOOKSHOP A ×

Publisher A buys **Online Bookshop A** to improve its brand presence and provide a direct channel for sales.

Forwards
(upstream)

Vertical integration

A publisher acquires two related businesses – a printer and a bookshop – so that it can have greater control over both the production of its books and their route to market.

• **PUBLISHER A** •

Backwards
(downstream)

× PUBLISHER/ ×
PRINTER A
× ×

Publisher A buys **Printer A** to improve print capacity and production costs, and provide more warehouse space.

PRINTER A

86%
of M and A deals do not exceed initial expectations for income or rate of return

MERGER AND ACQUISITION TYPES

Horizontal

When two firms in a similar field merge, usually to take advantage of economies of scale, share skills and resources, and reduce competition. The merger of Facebook and Instagram is one example of this.

Vertical

When firms in the same supply chain come together. It is sometimes done to ensure supply and control over raw materials. For example, when a garment manufacturer acquires a cotton producer.

Conglomerate

When firms in different industries come together. One advantage is the cross-selling of products or services to a larger customer base. One example is food corporation Danone's acquisition of Dutch company Numico, which helped it expand into the baby food and nutrition market.

Management buy-ins and buy-outs

A company's ownership may undergo a change, which can be driven either externally, known as a management buy-in, or internally, known as a management buy-out.

How it works

In a management buy-in (MBI), a group of managers or investors from outside the company raises the finance to buy a majority stake in the company and then takes over its management. This type of action occurs when a company appears to be either undervalued or underperforming. In a typical management buy-out (MBO), the company's existing management team purchases all or part of the company they work for. Despite the name, MBOs are not restricted to managers, and they can include employees from any level of the organization who wish to make the transition from employee to owner.

Buy-in

Some companies, such as investment banks or venture capitalists, can make sizeable profits by purchasing undervalued businesses and transforming them.

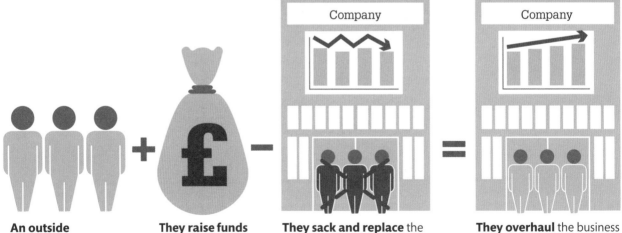

An outside management team or investment group sees that a company is undervalued.

They raise funds to buy a majority shareholding.

They sack and replace the previous management team.

They overhaul the business to improve performance and realize its true value.

BUY-IN MANAGEMENT BUY-OUT (BIMBO)

In this type of transaction, the existing management of a company stages a buy-out, but additional external management is brought in by financers to strengthen the company's leadership and to provide expertise in particular areas that might be lacking in the original team.

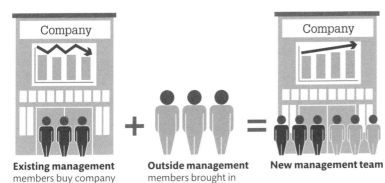

Existing management
members buy company

Outside management
members brought in

New management team

9:1
the typical ratio of debt to equity in a leveraged buy-out

Buy-out

A buy-out allows a company to sell off all or a part of the business, or it helps a small business owner to retire or move on.

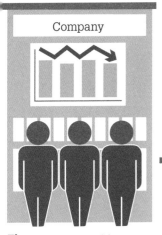

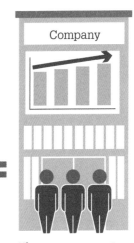

The management team sees an opportunity to take ownership when their corporate division is put up for sale.

They raise funds via bank loans, private investors, their own capital, or a loan from the seller.

They buy the business.

The management team who now own the company streamline the business to make it more profitable.

Who's who

A company's structure and hierarchy will develop as the business grows. The tendency now is to cut down on unnecessary layers of management, and to ensure that everyone in the organization knows what their role is and to whom they report. Most important is that the hierarchy fits the type of business and that authority is delegated to the appropriate level to enable timely decision-making.

Who's who in an organization

Stakeholders and shareholders

Stakeholders are anyone with a vested interest in the company. Shareholders are stakeholders who have bought stock in the company. *See pp.60–63.*

Board of directors

The board of directors makes sure the company is run profitably to provide returns to shareholders. The board votes in a chairman, who is sometimes also the chief executive officer (CEO). *See pp.52–55.*

C-suite executives

The top level operates the company day to day and sets strategy. Known as the C-suite as all job titles begin with a "C" for chief, it is headed by the CEO. *See pp.56–59.*

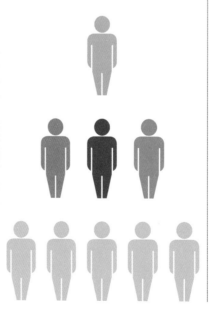

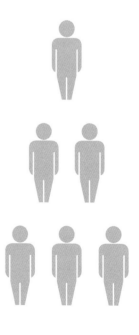

1/3

of global employees would strongly agree that they **trust the leadership** of their organization

FRONT LINE AND BACK OFFICE

Some employees are directly involved in operational activities, such as making goods and delivering services, or marketing and selling them. They are sometimes said to be working on the front line. Their work is important, but they cannot function without the support of back-office staff. These staff include people working in roles such as finance, IT, and human resources. It is important to ensure that both groups work well together to enable the smooth running of the business.

Mid-level management

Division and department heads are usually called directors or managers. Jobs at this level are often the first to go when a company downsizes or restructures. *See pp.56–59.*

Junior management

Supervisors, managers, or team leaders directly manage groups of employees carrying out specific tasks. Examples include a head nurse or foreman. *See pp.56–59 and pp.74–75.*

Non-management employees

These include skilled and non-skilled workers but also people recruited for their expertise, such as tax specialists and scientists involved in research. *See pp.56–59 and pp.74–75.*

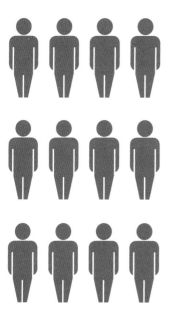

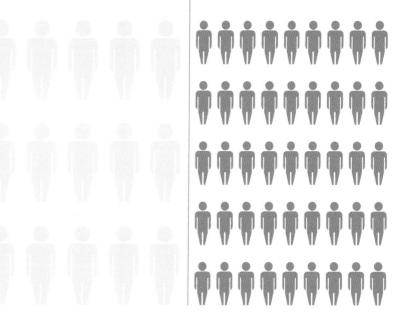

Board of directors

Public companies are obliged by law to appoint a board of directors to provide oversight.

How it works

All companies must have at least one director. If a company goes public and issues shares, it is legally required to have a board of directors. The board is made up of experienced business advisors who provide independent oversight of the company for shareholders and are mandated by law to govern the company responsibly.

Board members may come from within the company or be independent outsiders, and should cover a range of expertise – legal, financial, and marketing – or have specialist industry knowledge. Networkers are also highly prized for their ability to build connections with influential figures in the corporate and governmental spheres. Shareholders or board members elect roles such as chair (president in some organizations), vice-chair (or vice-president), secretary, and financial director – though the exact structure will vary from company to company.

Board of directors

The board of directors of a publicly listed company sits between the company and its shareholders.

REPORTS TO

Secretary

Appointed by

The board or shareholders

Responsible for

❯ Keeping records and other administrative tasks
❯ Assuring rule compliance

Financial director

Appointed by

The board or shareholders

Responsible for

❯ Producing annual accounts and financial strategy of the business

EVALUATES

Shareholders

Any person or institution that has bought shares in a publicly listed company is a shareholder. The board works for the shareholders, who effectively own the company.

Chair

Appointed by
The board or shareholders

Responsible for
> Publicly representing the company's policies
> Leading the board, conducting board meetings
> Determining the composition of the board
> Mentoring and monitoring the CEO or managing director (MD)
> Communicating with shareholders

16
the average board size in Austria, compared with 10 in the UK

Company
Responsible for day-to-day production, sales and marketing operations, and finance. The company reports to the board via its chief executive officer (CEO), who executes the board's decisions.

Vice-chair

Appointed by
The board or shareholders

Responsible for
> Standing in for chairman
> Undertaking special projects for chairman
> Assisting chairman to balance the experience, personality, and age of directors on board

REPORTS TO **EVALUATES**

CEO

Appointed by
The board or shareholders

Responsible for
> Performance of the company
> Implementing board strategy
> Leading senior management
> Reporting back to chairman and board

Directors

Appointed by
The board or shareholders

Responsible for
> Determining strategy
> Monitoring achievement of implemented policies
> Appointing managers
> Accounting for company's activities to shareholders and other stakeholders
> Non-executive directors are not employees of the company and offer objective advice and expertise

REPORTS TO   **EVALUATES**

Management
Managers pass the CEO's decisions down to employees.

Balancing the board

The board has three clear areas of responsibility: developing business strategy, advising the company, and overseeing how the firm is run. Selecting the right mix of directors to fulfil these functions is crucial.

Board members may come from inside or outside the company. Those who work for the company (executive or internal directors) have more expertise in running the business, but independent members (non-executive or external directors) are better placed to offer perspective, scrutinize the actions of company executives, and call them to account. When potential conflicts of interest arise between management and shareholders, independent directors can weigh decision-making in favour of acting in the company's best interests.

The ideal balance is a hot topic in corporate governance. In US companies, CEO and chairman roles have traditionally been combined, but following a spate of corporate scandals, the roles are now more often vested in two individuals. In Europe, keeping the roles separate has long been seen as best practice.

✓ NEED TO KNOW

> **NEDs** Non-executive directors, also known as independent, external, or outside directors

> **Executive directors** Board members who also work for the company – not to be confused with the term executive director when used as a title for the CEO

> **Companies Act** Corporate legislation in some countries, which may specify the proportion of inside and outside directors

Board structure variations

Independent board of directors

The board sits between shareholders and company. The CEO is the main channel of communication between board and company, while the chairman is the principal conduit between shareholders and board. This structure gives the board most independence.

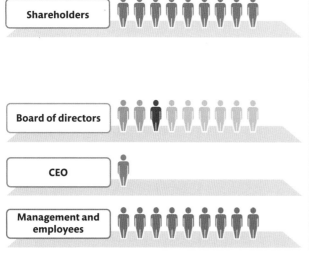

CEO as chairman

A set-up in which the company's CEO serves as the board's chairman. While this offers less independent scrutiny of finances, strategy, performance, and pay, it avoids duplication of roles. This set-up is usually found in small- and medium-sized companies and in US corporations.

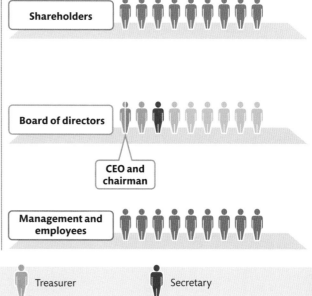

Key　Shareholders　Chairman　Treasurer　Secretary

WHAT DO BOARD MEMBERS DO?

The board exists to ensure the success of the company and to meet the appropriate needs of its stakeholders. It must enable the business to move forward but also exercises control. Some tasks are carried out by the members of the board themselves – these include establishing the vision and values for the company and setting strategy. Others are delegated to senior managers, such as deciding how to implement a particular strategy.

Different companies face different legal requirements for their boards, depending on whether the company is public or private, and where it is located globally. These requirements typically relate to matters such as the filing of accounts and the accurate recording of board meetings. Company board members are answerable to both shareholders and to regulators.

97%
of French boards have at least 30% female directors, compared with 43% in the US and 3% in Japan

Senior management as directors

A structure in which senior managers also sit on the board. The chief finance officer (CFO) is appointed board treasurer and the chief operations officer (COO) is vice-chairman. In some countries (Germany, for example), employees must be included on the board by law.

Two-tier board

An arrangement that is made up of separate supervisory and executive boards. The supervisory board is composed of outside directors, led by a chairman. The executive board comprises senior managers, including the CEO. The two boards always meet separately.

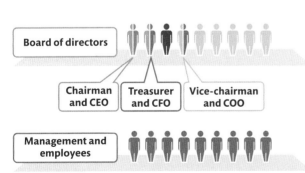

Shareholders

Board of directors

Chairman and CEO | Treasurer and CFO | Vice-chairman and COO

Management and employees

Shareholders

Supervisory board

Executive board

CEO and director | Employee and director

Management and employees

 Vice-chairman   Other directors   CEO   Management and employees

Company hierarchy

Almost every organization has a structured arrangement of levels for members, from the board of directors at the top to junior employees at the bottom. There is a trend towards reducing the number of levels.

How it works

There are five levels in the conventional corporate structure with a line of authority from top to bottom. The chief executive officer (CEO) is the highest-ranking person in the company, reporting to the board of directors and sometimes also sitting on the board. Reporting to the CEO are a number of high-level executives, known as C-level executives, as their job titles often begin with a "C". Below the C-level is management, in tiers that differ from company to company, with employees forming the bottom level. As well as skilled and unskilled employees, there may be staff on fixed-term contracts, taken on for the duration of a project or for a set length of time, in addition to consultants brought in for special purposes. There could also be casual temporary workers, as well as outsourced workers – the employees of an external company contracted to operate in a certain area of the business.

C-SUITE VARIATIONS

The range of C-level positions varies for each company. As well as the three top posts, there may be:

CAO Chief Administrative Officer

CIO Chief Information Officer

CTO Chief Technology Officer

CPO Chief Product/Production Officer, responsible for overseeing product development and production

CMO Chief Marketing Officer, responsible for marketing strategy and business development

C-level positions are evolving, adapting to market conditions and business priorities. New roles are emerging while some traditional roles are disappearing. The role of COO, for example, is less popular in modern organizations. Some of the new roles include:

CPO Chief Privacy Officer

CSO Chief Sustainability Officer

CDO Chief Digital Officer

CKO Chief Knowledge Officer

CCO Chief Customer Officer

C-suite executives

These are the most senior jobs in the company, with the CEO at the top, the COO and CFO traditionally on the next level down, and other C-positions below that. In many companies, the C-level positions have equal authority and all report directly to the CEO.

Mid-level management

Responsible for overseeing specific functions in the organization, the most senior managers at this level head up different departments or divisions. These managers are often called directors (not to be confused with the board of directors) or, in the US, vice-presidents. The exact job titles, and the number of mid-level managers, vary depending on the company.

51%

of CIOs and CTOs say they are pioneering new digital approaches within their business

Junior management and other employees

Team leaders, such as supervisors and assistant managers, implement management plans. They also coordinate teams of skilled and unskilled workers in, for example, production, customer service, and sales to carry out the core tasks needed for the company to function efficiently and profitably.

CHIEF EXECUTIVE OFFICER (CEO)
Decides on corporate policy and strategy

CHIEF OPERATING OFFICER (COO)
Responsible for day-to-day operations; reports to CEO and acts as second in command

CHIEF FINANCIAL OFFICER (CFO)
Manages company's financial risk; reports to CEO

US$**21** million

the average salary of a US CEO in 2019

MARKETING MANAGER
Directs marketing department day to day

FINANCE MANAGER
Puts CFO's plans or directions into action, instructing junior managers

OPERATIONS MANAGER
Oversees operations division; may also direct production department

R AND D MANAGER
Heads up research and development (R and D) of new products

SUPERVISORS AND TEAM LEADERS

NON-MANAGEMENT EMPLOYEES

Flattening hierarchies

The trend in management over the past few decades has been to eliminate layers from company hierarchies, which means they are becoming flatter – in other words, there are not as many levels to go through in order to reach the top.

In most cases, this has involved stripping away management positions in order to increase communication and collaboration across all levels. For example, the role of chief operating officer (COO) has been disappearing in recent years, as have layers of middle management, with many more division heads now reporting directly to the CEO. In such cases, some degree of hierarchy is maintained, but other companies go even further, evolving completely flat hierarchies where there are no bosses at all. However, such approaches tend to work best for smaller firms, proving less scalable in larger organizations.

Sometimes companies decide to restructure the other way round instead – from flat to tall – by eliminating a number of senior management posts and replacing them with a greater number of junior supervisory roles.

✓ NEED TO KNOW

❯ **Span of control** The number of employees reporting to a manager or other senior level; the greater the span of control, the more workers reporting to an individual above

❯ **Line position** Job role with responsibility for achieving the goals of the organization

❯ **Staff position** Job role providing expertise to assist someone in a line position

Tall vs flat hierarchies

There are pros and cons for both types of hierarchy, and each company has to find the number of levels, and positions within each level, that suit the nature of its business.

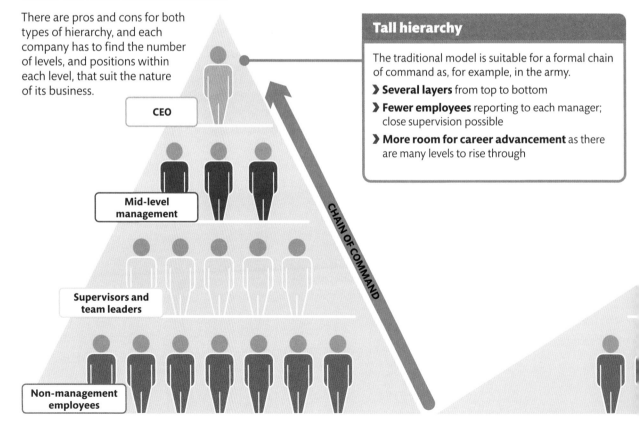

CEO

Mid-level management

Supervisors and team leaders

Non-management employees

CHAIN OF COMMAND

Tall hierarchy

The traditional model is suitable for a formal chain of command as, for example, in the army.

❯ **Several layers** from top to bottom

❯ **Fewer employees** reporting to each manager; close supervision possible

❯ **More room for career advancement** as there are many levels to rise through

CASE STUDY

Going flat at Valve

Valve is the developer behind such hit video game series as *Half-Life* and *Portal*. Feeling that its hierarchical structure was holding back innovation, it decided to switch to a flat structure. Now, Valve has no bosses, and staff are free to work on the projects they want. In return, they need to take responsibility for their mistakes and the products they create. While many people thrived in the freer environment, others struggled to adapt and departed. The firm also saw numerous projects abandoned after they failed to gain momentum. The experience led Valve to tweak its radical approach, maintaining its flat structure but uniting staff temporarily to focus on a new *Half-Life* title. As one developer admitted: "We were wrong on the premise that you will be happiest if you work on something you personally want to work on the most." Released in 2020, *Half-Life: Alyx* was immediately acclaimed as a landmark in virtual reality gaming.

14%
of executives believe a traditional hierarchical model makes their business highly effective

Flat hierarchy

This looser model is more flexible and suitable for companies that foster creativity.

> **Only a few layers** so mid- and low-level management are merged
> **Large number of employees** reporting to each manager; close supervision not possible
> **More freedom for employees** to make their own decisions

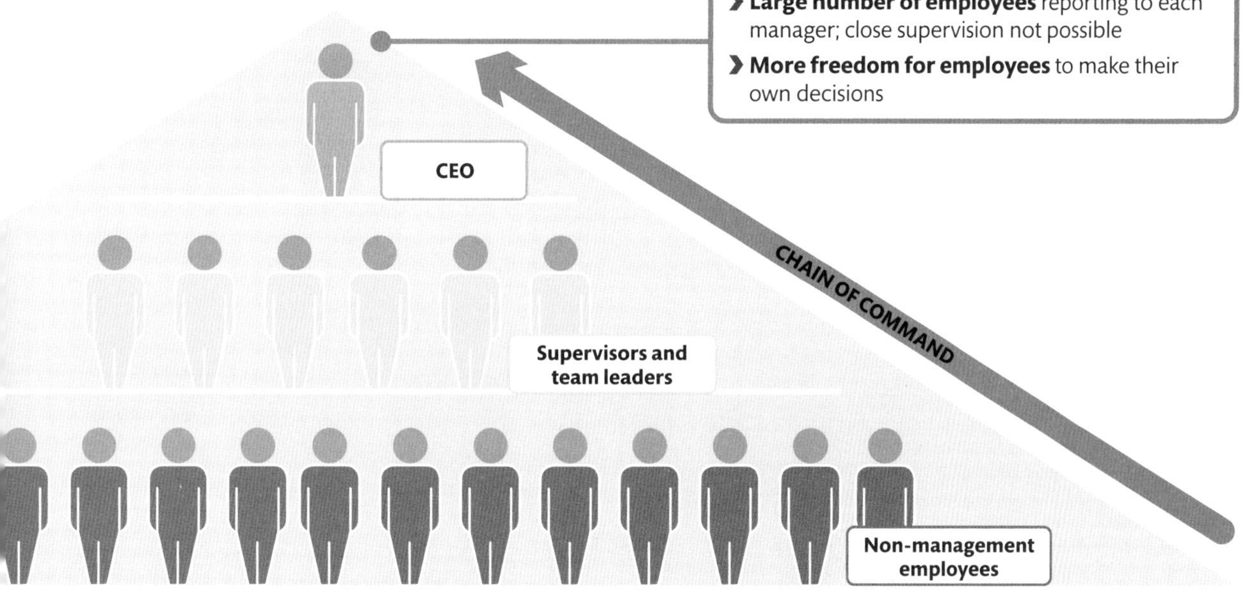

CEO

Supervisors and team leaders

CHAIN OF COMMAND

Non-management employees

Stakeholders

A stakeholder is anyone who is affected by the operations of the company, directly or indirectly. Stakeholders include groups, such as employees, shareholders, regulators, suppliers, and customers.

How it works

Companies have an impact on many groups of people through their operations. These include employees who rely on them to pay salaries and customers who want the products and services they supply. It is important for managers to understand what all these various stakeholders are looking for from them, whether they can meet their needs, and if so, how.

Sometimes the needs of stakeholders conflict. For example, a community may rely on a business to provide local employment opportunities, but will likely be less pleased if the operations of the business are noisy or cause pollution. In such cases, the managers of the company must find ways to maximize the benefits to stakeholders and minimize the drawbacks.

Stakeholders' areas of interest

Different stakeholder groups take different levels of interest in different factors. Some predominantly care about a company's environmental, social, and governance (ESG) factors. Others may be more interested in its financial performance, while still taking ESG concerns into account. Shareholders, for example, want profits, but they also understand how sustainability is key to long-term growth and may want to invest their money ethically.

Stakeholders with ESG concerns

Stakeholders have no direct involvement, but believe that companies have a responsibility to the communities they operate in, to respect the environment, human rights, and animal welfare.

US$**892**
million
the average drop in market value triggered by negative news about a company's human rights record

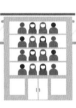

Non-governmental organizations
....
❯ Contribution to enviromental and social causes
❯ Legal compliance

Community
....
❯ Impact on local inhabitants
❯ Concern for broader social welfare

Stakeholders with economic and ESG concerns

Stakeholders use ESG – a recognized part of policy and reporting for most companies – to evaluate corporate behaviour and to determine future financial performance. Concerns range from profits to ethics.

Government
> Tax payments
> Legal compliance

Shareholders
> Ability to pay dividend
> Increase in share value

Customers
> Quality product
> Value for money
> Customer service

Trade unions and labour unions
> Treatment of workers
> Fair pay, benefits, and working conditions

Suppliers
> Ability to pay debt
> Enough liquidity

Employees
> Pay and benefits
> Longevity of the company
> Employment prospects

Lenders
> Ability to repay loans
> Integrity of management
> Financial strengths of the company

Stakeholders in action

Compared with other stakeholders, shareholders have the most interest in the financial performance of a company. They are also forced to take an interest in how seriously the company takes its corporate responsibility (CR), whether or not they are socially and environmentally conscious themselves. Several high-profile cases have shown how stakeholder reaction has caused a significant decline in share prices. By using social media, stakeholders can generate a storm of public disapproval, leading to angry consumers and nervous investors.

How stakeholders affect share value

In April 2010, an offshore oil rig owned by British Petroleum (BP) exploded in the Gulf of Mexico. BP attempted to alleviate stakeholder concerns but stakeholders responded negatively, starting their own social media campaigns to shame the company. Sixty-six days after the oil spill, BP's share value on the New York Stock Exchange had dropped by 52 per cent.

BP shares trading at
US$60.57
on 20 April 2010

News breaks that spill is worse than BP claims.

Stakeholder social media campaign intensifies.

News media report on the stakeholder backlash.

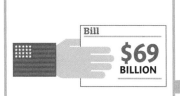

Bill
$69 BILLION

US government's Obama administration criticizes BP and sends company US$69 billion bill for clean-up.

Obama administration advises it could take legal action to stop BP paying dividends to shareholders.

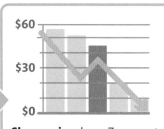

Share price drops 7 per cent in London trading.

US$**132** billion invested in European ESG funds in 2019

Oil rig explodes, killing 11 employees and spewing millions of gallons of oil into the Gulf of Mexico.

News media report on the event.

BP starts social media campaigning on Twitter, initially to minimize the impact of the spill.

Stakeholders of the BP oil spill

> Inhabitants along the affected coastline
> Local fishermen
> Oil spill clean-up workers
> Environmental activists
> BP employees

> BP shareholders
> Petrol customers
> Tourists and tourist businesses
> Media
> Government
> General public

Stakeholders use social media to voice anger and concern over perceived lack of responsibility by BP. Conservationists warn of wildlife devastation. Celebrities offer to help in the clean-up. Stakeholders call for more disclosure from BP.

Five of BP's top 10 shareholders sell off stock.

By 25 June, BP's share price has more than halved; more than 34 billion shares have been bought and sold.

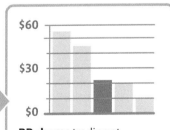

$60
$30
$0

BP shares trading at
US$23.91
on 25 June 2010

Business cultures

Every organization has a particular workplace culture, consciously or unconsciously shaped by the personalities, values, and behaviour of the people leading it and working in it.

How it works

The organizational culture of every business is different, reflecting the ethos of the company, the workplace habits, and the image the company projects. It is also tied to the type of work that is done. In a high-stakes financial trading company, the pace and pressure of the work makes the atmosphere crackle, whereas in a firm relying on creativity for its products, the mood is likely to be more relaxed. The type of incentives offered to management and employees may also affect the workplace, creating either a competitive or collaborative culture, or a mix of both. The rise of remote working is also leading to many changes in cultures.

Types of corporate culture

Management experts have tried to explain how organizational cultures work. Charles Handy, a former professor at the London Business School, describes them in terms of four major types: power, task, role, and person.

Role culture

Where a company is based on the structural support of specialized roles. Each role is crucial and will persist even if the person occupying it leaves. Procedures and systems are strictly followed, as in a government department.

Power culture

Driven by a powerful individual at the centre of the organization, who is relied on for decision-making and the company's successes. Those closest to the centre have most influence. Typical of a family-owned business.

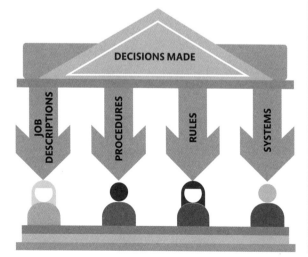

bureaucratic / controlling

WHAT SHAPES CORPORATE CULTURE?

Many factors reinforce a culture. To bring about change, the workforce needs to be inspired by different motivations, values, and types of role model.

Organization size
Big business, or small company

Company structure
Strict hierarchy, or power shared among many people

Founding values
Includes origination myths and stories

Leaders
Their personality and behaviour

Symbols
Titles, dress codes, interior aesthetic

Control systems
Rewards, incentives, performance assessment

84%
of senior managers in global organizations agree that organizational culture is critical to success

Task culture

Project-oriented work where a project's completion is the motivating force. Relies on teamwork and individuals' expertise, but results are more important than personal objectives. Found in technology companies, for example.

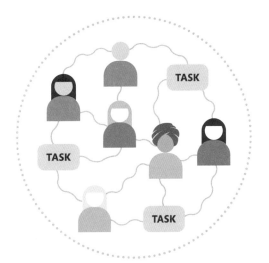

Person culture

Company power and influence is shared among individuals who work semi-autonomously. Individuals count for more than the company, which is made up of people with similar specialist training, such as in an architects' practice.

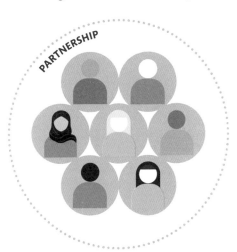

PARTNERSHIP

entrepreneurial / flexible

Corporate structure

A company's structure – the way in which it is organized – can have a major impact on the way it performs. There are several models of corporate structure typically used in the business world, and they continue to evolve – all the more so now as businesses embrace remote working. The first consideration is whether power should be centralized at the top, with decision-making in the hands of a few key senior employees, or decentralized, with more power in the hands of staff.

Choosing a structure

A company's structure changes as it grows. More complex structures will either evolve or are designed as a firm moves forward, depending on the nature and size of the business, the complexity of the work, any requirement for instant expertise, and the geographical location of parts of the business.

Centralized

Power rests in the hands of a few people, with a long chain of command.

> Power at the top
> Rigid
> Conventional
> Inflexible
> Slow response to change

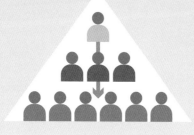

Functional

Good for strict control and formal relationships, as in the military.
See pp.68–69.

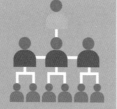

CEO COORDINATES

Divisional

Suits companies with many global offices or product lines.
See pp.70–71.

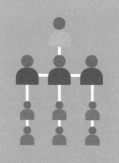

CEO COORDINATES AND EACH DIVISION IS RESPONSIBLE FOR GENERATING PROFIT

Matrix

Good for large corporations with complex projects in different locations.
See pp.72–73.

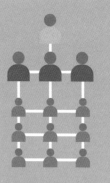

DIVISIONAL AND FUNCTIONAL MANAGERS COORDINATE

78%
of groups reach solutions to simple tasks faster in centralized structures

100%
of groups reach solutions to complex tasks faster in decentralized structures

When change is needed

Signs that a structure is not working include low morale and high staff turnover, no new products being developed, and profit suddenly accelerating or decelerating. Tools to amend poor structure include:

> **Business process reengineering (BPR)** Analyzing and redesigning the workflow within a company.

> **Altering the reporting line** In a traditional solid-line reporting relationship, one line manager oversees goals and performance. It can be beneficial to switch to the weaker chain of a dotted-line reporting relationship, in which a manager sets some but not all the objectives.

Network

Suits creative and technology companies in which everyone is online. *See pp.74–75.*

CORE COMPANY COLLABORATES WITH VIRTUAL COMMUNITY

Team-based

For companies that rely on innovation and are customer focused. *See pp.76–77.*

STAFF SELF-COORDINATE

Decentralized

Power is spread through the company, and staff make their own decisions.

> Power shared
> Organic
> Experimental
> Flexible
> Fast response to change

Functional structure

The classic way to organize a company is by dividing it into departments that reflect the main functions of the business, each headed by a director or manager.

How it works

The chain of command is straightforward. The business typically consists of a chief executive officer (CEO) or president at the top, with the various specialist departments or divisions, such as marketing and finance, aligned below.

Each department operates as an independent unit, with its own budget, and reports directly to the CEO, who takes responsibility for the operation of all the departments. A functional structure is the most common type of organization.

Typical departmental hierarchy

The departments operate independently, with the managers reporting to the CEO or president, who has overall command. The sales and marketing department usually takes responsibility for managing product lines.

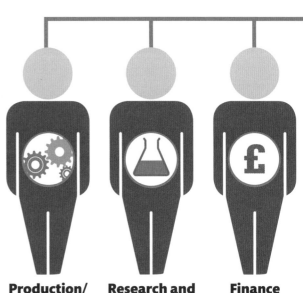

Production/ operations manager

Research and development manager

Finance manager

⚠ WARNING

Dangers of silo mentality

Silo mentality describes a scenario in which each department has a different, closed view of its role within the overall scheme and information does not get shared.

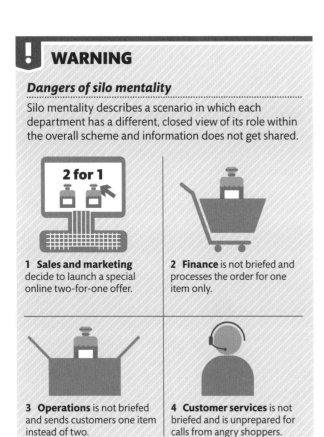

2 for 1

1 Sales and marketing decide to launch a special online two-for-one offer.

2 Finance is not briefed and processes the order for one item only.

3 Operations is not briefed and sends customers one item instead of two.

4 Customer services is not briefed and is unprepared for calls from angry shoppers.

Deciding what to sell

The marketing department is closest to the market and is best able to analyse which product lines may do well. The sales and marketing manager can suggest what new products the company could make.

PRODUCT A

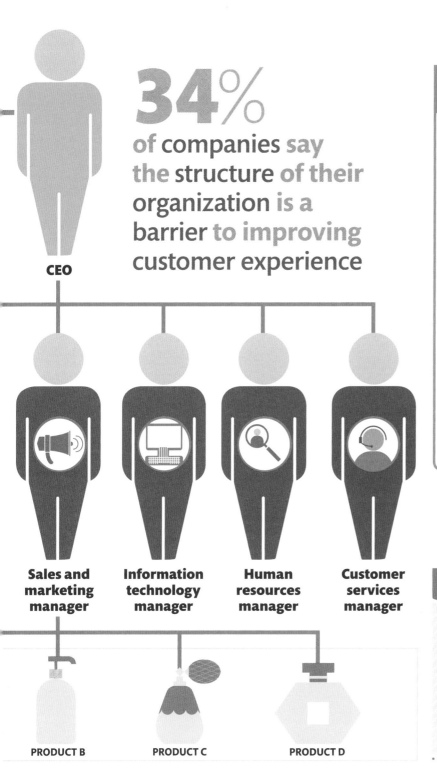

34%
of companies say the structure of their organization is a barrier to improving customer experience

CEO

Sales and marketing manager

Information technology manager

Human resources manager

Customer services manager

PRODUCT B

PRODUCT C

PRODUCT D

FUNCTIONAL: PROS AND CONS

Pros

❯ Allows for the development of specialization and expertise

❯ Enables efficient use of resources and potential economies of scale

❯ Offers obvious career path for employees in each department

❯ Simple, efficient structure for manufacturers producing a limited range of goods for sale

Cons

❯ Formal lines of communication; stifles innovation and creativity

❯ Departments fail to coordinate with one another efficiently

❯ Response time on problems and queries between different departments slow

❯ Many decisions referred up to the top, creating a backlog

✓ NEED TO KNOW

❯ **Line relationship** Chain of command down the structure

❯ **Reporting structure** Who reports to whom

❯ **Silo** Pejorative term for a department that works in isolation: a vertical, closed structure like a grain silo

Divisional structure

Some companies arrange their staff into divisions devoted to a specific product or market. Each division is a self-sufficient team employing the personnel for the various functions within it.

How it works

Under the overall control of a CEO or president, several divisions work alongside one another to design, research, produce, and sell a particular product, or to service a specific market. Each division may run its own specialist functions, such as operations or sales, though some, such as finance, may remain centralized to save on costs. A firm may arrange its divisions according to the types of product it makes, the regions in which it operates, or the customers to whom it sells. Large companies may adopt hybrid structures – by product and geography, for example.

DIVISIONAL: PROS AND CONS

Pros

> If one division fails, no threat to the rest of the business

> Can respond quickly to changes in the market

> Focused on customer needs

> Performance of each division clearly measurable

Cons

> Doubling up on resources, for example, each division employing finance personnel

> Lack of expertise-sharing between divisions

> Career path for staff restricted

> Heightened sense of competition among divisions

Division by geography

For businesses with products that need to be adapted to local markets, an organization can be structured according to each of the regional markets it serves. These may be domestic or international. Food and drink corporation PepsiCo broadly follows this structure, with seven divisions serving five regions (*see case study, right*).

North America
Three divisions: PepsiCo Beverages, Frito-Lay, and Quaker Foods

Latin America
Miami HQ

Division by product

Businesses selling different types of products may pick a structure by which each division handles one category. Samsung Electronics, part of South Korea's larger Samsung Group, is organized by product division.

CEO

CONSUMER ELECTRONICS
TVs, appliances, medical equipment

IT & MOBILE COMMUNICATIONS
Phones, tablets, PCs, networking

DEVICE SOLUTIONS
Chips, processors, sensors

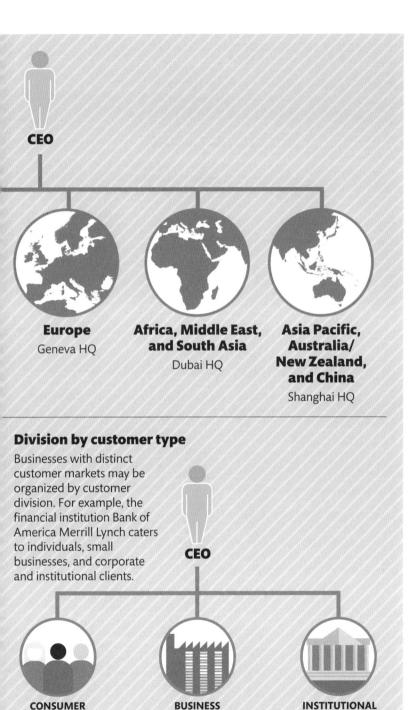

CEO

Europe
Geneva HQ

Africa, Middle East, and South Asia
Dubai HQ

Asia Pacific, Australia/ New Zealand, and China
Shanghai HQ

Division by customer type

Businesses with distinct customer markets may be organized by customer division. For example, the financial institution Bank of America Merrill Lynch caters to individuals, small businesses, and corporate and institutional clients.

CEO

CONSUMER
Typically the original market

BUSINESS
Products adapted or favourably priced

INSTITUTIONAL
Large-scale provision to a single client

CASE STUDY

PepsiCo

Food and beverage company PepsiCo's global operations have undergone various transformations over the decades, as it has acquired new brands and expanded around the world. Today, it comprises seven divisions in a hybrid structure arranged by product and geography.

Three divisions are in North America – PepsiCo Beverages North America (drinks), Frito-Lay North America (snacks), and Quaker Foods North America (cereals and snacks) – while the remainder look after both food and drink products in four global regions.

This allows those making the decisions about popular local brands – including Walkers in the UK and Pioneer Foods in South Africa – to be close to the customers who buy them.

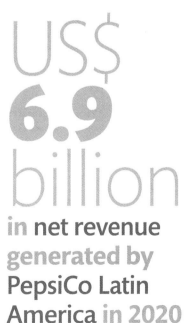

US$
6.9
billion
in net revenue
generated by
PepsiCo Latin
America in 2020

Matrix structure

Unlike a conventional company hierarchy organized either by function or division, a matrix combines the two approaches so that staff work in both functional and divisional units, and report to two bosses.

How it works

A business that uses a matrix set-up often begins with the more traditional functional structure. As the business develops, it may make sense to overlay a divisional structure to meet changes in business conditions – for example, if a company is managing several large projects for a client or expands globally and is selling its products in several regions. A matrix grid may start out as temporary – perhaps formed to manage short-term projects – and become permanent.

The two chains of command in a matrix create the grid. Staff report along a vertical line to a functional manager, such as the marketing director, and along a horizontal line to the project manager of a specific business line, brand, project, or region.

FOUR BIG MATRIX ORGANIZATIONS

Each of the following companies has been cited as a model for making the matrix structure work:

❯ **Procter & Gamble (P&G)** To help it innovate and respond faster to the market, the consumer-product company is segmented into baby and feminine care, beauty, family care and P&G ventures, health care, grooming, and fabric and home care.

❯ **Nestlé** The Swiss conglomerate is managed by geographical divisions across most of its food and drink business, though some product-centred businesses, including Nespresso and Nestlé Health Science, are managed globally.

❯ **Sony** The Japanese media, tech, and financial services conglomerate is primarily organized around business-/product-type divisions and function-based groups, such as research and development, though it also uses geographic divisions. This flexible structure allows it to effectively address market challenges.

❯ **Starbucks** The global coffee-shop chain is arranged by product, geographic, and business function divisions to ensure quality and innovation meet customers' expectations and anticipate their desires.

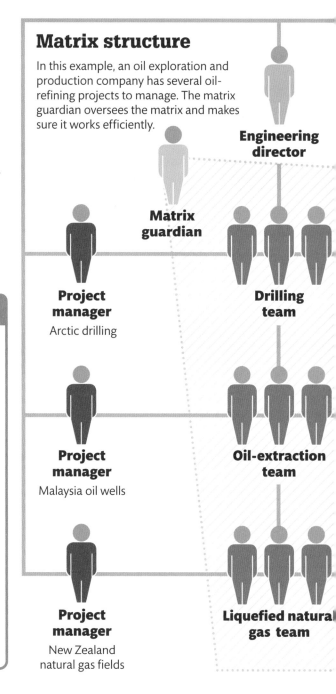

Matrix structure

In this example, an oil exploration and production company has several oil-refining projects to manage. The matrix guardian oversees the matrix and makes sure it works efficiently.

Engineering director

Matrix guardian

Project manager
Arctic drilling

Drilling team

Project manager
Malaysia oil wells

Oil-extraction team

Project manager
New Zealand natural gas fields

Liquefied natural gas team

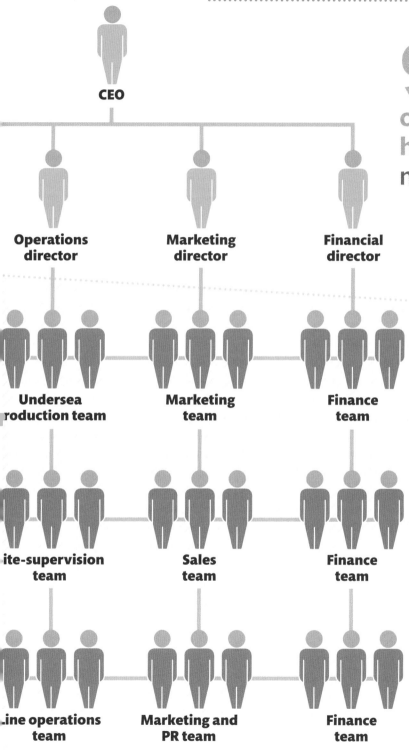

CEO

Operations director

Marketing director

Financial director

Undersea production team

Marketing team

Finance team

...ite-supervision team

Sales team

Finance team

...ine operations team

Marketing and PR team

Finance team

90%
of top multinationals have adopted a matrix structure

✓ NEED TO KNOW

- **❯ Matrix guardian** Senior professional appointed to oversee the matrix and make sure it works efficiently
- **❯ Mature matrix** Matrix structure in which functional and divisional bosses have equal power
- **❯ Solid-line reporting** A direct reporting relationship between a worker and primary supervisor
- **❯ Dotted-line reporting** A more indirect reporting relationship with a secondary supervisor

MATRIX: PROS AND CONS

Pros
- ❯ Faster decision-making
- ❯ Potential for improved productivity
- ❯ Flexible use of staff

Cons
- ❯ Expensive to set up and run
- ❯ Possible confusion as to the reporting line
- ❯ More potential for interpersonal conflict as team goals conflict

Network structure

Also called a virtual organization or virtual corporation, a network structure is centred on a streamlined company, with digital connections linking it to external, independent businesses.

How it works

The company at the centre of the structure is stripped back to basic functions that are essential to the type of business being operated – research and development, for example, in the case of a technology company. All other functions are outsourced to external specialists.

The various parties often work remotely around the globe and are connected by the internet. Together, they provide all the services needed for the network to function as one entity. This type of business structure is based on the idea of the social media network, and so is known as a network enterprise.

✓ NEED TO KNOW

> **Agile business** Term to describe a networked organization; the opposite of a traditional bureaucracy

> **Decentralized** Organization with a wide span of control and often an upward flow of ideas

Network structure in practice

A small film production company based in Los Angeles, California, is operating from a studio space with two employees – a producer and an assistant. For each project, the producer connects with outsourced talent around the world and everyone collaborates to create the finished film. The producer contracts and pays these external suppliers.

VARIATION: MODULAR STRUCTURE

In a business with a modular structure, parts of a single product are outsourced (it is functions or processes, not products, that are outsourced in a network structure). A modular structure is especially suitable for organizations producing appliances, computers, cars, and mechanical consumer goods. Toyota is an example of a company with a modular structure, managing hundreds of external suppliers to produce its finished vehicles.

Pros

> Potential for round-the-clock work because of global locations
> Can source the best expertise wherever it is in the world
> Low overheads as there are minimal staff in the core company
> Can develop a flexible and highly creative environment

Cons

> Extreme reliance on technology means network errors can stop effective performance of the business
> Potential for less control and missed deadlines
> Difficult to find common time across different time zones for virtual meetings

27%
of networked organizations report higher profit margins than their competitors

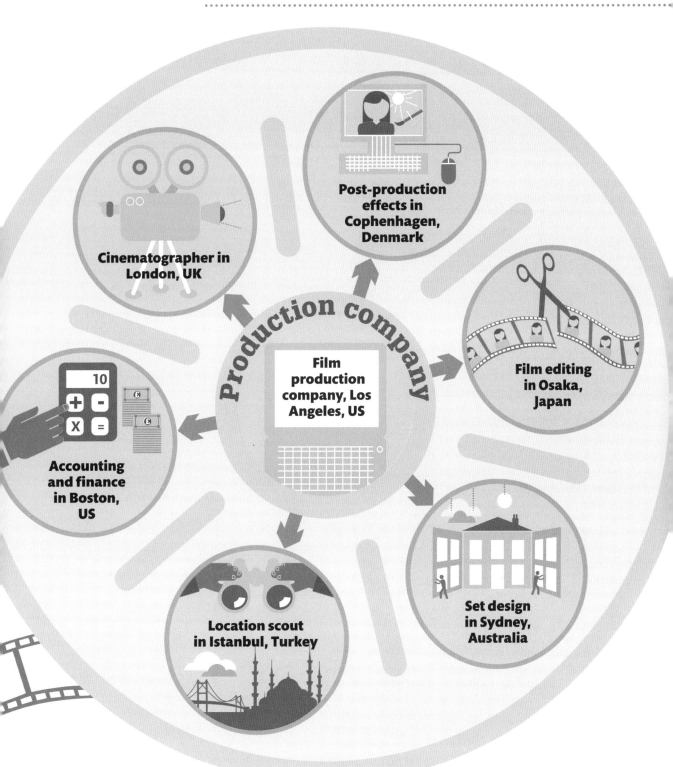

Cinematographer in London, UK

Post-production effects in Cophenhagen, Denmark

Production company

Film production company, Los Angeles, US

Film editing in Osaka, Japan

Accounting and finance in Boston, US

Location scout in Istanbul, Turkey

Set design in Sydney, Australia

Team-based structure

As its name implies, a team-based organization (TBO) is made up entirely of teams. Managers and staff from different departments join to form teams handling specific projects, in the short or long term.

How it works

In a TBO, teams reach decisions through brainstorming and mutual agreement among team members, rather than a senior management member issuing orders from the top down the chain of command as in a traditional organizational structure. Communication is less formal in TBOs, often carried out using messaging apps and social media, as well as online collaboration tools, such as Slack, and video conferencing software including Zoom and Microsoft Teams. One step beyond the team-based structure is a Holacracy (*see box, right*), an unconventional type of organization in which there are no managers, and even the CEO relinquishes power, allowing employees to self-govern through regular committee meetings, which they organize themselves.

✓ NEED TO KNOW

> **Cascading** Successful passing of information or objectives down through the workforce

> **Lateral structure** Decentralized structure in which departments work to a common goal

> **Flat lattice** Structure with no chains of command, in which workers choose to follow leaders

Team-based hierarchy

While TBOs still have a CEO, little other hierarchy exists. Team leaders are part of the team rather than above it in a chain of command. At its best, a team-based model fosters a culture of trust, so individuals take pride in their work and responsibility for carrying out tasks well and on time and budget.

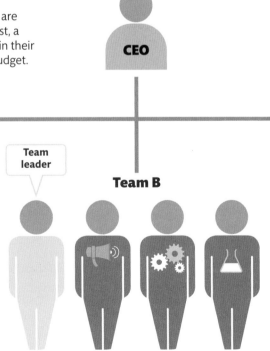

CEO

Team leader

Team A

Team leader

Team B

HOLACRACY – BREAKING BOUNDARIES

In a Holacracy, staff are grouped into teams that set their own roles and goals and choose their own leaders. The idea is that if power and responsibility are shared, employees will give their very best. In 2014, the Las Vegas-based online shoe and clothing shop Zappos adopted the model for its 1,500 staff. The term "Holacracy" is a trademark of HolacracyOne, the company spearheading the adoption of the management system. It follows the same principle as a flat lattice, but takes the idea one step further by presenting a comprehensive management structure with clear processes for internal operations and governance.

TRADITIONAL HIERARCHY

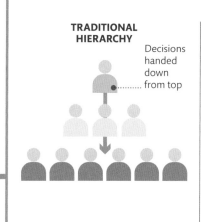

Decisions handed down from top

HOLACRACY – A STRUCTURE OF SELF-MANAGED TEAMS

Decision-making by committee

74%

of global organizations have seen improvements in performance since switching to a team-based structure

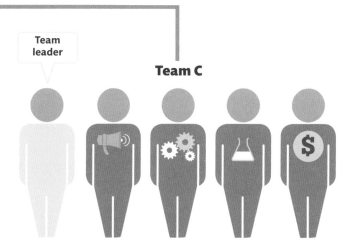

Team leader

Team C

TEAM-BASED: PROS AND CONS

Pros

❯ Quick decision-making and rapid response to problems and challenges

❯ Reduced overheads as there is no heavy management structure

❯ Open communication since there is no fear of management reaction

Cons

❯ If staff lack expertise, decisions may be flawed

❯ Limited sharing between teams may affect business performance

❯ Decisions by consensus harder to reach

Human resources

The human resources (HR) department is responsible for all policies and processes relating to the people employed by a business. To help the firm achieve its goals, HR has to make sure it employs a diversity of people with the right skills, irrespective of their gender, race, or faith. It must treat them consistently and fairly, providing a framework to look after their wellbeing, supply training, and foster their progress.

HR framework

The starting point for any decision in an organization is its business goals. HR supports the delivery of these goals by ensuring that there is a staffing strategy to support the business plan. Typically, an HR framework sets out a people strategy including the competencies of the people who best suit the organization. This is then implemented in a range of areas, from recruitment and selection to learning and development. Diversity and inclusion (D&I) is increasingly important, with firms that have higher levels of gender, ethnic, and cultural diversity consistently performing better. HR professionals work closely with business leaders and line managers to design and implement HR systems that back up strategic business aims.

Business goals

Business goals are the driver for every business decision, and HR polices support them.

SELECTION AND RETENTION
See pp.82–83.

SUCCESSION AND TALENT PLANNING
See pp.82–83.

PERFORMANCE MANAGEMENT
See pp.84–85.

LEARNING AND DEVELOPMENT
See pp.82–83.

Values and culture HR helps to determine principles, behaviour, and how tasks are done in a business.

Organization design HR formulates the structure and formal reporting relationships that define a company's shape.

People and performance HR is responsible for employees' welfare and their contribution to business goals.

36%

more profitability **is achieved by** the most ethnically **and culturally** diverse **companies**

DIVERSITY AND INCLUSION
See pp.82–83.

REWARDS AND BENEFITS
See pp.86–87.

EMPLOYEE ENGAGEMENT
See pp.92–93.

ESSENTIAL PEOPLE SKILLS

As well as recruiting effectively and ensuring employees deliver, HR plays a role in nurturing essential people skills across the organization.

Relating to others

❯ Some people are natural leaders, but most leaders can benefit from objective thinking about the leadership strategy they wish to follow. *See pp.88–89.*

❯ Even in flattened, team-based hierarchies, team leaders need to develop leadership skills to guide and support their teams. *See pp.90–91.*

❯ Despite the revolution in technology, people remain vital to organizations, as skills and knowledge are central to success. As a result, HR has an expanding role. One example is Google, which calls its HR function People Operations (POPS) and treats its staff as a valuable asset, offering a range of attractive perks to "find them, grow them, and keep them". *See pp.92–93.*

Managing projects

❯ Project management is an essential skill for managers at all levels, whether they are running regular day-to-day activities or special projects. *See pp.94–95.*

Negotiating

❯ The ability to negotiate successfully is an essential skill. Awareness of strategies and styles is key to success. *See pp.96–97.*

The human resources cycle

From the moment a company starts the process of recruiting an employee to the time that person leaves the company, the individual is in a cycle that is managed by the human resources (HR) department.

How it works

People are a significant cost to any organization and of great value – both those who work on the premises and those who work remotely. Many CEOs talk about staff as their most important business asset, and US industrialist Henry Ford famously said: "You can take my factories, burn up my buildings, but give me my people and I'll build the business right back again." The HR department is there to ensure that the right people are in the right roles so that the company can deliver the business strategy and maintain a competitive edge. The complexity of the business influences the stages in the HR cycle, but the basic elements are the same.

NATIONAL EMPLOYMENT LAWS

Employment practice is regulated by a raft of legislation covering everything from gender and racial discrimination, to holiday entitlement and dismissal. Laws that once only applied to full-time staff are being increasingly extended to part-time workers and those on contracts.

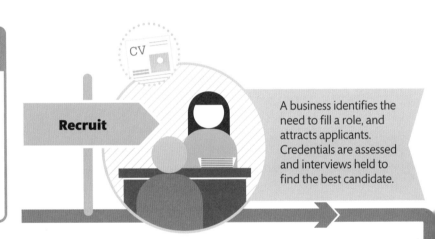

Recruit

A business identifies the need to fill a role, and attracts applicants. Credentials are assessed and interviews held to find the best candidate.

Employ

Once terms are agreed and a contract signed, the candidate becomes the firm's employee.

"Hire people smarter than you and get out of their way."

Howard Schultz, *former Starbucks CEO*

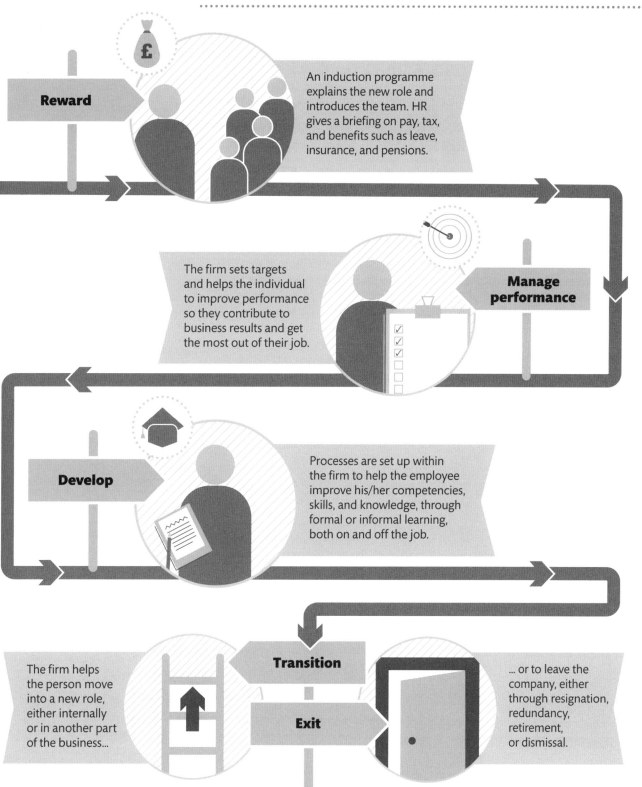

Reward

An induction programme explains the new role and introduces the team. HR gives a briefing on pay, tax, and benefits such as leave, insurance, and pensions.

Manage performance

The firm sets targets and helps the individual to improve performance so they contribute to business results and get the most out of their job.

Develop

Processes are set up within the firm to help the employee improve his/her competencies, skills, and knowledge, through formal or informal learning, both on and off the job.

Transition

Exit

The firm helps the person move into a new role, either internally or in another part of the business...

... or to leave the company, either through resignation, redundancy, retirement, or dismissal.

Recruitment and selection

Placing the right person in the right job is vital for the success of the organization – this is the process of recruitment and selection. Technology is changing traditional hiring pathways.

How it works

Human resources and line managers usually work together to organize the process of recruitment and selection. Recruitment starts with the company identifying a vacancy – the need for someone to do a job, and pulling together information about the exact nature of the role, and the skills, abilities, and experience required to do it. Aspects to consider include the job's purpose, tasks required, and the outputs or deliverables of the job holder, as well as how the role fits into the organization's structure. This information forms the basis of a job description and person specification. The search can then begin. The company's own website, recruitment agencies, social media, networking sites, commercial job boards, and advertisements in the press are traditional ways of attracting the attention of people outside the organization. Today, application forms are often directly submitted online, triggering automatic responses and sorting of candidate details.

BOOSTING DIVERSITY

A diversity and inclusion (D&I) strategy is an essential part of any HR framework. Recruiting from a range of backgrounds, regardless of gender, race, culture, and age, and making all staff feel safe and included in the workplace, helps firms innovate, connect to more customers, and get the most out of their workforce, ultimately leading to higher profits. Casting a wide recruitment net, communicating D&I commitments, assessing candidates' competencies over skill sets and experience, removing bias in the selection process, and providing D&I training can all help boost company diversity.

3
people are hired every minute on professional networking website LinkedIn

Job description and person specification

☑ Clear, bias-free written statement of the role, including job title, purpose, duties, responsibilities, scope, and reporting structure, as well as qualities and competencies required. It is used in the recruitment process to provide a clear guide for both applicants and interviewers.

Person specification

Summarizes the necessary or desired criteria for candidate selection using inclusive language, including skills and/or competencies for the role, experience, and educational qualifications.

Internal search

Looking at internal resources first creates opportunities for career development and progression, improving employee engagement and retention.

Personal recommendation

Some companies encourage existing employees to introduce friends as candidates.

External search

Increasingly, companies and candidates use professional networking sites such as LinkedIn and social media such as Facebook or Twitter. External candidates diversify the workforce but cost more to attract.

Applications

The curriculum vitae (CV) or résumé is the essential document, often with a covering letter. Companies may use an application form instead.

✓ NEED TO KNOW

> **Psychometric tests** Often used as an initial screening method, these aim to assess attributes such as intelligence, aptitude, and type of personality, using verbal and non-verbal reasoning tests and behaviour questionnaires.

CONTRACT

Selection

After HR has drawn up a shortlist using nondiscriminatory criteria, candidates may be assessed by interviews, group assessment, and psychometric testing, either online or in person.

Appointment

Companies may take up references for the chosen candidate. The employment offer is a legally binding contract that sets out the terms and conditions of the job.

Evaluating staff

For a business to achieve its goals, it needs to have a process that measures the contribution and performance of each individual against those goals.

How it works

The way in which tasks are done is becoming as important as what tasks are done, as organizations recognize the importance of creating the right culture to enable workers' performance. For any company, effective evaluation of the performance of employees should be strategic and is aimed at ensuring the maximum productivity of individuals, teams, and the organization as a whole.

Traditional performance-management cycle

Performance management is an ongoing, continuous process. Many companies use "360-degree feedback" to collect information about an employee's performance anonymously from a range of people, including their boss, colleagues, customers, and staff members.

Individual goals
Personal goals are set to align with business strategy

> **Business goals** drive tasks and activity.
> **Culture** enables teams and individuals to deliver.
> **HR policies** give clear benchmarks.

WINNER!

Rewards
Promotion and pay rises in line with performance

A WIN-WIN SITUATION

Evaluating performance is good for both the business and the individual.

Business

> Aligns individual goals with company goals.
> Offers consistent approach, with benchmarks.
> Continuously enables improvement.
> Fosters the right behaviours and relationships.

Individual

> Understands what is expected of them.
> Has the skills to deliver on these expectations.
> Is supported to fill any gaps in capability.
> Is given feedback and allowed to discuss aims.

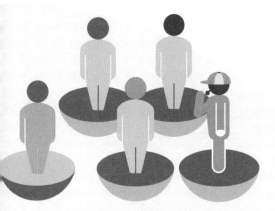

UNCONSCIOUS BIAS

Companies should be aware of the role unconscious bias can play in performance appraisals. An appraiser's subconscious prejudices about employees' race, gender, age, class, sexuality, or disability can see talented individuals repeatedly denied promotion or having their attitude questioned. Conduct unconscious bias training to make staff more aware of the issue, and oblige appraisers to use objective criteria to identify job competencies and to justify their appraisal scores with evidence.

2 Discussion
Ongoing communication on standards of work and behaviour to improve working relationships

✓ NEED TO KNOW

> **Balanced scorecard** Framework to measure performance against strategic goals, devised by Drs Kaplan and Norton

> **Competencies** Defined behaviours and attributes that individuals must have to perform effectively at work

> **Performance appraisal** Process via which individual employee and their manager can discuss performance and development

3 Coaching
Discussion of performance issues and ways to tackle challenges

360-degree feedback
Gives a rounded picture with better information about working relationships

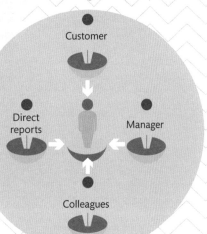

Customer

Direct reports

Manager

Colleagues

4 Appraisal
Formal feedback from the line manager, with an opportunity for individuals to contribute

INPUT FROM COLLEAGUES

Motivation and rewards

People work for money, but they are also motivated by other factors, such as doing a good job and being valued. Non-financial rewards drive day-to-day motivation more strongly than pay and benefits.

How it works

In the past, tangible pay and benefits were the key motivational tools for employees. These financial rewards are termed extrinsic because they are external to the actual work and others control the amount, distribution, and timing. Employers now recognize that while extrinsic incentives are clearly important, intrinsic (psychological) rewards are crucial.

Understanding motivation in the workplace

Happy staff work well, and job satisfaction comes from subtle feelgood factors as much as a pay cheque. Employees who enjoy their work tend to stay – job satisfaction makes for lower staff turnover.

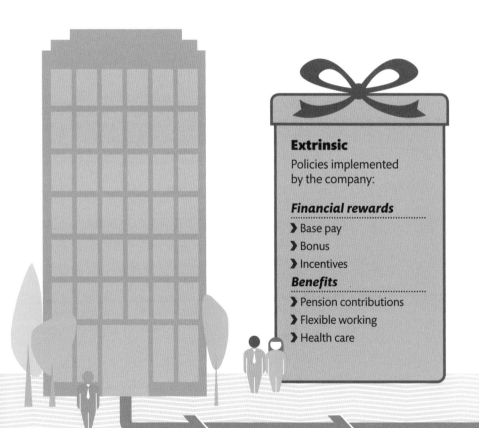

Extrinsic
Policies implemented by the company:

Financial rewards
> Base pay
> Bonus
> Incentives

Benefits
> Pension contributions
> Flexible working
> Health care

Individual motivation
Employees obtain psychological benefits from doing meaningful work and performing it well. Only one in eight workers (about 180 million employees in 142 countries studied) are committed to their jobs and make a positive contribution to their organization.

15%
of employees around the world are fully committed to their jobs

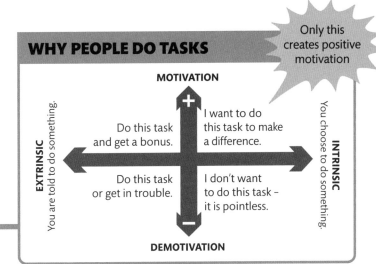

WHY PEOPLE DO TASKS

Only this creates positive motivation

MOTIVATION

+

EXTRINSIC
You are told to do something.

INTRINSIC
You choose to do something.

Do this task and get a bonus.

I want to do this task to make a difference.

Do this task or get in trouble.

I don't want to do this task – it is pointless.

−

DEMOTIVATION

Intrinsic
Feelings that an individual has:

> **Purpose** A sense of being able to accomplish something of value
> **Choice** Clear ownership and feeling responsible for outcome
> **Progress** As an individual, feeling and seeing evidence of moving things forwards
> **Competence** Pride and satisfaction in own work

Fostering intrinsic rewards
Businesses that are successful engender trust and so have employees who are passionate about what they do. All these factors contribute:

Purpose for organization and individual
> Clear vision for organization
> Understanding of where individual fits in to achieve that purpose
> Clear goals and expectations for individual

Recognition
> Continuous feedback
> Ongoing engagement
> Non-cash rewards, such as praise

Career development
> Progression and promotion
> Mentoring and coaching
> Learning opportunities

Culture
> Strong teamwork and consistent behaviours
> Open communication
> Sharing of knowledge and information

INCREASING MOTIVATION

Leadership strategy and styles

Top-down leadership, in which managers give orders, is not always the best way to get results. A number of different leadership styles have been identified by business experts.

How it works

Every leader is an individual with his or her own approach. However, over the years, management gurus have identified key leadership styles that can be used to achieve different results, depending on the environment. Many frameworks are based on the ideas of psychologist Kurt Lewin, who developed his theories in the 1930s with three major styles: autocratic, democratic, and laissez-faire (non-interference).

In 2007, for example, business authors Eric Flamholtz and Yvonne Randle developed a leadership matrix based on Lewin's theories, which shows the best style to use in any given situation, ranging from autocratic (one all-powerful leader) to consensus (decisions reached by general agreement). Truly inspirational leaders encourage people to believe in themselves so that they achieve results beyond even their own expectations.

> "Outstanding leaders go out of their way to boost the self-esteem of their personnel."
>
> Sam Walton, *Walmart founder*

TRANSFORMATIONAL LEADERSHIP

While different styles can suit different situations, transformational leadership, in which leaders and their followers raise one another to higher levels of integrity and motivation, was identified by guru James MacGregor Burns as the most effective. This has been developed by others, including industrial psychologist Bernard Bass, who listed the qualities of a transformational leader.

Is a model of integrity and fairness

Sets clear goals

Has high expectations

Encourages others

Provides support and recognition

Stirs the emotions of people

Gets people to look beyond their self-interest

Inspires people to reach for the improbable

When to use which leadership style

A three-year study of 3,000 managers led psychologist Daniel Goleman to identify six distinctive styles of leadership. Each style has a significant impact on how people feel about their work. The most effective leaders master a number of styles and use them appropriately according to the situation.

	Style	When to use	Drawbacks
Affiliative	**"People come before task."** Focuses on creating emotional bonds within a team and a sense of belonging within an organization.	Use in times of stress, when team-mates need to recover from trauma, or when the team needs to rebuild trust.	Praise and nurturing can foster mediocre performance and lack of direction.
Coaching	**"Try this."** Helps people find their strengths and weaknesses, linking these to career aspirations and action.	Use to help team-mates build lasting personal strengths that make them more successful.	Coaching is ineffective when team-mates are defiant and/or unwilling to change or learn, or if a leader lacks ability.
Commanding/ coercive	**"Do what I tell you."** Demands immediate compliance, without discussion or negotiation.	Only use in times of crisis or to control problem employee when all else fails.	Insistence should only be used when essential; it can alienate people, stifle inventiveness/flexibility, and tauten atmosphere.
Democratic	**"What do you think?"** Aims to build consensus through participation.	Use when it is necessary for the team to buy into or have ownership of, a decision, plan, or goal.	This is not for use in crisis or when team-mates are not well enough informed to be able to offer suitable guidance to the leader.
Pace-setting	**"Do as I do, now."** Expects and models excellence, creating challenging and exciting goals for the team.	Only use when the team is already motivated and competent, and when fast results are necessary.	Style can overwhelm some team members and adversely affect employee commitment; it may stifle creativity and innovation.
Visionary/ authoritative	**"Come with me."** Mobilizes the team towards a common vision and goal, leaving the means up to the individual.	Use when the team needs a new vision because circumstances have changed, or when explicit guidance is not required.	This is not effective when a leader is working with a team of experts or better-informed group.

Leadership for team building

Just as generals have to get the best from their troops, so business leaders must make the most of their teams. The key is ensuring that individuals work together to achieve a common goal.

How it works

From statesmen, such as former British prime minister Winston Churchill, to Facebook executive Sheryl Sandberg, great leaders recognize that to achieve a long-term goal, they must not only use their own capabilities but also maximize the combined strength of other people. They have a passion that sweeps people along with them; they learn from mistakes and are prepared to alter course to meet changing circumstances. Much academic work has been done to study the traits and strategies of such leaders.

How leaders inspire their teams

Academic Carl Larson and organizational effectiveness expert Frank LaFasto conducted a three-year study of more than 75 diverse teams. They identified six characteristics of leadership that steer a team towards optimum results.

Focusing on goal
› Defines goal in clear and inspirational way
› Helps each team member see how they contribute to goal
› Does not play politics

Encouraging collaboration
› Allows open discussions
› Demands and rewards collaboration
› Involves and engages people

Building confidence
› Accentuates the positive
› Shows trust by assigning responsibility
› Says "thank you"

> "Leadership is the art of getting someone else to do something you want done because he wants to do it."

Dwight D. Eisenhower,
former US president

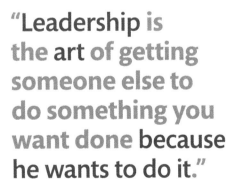

BUILDING AN EFFECTIVE TEAM

In their book *The Wisdom of Teams* (1993), Jon Katzenbach and Douglas Smith make a distinction between teams and ordinary groups of people who work together. They define a team as "a small number of people with complementary skills who are committed to a common purpose, set of performance goals, and approach for which they hold themselves mutually accountable". They found that leaders who manage to build successful teams tend to:

> Select members for skill and potential, not personality.

> Focus on a few immediate tasks and goals at the beginning, to help the team to bond.

> Set boundaries and behavioural norms.

> Stimulate the team regularly with new information, encouraging open discussions and active problem-solving.

> Ensure that the team spends lots of time together, both in and outside of work.

> "Don't find fault – find a remedy"

Henry Ford,
US industrialist

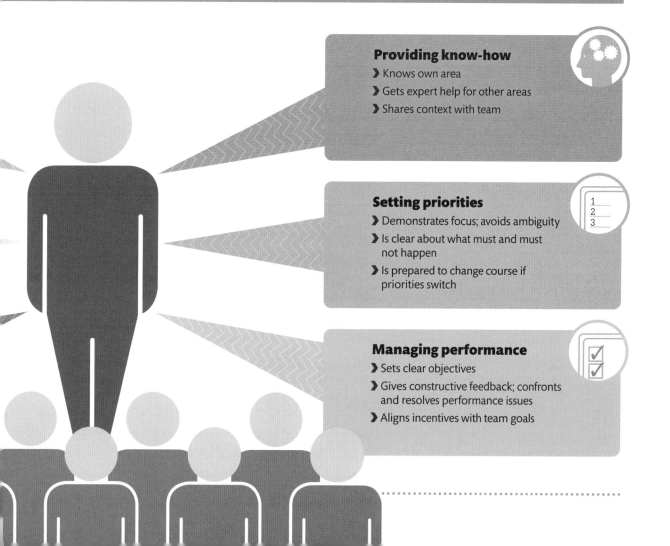

Providing know-how
> Knows own area
> Gets expert help for other areas
> Shares context with team

Setting priorities
> Demonstrates focus; avoids ambiguity
> Is clear about what must and must not happen
> Is prepared to change course if priorities switch

Managing performance
> Sets clear objectives
> Gives constructive feedback; confronts and resolves performance issues
> Aligns incentives with team goals

Employee relations and communications

Thriving organizations recognize the importance of harnessing people's ideas and energy to provide a competitive edge, while managers are keen to gain, retain, and build employee commitment and engagement.

How it works

Whether managed by human resources (HR) or as a function in their own right, employee relations and communications are increasingly sophisticated. Rather than just relying on face-to-face talks and word of mouth, successful firms use a range of communication tools to help people understand the business goals and their contribution to results. In particular, leaders no longer send only one-way messages but harness interactive media, such as video-conferencing. In turn, this has paved the way for effective remote working. Workers can use intranets and online collaboration tools, such as Slack, to share knowledge, but may still opt to meet in formal settings, such as councils and forums.

The art of communication

In this example, a company is establishing weekly employee forums to facilitate communication and build trust throughout the business. To strengthen employee awareness, engagement, and commitment to the idea, various media are used, from email to webinars and discussion. Managers focus ever more on collaboration rather than just imparting information.

EMPLOYEE FORUMS

In many countries, employee communication used to focus on structured industrial relations, managed by HR. Employee relations are now based more on trust and building strong relationships. Many firms create formal works councils or employee forums.

At their best, employee forums:

❯ Allow representatives from across the business to share and generate ideas for improving performance.

❯ Encourage discussions on vision, changes, and plans for business.

❯ Recognize the value of employees.

Commitment

Engagement and involvement

Awareness and understanding

DEGREE OF COMMITMENT

TIME

CONTACT
An email is sent to all employees with a short video informing them an employee forum is to be set up.

CASE STUDY

John Lewis

The John Lewis chain of department stores in the UK is famous for its unique employee-owned structure, in which every worker is a partner in the business. It has a number of employee-communication policies:

> **Gazette** Employees can send letters directly to management through the weekly gazette. Managers publish their responses in the gazette for all to read.

> **Partnership council** Made up of 58 elected partners from across the business, the council meets several times a year. The chairman and directors report to the council, which can remove the chairman.

> **Forums** Elected by employees on a three-year basis, forum representatives serve to reflect the views of the partners in a specific region, community, or business area.

£1.5 billion
spent on basic pay by John Lewis in 2020/21

REINFORCE AND INTERNALIZE
Regular face-to-face updates show employees how forums have made a difference.

ESTABLISH PRACTICE
A company-wide awayday illustrates to employees how the forums have changed working practices.

STIMULATE POSITIVE PERCEPTION
An inspirational seminar illustrates the benefits of the new councils.

ADOPT AND SHARE
Employees attend forums and then share their opinions on Twitter and Slack so they feel involved and collaborate with managers.

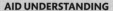

AID UNDERSTANDING
Resources placed on the company intranet detail how employee forums will work.

CREATE AWARENESS
The purpose of employee forums is explained at a company-wide video conference.

Project management

Besides day-to-day activities, a business may have projects – one-off, specific pieces of work. Projects need to be well managed so they deliver the benefits they were designed to achieve, on time and to budget.

How it works

The process of project management takes a complex project from start to finish. It requires a different set of knowledge, experience, and skills from a mainstream operation because the goals set up have to be achieved within defined limitations. These constraints include scope, time, quality, and budget. A project team might include people from different organizations, diverse disciplines, and multiple locations. Successful project management involves not only overseeing the people working towards the particular objective, but also managing the risks, schedule, relationships, individual and team input, range of stakeholders with a vested interests in the project, and financial resources.

Effective project management is increasingly viewed as a strategic competence (*see p.85*) for any business because it enables the introduction of new products, new methods, and new technology.

(*see p.85*)

 **NEED TO KNOW**

Project management tools

There are many different project management tools, with each suiting certain types of project and skill levels better than others. Specialist software, such as Wrike and LiquidPlanner, offer powerful feature sets, while more user-friendly tools, such as Trello, are good for simpler projects.

Steps in project management

There are many workable project management systems, using various definitions for the key stages, all of which are encompassed in five main elements.

Initiation
> Project charter, including business case, objective, scope, budget, deliverables, and schedule
> Roles and responsibilities
> Resource allocation

Planning
> Detailed plan of work
> Critical path analysis
> Risks

Execution
> Coordinating people and resources
> Quality assurance
> Communication to team and stakeholders

HURDLES AND HOW TO OVERCOME THEM

Every project comes up against challenges. These are some of the common ones, and the ways that effective management can keep the project on track.

Obstacle	Project managment	Options
Project is not on schedule, or running short of time	❯ Map out timeline of work and critical paths using tools and techniques. ❯ Review remaining work and identify risks, barriers, and mitigating strategies.	❯ Negotiate scope, budget, and resources of the project. ❯ Inform other teams and see if any changes can be factored in.
Unclear vision or lack of clarity	❯ Review project charter and revisit vision and objective. ❯ Involve team so everyone understands direction of work and avoids stalling.	❯ Seek clarity from sponsors and/or senior management.
Scope creep – project changes once under way	❯ Manage requests for change against business case and project objective.	❯ Communicate to identify why change is important and how to incorporate, or find alternative.

Monitoring and control
❯ Measuring effort and progress
❯ Managing and mitigating risk
❯ People management

Closure
❯ Finalizing all activities
❯ Communication
❯ Learning – project review

97%
of managers from 38 countries believe project management is critical to success

Negotiating strategy

Skilful negotiation is vital in business when two or more sides have different viewpoints, and each one wants to press for their own advantage. The ideal outcome is a compromise that delivers the best result for both parties.

How it works

Like many aspects of business, negotiation is a process to find a mutually acceptable solution. Before any discussion, each party must work to understand the other's interests and decide on a strategy, otherwise talks can end in stalemate, bad feeling, and loss of business. Being able to negotiate is vital to build strong working relationships, deliver sustainable, well-considered solutions (rather than a short-term fix), and avoid future conflicts.

Reaching agreement

Any strategy, from a wage negotiation between a trade union and employer to a sales negotiation between a customer and supplier, depends on the relationship between the two parties. Good negotiation should leave each party feeling satisfied with the outcome of the discussion and ready to do business again.

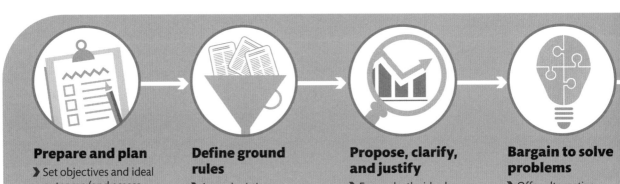

Prepare and plan

› Set objectives and ideal outcome (and assess those of other party).
› Rank and value issues and think of possible concessions.
› Consider ideal agenda and meeting place. Rehearse.

Define ground rules

› Agree logistics – location, room set-up, agenda, schedule, number of negotiators.
› Define etiquette, such as no mobile phones, one person speaks at a time, formal breaks.
› Agree how information is to be presented and recorded.

Propose, clarify, and justify

› Ensure both sides have equal opportunity to put forward their case.
› Clarify any points of disagreement.
› Focus discussion on understanding rather than resolving.

Bargain to solve problems

› Offer alternative proposals and concessions.
› Discuss what is acceptable to each side.
› Aim to find win-win solutions.

65%
of face-to-face communication
is through non-verbal signals

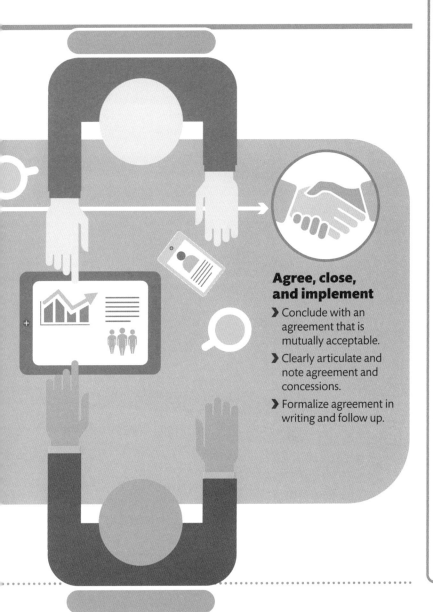

Agree, close, and implement
❯ Conclude with an agreement that is mutually acceptable.
❯ Clearly articulate and note agreement and concessions.
❯ Formalize agreement in writing and follow up.

BODY LANGUAGE IN DIFFERENT CULTURES

With international negotiations, it can be hard to read body-language signals, particularly as the meaning of gestures can vary.

Eye contact Chinese people avoid direct eye contact to show respect while American people see lack of eye contact as a sign of shiftiness.

Facial expressions When emotions are high in the US, it is acceptable to frown, even to swear, but not to cry. Japanese people might smile or laugh, but never frown or cry.

Head movements In much of Europe and the US, people nod to mean yes and shake their head to mean no. But in some parts of the world, such as in Bulgaria, it is the opposite way round.

Gestures Western cultures use a hand extended towards a person to indicate "Come here". Chinese people would see this gesture as offensive.

Posture In the US, being casual is valued; people might slouch when standing or sitting. In some European countries, such as Germany, a slouching posture is considered rude. Formality is also valued in Japan, particularly the ability to sit upright and still.

Flexible working

Businesses are taking a more flexible approach to how and where their staff work. Faster internet connections, cloud computing, and better apps have made it possible for workers to collaborate effectively at a distance, and many companies are recognizing the benefits of allowing them to do so. Are shared workspaces becoming a thing of the past?

How it works

Advances in communications technology have made it easier for businesses to allow employees to work in ways that suit their particular needs. In the UK, any employee who has been with their employer for more than 26 weeks has the legal right to request flexible working – whether that means choosing their own hours or working from home. The COVID-19 pandemic has accelerated this process. As countries around the world put lockdowns into force to curb the spread of the virus, businesses and employees scrambled to adapt to the new reality of doing what they used to do in person over the internet via video call, email, instant messaging, and other means. The result is that businesses now have a clear understanding of the benefits – and drawbacks – that flexible working can create, and most are unlikely to insist on every member of staff working in the same physical space all the time.

Working remotely: pros and cons

Pros

 Fosters a better work/life balance, creating happier, more productive employees

 Gives staff time to focus on their work, with fewer distractions

 Frees up room in company workspaces, allowing businesses to save on rents

 Gives organizations access to a global talent pool

Cons

 Not suitable for every business – many still need staff to collaborate in person

 More time needs to be spent to ensure clear communication

 Workers can end up feeling isolated; team culture is harder to foster

 Business operations completely reliant on technology functioning properly

25% of workers in **advanced economies** can **work from home** three to five days a week with **no loss of productivity.**

Going remote: what you need

 Maximizing the benefits and minimizing the problems of flexible working requires the right set-up. This not only means making sure the appropriate tools and technology are in place for all staff members, but also adjusting work practices and developing skills.

Tools

Workspace

Wherever they choose to do their job, staff need a suitable space to work: somewhere with good lighting, free from excessive distractions, and furnished with a comfortable desk and chair.

Hardware

Minimum requirements are a laptop and a reliable internet connection. An ergonomic wireless mouse, good headphones, a webcam, a microphone, a footrest, and a document holder can be handy extras.

Communication tools

Alongside email, video-call platforms, such as Zoom and Skype, are indispensable for providing face-to-face contact, while instant-messaging apps, such as Slack, help people ask questions and share documents. Other collaboration tools, including online whiteboards and project management apps, are also useful.

File-sharing services

Staff need to be able to read and edit company documents, and exchange them with colleagues. This might be through remote access to the company server or via online file-sharing services, such as Microsoft 365 or Google Drive. Such services store data on remote servers in the "cloud", allowing workers to share documents, track changes, manage different versions of them, and tag other users wherever they are.

Specialist software

Workers may also require access to software specific to their roles or unique to the business. Cloud-based subscription packages can make professional software easier to deploy.

Skills

Communication skills

Working remotely prevents people from picking up on – or giving out – many of the non-verbal cues that we use when communicating, so extra effort is required to communicate clearly.

People-management skills

For the same reason, interpersonal skills are also important. Reaping the benefits of flexible working means taking time to understand people's individual circumstances: keep in regular contact, listen carefully, show empathy, and offer support if needed.

Technology skills

People must know how to use the technology they need to work remotely to do their jobs properly. Understanding how to protect data to prevent security leaks is also key.

Time-management skills

Boundaries between work and home life can blur when working from home, so maintain a structured timetable. Start and finish on time, take regular breaks, and organize work hours carefully, keeping meetings to a minimum and blocking off enough time to get work done.

Flexibility

By its nature, flexible working means adapting to constant change. The key is to stay receptive, take the time to understand new problems, requirements, and technologies, and adopt fresh approaches.

HOW
FINANCE
WORKS

Financial reporting ❯ Financial accounting
Management accounting ❯ Measuring
performance ❯ Raising finance and capital

Financial reporting

Financial reports are everywhere: a bill at a restaurant is a financial report, as are sales receipts and bank statements. In business, however, financial reporting refers to the financial statements that make up a company's annual review and accounts. Compiled by accountants, they provide investors and lenders with information to assess a company's profitability, and enable company managers, government, tax authorities, and other stakeholders to evaluate the business.

Types of financial report

Financial reports take many forms and can contain a vast amount of information about a company's finances, work, core business values, performance, employees, and its compliance with local, logistical, domestic, and international laws. The most important financial report, or statement, is usually the annual review (also called the annual report) – essentially a collection of many other, smaller reports – which sums up how the business has performed in the last year. A multitude of laws, regulations, and guidelines govern what should be put into this report.

THE ACCOUNTING CYCLE

The eight steps of the accounting cycle are used by nearly all accountants. The cycle helps by standardizing processes and makes sure that accounting jobs are performed correctly and in the same way and order for every activity.
See pp.102–103.

The annual review

Financial statements usually appear in a company's annual review and sum up its financial activities in a standardized way for different audiences to interpret quickly and clearly. These statements take various forms, and being able to deconstruct them is a vital skill for accountants and business people, as it enables them to easily see how well a business is performing and why.

50%
of **accounting students worldwide are women**

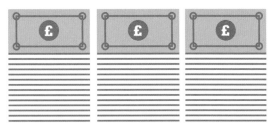

TYPES OF ACCOUNTING

There are seven widely recognized types of accounting:

 ❯ **Financial** Drawn up by accountants; used by investors, creditors, and management. *See pp.110–129.*

 ❯ **Management** Used by managers to control cash flow and budgets, and forecast sales. *See pp.130–143.*

 ❯ **Governmental** Also called public finance accounting; used by public sector for non-commercial accounting

 ❯ **Tax** Dictates exact rules that companies and individuals must follow when preparing and submitting tax returns

 ❯ **Forensic** Engages in disputes and litigation, and in criminal investigations of fraud. *See pp.152–153.*

 ❯ **Project** Deals with a particular project; a useful aid for project management.

 ❯ **Social** Shows how a company is making a positive difference to the community and environment.

Financial statements

❯ **What's in an annual review?** A full record of company performance according to various criteria, as well as accounts. *See pp.104–105.*

❯ **What are the statements?** The main one is financial; others include sustainability, directors' pay, and charitable donations. *See pp.106–107.*

❯ **Who reads which statements?** Sections are relevant to banks, shareholders, government, auditors, staff, and media. *See pp.108–109.*

❯ **What do the notes mean?** Main statements are annotated in more detail. *See pp.104–109.*

❯ **What are the rules?** Accounting principles regulate financial reports. *See pp.112–113.*

❯ **Which are the most important financial statements?** Profit and loss statements, balance sheets, and cash-flow statements contain key facts. *See pp.114–121.*

The accounting cycle

The accounting cycle is a step-by-step process book-keepers use to record, organize, and classify a company's financial transactions. It helps to keep all accounting uniform and eliminate mistakes.

How it works

The cycle works as an aid to organize workflow into a cyclical chain of steps that are designed to reflect the way assets, money, and debts have moved in and out of a business. It progresses through eight different steps, in the same order each time, and restarts as soon as it has finished. The cycle can be based on any length of time – this is known as an accounting period – and usually lasts a month, a quarter, or a year. Accounts that deal with revenues and expenses return to zero at the end of each financial year, while accounts showing assets, liabilities, and capital carry over from year to year.

The eight-step cycle

The processes shown here are repeated in the same way for every accounting period. All businesses go through different phases, and the accounting cycle works by reflecting that. The financial statement, which is prepared towards the end of each cycle, is helpful in showing how strongly the business has performed during each period of time.

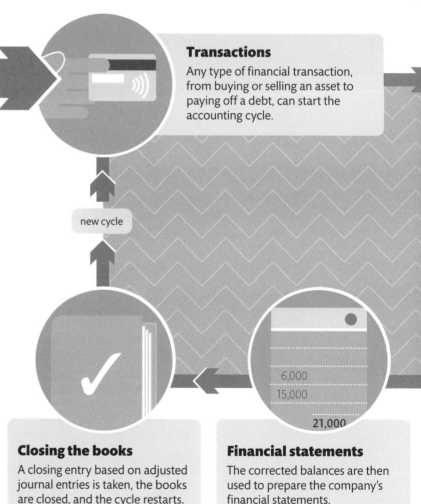

Transactions
Any type of financial transaction, from buying or selling an asset to paying off a debt, can start the accounting cycle.

new cycle

6,000
15,000
21,000

Closing the books
A closing entry based on adjusted journal entries is taken, the books are closed, and the cycle restarts.

Financial statements
The corrected balances are then used to prepare the company's financial statements.

BOOK-KEEPING AND ACCOUNTING

> **Internal controls** A method of deploying, measuring, and monitoring a business's resources. This helps to prevent fraud and keep track of the value of assets.

> **Double-entry book-keeping** The process of recording all transactions twice – as a debit and as a credit. If a company buys a chair for £100, its debit account increases by £100 and its credit account decreases by £100.

> **Bad debts** Debts that cannot or are unlikely to be recovered, so are useless to the creditor (lender), who writes them off as an expense.

Journal entries

Accountants then analyse the transaction and create a record of it – a journal entry – in the company's accounting system.

Posting

Journal entries are then transferred to the general ledger – a digital record logging all the company's accounts.

72%
of UK self-employed contractors do their own accounts

Trial balance

A list of all the company's accounts is prepared at the end of the accounting period, usually a year, quarter, or month.

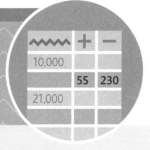

Worksheet

Often, trial balance calculations don't accurately balance the books (*see pp.116–117*). In such cases, changes are made on a worksheet.

Adjusting journal entries

Once the accounts are balanced, any adjustments are noted in journals at the end of the accounting period.

Financial statements

The formal records of a business's financial activities are presented as financial statements. Most jurisdictions require accurate information by law, and finance directors and auditors are liable for its contents.

How it works

Financial statements summarize a company's commercial activities clearly and succinctly, with details of the business's performance and changes to its financial position. They are aimed at several parties so they need to be detailed but also comprehensible to the general public. The statements are usually presented together in the form of an annual review, with in-depth accounts and footnotes to give detail. Legal requirements vary, but accounts must be exact.

What's in an annual review

The contents page is laid out as in a book and shows where to find the big three statements – the balance sheet, cash-flow statement, and profit and loss statement – and softer information such as stories about staff and opinions of other stakeholders. Overall, the annual review gives the company an opportunity to impress shareholders and lenders as well as fulfil legal reporting obligations.

Chair's introduction
It is common for the chair to write an introduction focusing on the positives and explaining any negative parts of an annual review for the benefit of stakeholders.

Our environment
These pages contain much of the company's information on its environmental protocols, most of which are industry-specific. *See pp.122–123.*

Our customers and community
This section underlines a company's social ethos, in particular its community involvement. Different types of companies may focus on different values.

Our employees
A section on employees details areas such as staff development and training, health and safety, and key statistics on staff satisfaction.

Our finance
A brief overview summarizes key areas of finance for the company, including overall performance, turnover, operating costs, capital investment, depreciation, interest charges, taxation, and dividends. *See also pp.114–121.*

Our infrastructure
The infrastructure pages of an annual review are a good place to include more detail about the company's fixed assets and explain why the company is an attractive investment for investors.

CONSOLIDATED FINANCIAL STATEMENTS

In an era of globalization, large corporations are now commonly made up of multiple companies. Companies owned by a parent company are known as subsidiaries, and continue to maintain their own accounting records, but the parent company produces a consolidated financial statement, which shows the financial operations of both companies. Depending on the jurisdiction's reporting requirements, however, if a company owns a minority stake in a second company, then the latter will *not* be included in the former's consolidated financial statement.

✓ NEED TO KNOW

> **Subsidiary** One company that is controlled by another, usually a holding company
> **Holding company** Company set up to buy shares of other companies, then control them
> **Globalization** Process of businesses developing such a large multinational presence that they transcend international borders and government controls

Our performance indicators

Performance indicators are common across all industries. They measure areas such as customer satisfaction and the quality of goods or services provided by the company.

Directors' report

In the directors' report, members of the board of directors give their professional opinions on how the business has performed over the last year.

Environmental accounting

The environmental accounting section contains figures that pertain to the environment, often those stipulated by law – for example, greenhouse gas emissions.

Independent auditor's report

Auditors are independent and check the accuracy of companies' accounts. This helps to eliminate mistakes and track fraud.

Board of directors

The board of directors, governance report, and statement of directors' responsibilities sections indicate who is leading the company, showcases their credentials and roles, and reveals their pay.

Notes to the accounts

Notes to the accounts are a key part of financial statements. They provide extra detail, insight, and explanation of the bare-bones figures supplied in earlier pages of the review.

Deconstructing a financial statement

The profit and loss account shows revenues, costs, and expenses – how much money the business makes – over an accounting period. The balance sheet shows what a business is worth at the time it is published, and is relevant to investors as it reveals assets, liabilities, and shareholders' equity – all useful for gauging business health. The cash-flow statement shows the movement of cash within a business – its liquidity. However, along with the big three financial statements, an annual review contains a wealth of information about a company's performance, of interest to its stakeholder groups. It is often the notes that bring statements to life.

TAXES

The percentage of business taxes taken by governments varies from country to country but the generic types remain similar:

> **Direct taxes** are levied directly on profits or income and include income taxes, and taxes relating to sales or purchase of property and other capital assets.

> **Indirect taxes** are paid on goods or services – value added tax (VAT), for example. Indirect taxes are often targeted to reduce consumption of harmful goods, a factor relevant to companies working in the alcohol and tobacco industries.

> **Green taxes** are increasingly common and are often indirect. They are generally used as a way of prohibitively increasing the price of goods or services harmful to the environment, such as air travel, landfill sites, or fuel, to diminish their use.

> **Corporation tax** is only paid by companies, not by sole traders or partnerships. It is levied as a percentage of the company's total profit.

Case study: the detail

Financial statements are presented as part of the annual review, which also publishes case studies, profiles of customers, suppliers, employees, and directors, quotations, and statistics. The notes, often running to 20 pages or so, contain tables and text that flesh out the financial information. This example shows the sustainable investment figures in the annual report of a fictional utility company.

Our finance

This section contains the headline financial figures of the business, such as profit, tax paid, assets owned, liabilities, and dividends paid out, as well as some more detailed explanation of the figures.

Sustainable investment

The utility company's investment in sustainability includes mandatory expenditure and extra discretionary expenditure.

	2021 £m	2020 £m
CUSTOMERS AND COMMUNITIES	130	110
ENVIRONMENT	115	102
EMPLOYEES	91	88
TOTAL	336	300

NEED TO KNOW

❯ **Monopoly** Situation in which there is just one supplier of a particular product or service; without government control, a company with a monopoly could make prices high and quality low, as consumers would have no alternative

❯ **Oligopoly** Industries that have a small number of suppliers; the competition is not as intense as in the free market, so governments often impose regulations on companies to ensure quality and fair prices

❯ **Remuneration** Money paid for work or a service provided – the financial term for pay; may include bonuses or share options

BOARD OF DIRECTORS

Much of what might be considered personal information about directors of public companies is in the public domain. It is usually a legal obligation to disclose:

❯ Names of executive directors

❯ Names of non-executive directors, and whether they are independent or shareholders

❯ Shareholding

❯ Board attendance record

❯ Dates of directors' terms of office

❯ Remuneration, including bonus, share options, pension plans, and benefits

❯ Notice period

❯ Termination payment

❯ Potential conflicts of interest

Charitable donations

Companies vaunt their philanthropy in the annual review, detailing how much they have given away and how it has helped. They may support charities relevant to the nature of their business or let employees vote on recipients.

Customer satisfaction

Overall, this section shows how the company works with customers to improve service and support. In monopoly and oligopoly industries, customer satisfaction is particularly important, as governments often set high targets.

71%
of CEOs feel
personally responsible for ensuring that their organization's sustainability policies reflect their customers' values

Financial statements for users

The many financial statements included in the annual review are a goldmine of information for those who know how to read them. They provide headline profit figures, explanations of issues from directors, detailed financial data, and information about companies' operations and policies. For this reason, financial statements are useful to a wide range of stakeholders, from the company's employees, customers, and shareholders to potential investors, governments, tax authorities, journalists, credit-rating agencies, banks, and the general public.

Who reads what

Different stakeholders are interested in different parts of the annual review. Customers of a service provider, for instance, may look at the section on customers and community while potential lenders go to the financial statements.

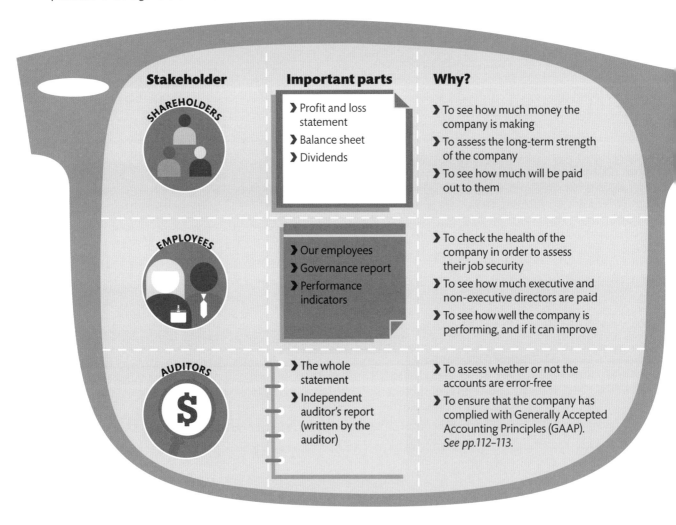

Stakeholder	Important parts	Why?
SHAREHOLDERS	❯ Profit and loss statement ❯ Balance sheet ❯ Dividends	❯ To see how much money the company is making ❯ To assess the long-term strength of the company ❯ To see how much will be paid out to them
EMPLOYEES	❯ Our employees ❯ Governance report ❯ Performance indicators	❯ To check the health of the company in order to assess their job security ❯ To see how much executive and non-executive directors are paid ❯ To see how well the company is performing, and if it can improve
AUDITORS	❯ The whole statement ❯ Independent auditor's report (written by the auditor)	❯ To assess whether or not the accounts are error-free ❯ To ensure that the company has complied with Generally Accepted Accounting Principles (GAAP). See pp.112–113.

UNDERSTANDING REVIEW JARGON

An annual review includes essential information about the financial health of the business, such as:

Post-tax return on capital
❯ A percentage figure estimated by dividing income after tax by the amount of investment. It is useful for showing shareholders the kind of returns they can expect on their investments.

Gearing
❯ Gearing is a company's debt compared to its equity and is expressed as a percentage. The higher the gearing, the more risk a company is taking. *See pp.174–175.*

Credit rating
❯ Credit ratings assess the likelihood that individuals, businesses, or governments will be able to pay back money lent to them. Credit rating agencies often give ratings in the form of letter grades, with AAA being the highest, indicating that a company has a strong capacity to meet financial commitments. C and D grades are the lowest.

Stakeholder	Important parts	Why important?
GOVERNMENT/TAX AUTHORITIES	❯ Taxation ❯ Independent auditor's report ❯ Environment section and environment-related notes	❯ To check that the figures are correct and the correct amount of tax has been paid ❯ To check the audit, and that they are satisfied with the accounts ❯ To check that environmental law has been adhered to
FINANCIAL INSTITUTIONS/BANKS	❯ Balance sheet	❯ To see the company's assets and liabilities and assess its strength, and whether or not it is wise to lend to the company
JOURNALISTS	❯ Chair's introduction ❯ Accounts and notes	❯ To find elements to quote ❯ To see how strongly the company has performed ❯ To analyse why a company has been performing well or poorly, and see if there is a story to write

Financial accounting

A company's financial accounts classify, quantify, and record its transactions. They are extremely useful for people outside the business, such as creditors and potential investors, as well as those currently involved with making investment decisions. For this reason, the accounts should be concise and clearly present the timing and certainty of future cash flows, so that people looking at the company can decide whether or not to invest in, lend money to, or do business with it.

Key elements

The profit and loss account, balance sheet, and cash-flow statements are the most important financial statements in an annual review, supplemented by the report's notes. To understand these statements, a knowledge of accounting principles, depreciation, amortization, and depletion is vital. Accountants also need to understand the legal requirements that the statements must satisfy and how environmental laws can affect a business and its accounts.

Accounting standards

Generally accepted principles standardize practice worldwide to ensure accuracy and prevent fraud. *See pp.112–113.*

❯ International standards simplify account reporting.

❯ Companies must meet environmental accounting rules and regulations. *See pp.122–123.*

Profit and loss statement

Shows how much money a company is making and is especially useful for potential investors and stakeholders. *See pp.114–115.*

❯ Outlines revenues and gains minus expenses and losses or operating costs.

❯ Informs a company if a profit warning is needed.

Balance sheet

Gives a snapshot of how much a business is worth at a certain time and is a good indication of its long-term health. *See pp.116–119.*

❯ Balances company's assets against its equity and liabilities.

❯ Lists different types of assets, including tangible fixed assets and current assets.

US$74 billion

the total value lost by shareholders in the 2001 Enron accounting scandal

AUDITING

The accounts of public companies are given unbiased scrutiny by external accountants to check that they are accurate and clear. This is a legal requirement in most countries, designed to ensure market confidence in the business world and transparency in corporate finance. A company may also have an internal audit process, which means that its accounts are checked before being submitted to an external auditor.

Cash-flow statement

Reveals a company's liquidity by tracking the flow of cash – money or short-term investments – in and out of the company. *See pp.120–121.*

❯ Shows if a company can sustain itself, grow, and pay debts.

❯ Details cash flow from operating, investing, and financing activities.

Environmental accounting

Accounts for myriad environmental rules and regulations that oblige companies to mitigate the impact of business activities. *See pp.122–123.*

❯ Showcases green credentials in financial statements.

❯ Reveals compliance with environmental, social, and governance criteria.

Depreciation

Accounts for the decrease in value over time of tangible fixed assets in order to spread the cost of assets over their economic life. *See pp.124–127.*

❯ Can be calculated using a number of different methods.

❯ Tangible fixed assets include buildings, plant, and machinery.

Amortization and depletion

Account for the decrease in value over time of a range of intangible assets, loans, and natural resources. *See pp.128–129.*

❯ Intangible assets include patents, trademarks, logos and copyright.

❯ Natural resources include minerals and forests.

Profit and loss statement

A profit and loss statement is a financial statement that shows all revenues, costs, and expenses during an accounting period. It is also known as an income statement, or an income and expense statement.

How it works

The purpose of the profit and loss statement is to show the profitability of a business during a given period. Along with the cash-flow statement and the balance sheet, it is the most important financial statement businesses produce, as it shows investors how profitable the company is. The statement usually works by showing revenues and gains, less expenses and losses from business activities, as well as on the sale and purchase of assets. By law, limited companies must produce a profit and loss statement every year; sole traders and partnerships are not obliged to do so.

How to read a profit and loss statement

Profit and loss statements commonly illustrate the financial performance of a business over a particular month, quarter, or year. The key pieces of information are the figures for turnover (or revenue) and operating profit. If profits are going to be lower than expected, the company may put out a profit warning in advance of releasing the statement.

Case study: profit and loss statement
This example of a profit and loss statement for a fictional utility company shows that it is making a profit.

	Year 2021 £m	Year 2020 £m
Turnover	607.5	575.9
Operating costs	–372.7	–354.2
Operating profit	234.8	221.7
Financial income	0.6	0.2
Financial expenses	–98.1	–100.3
Net financing expense	–97.5	–100.1
Profit before tax	137.3	121.6
Taxation	61.2	20.8
Profit after tax	76.1	100.8

Amount of money taken by the business over a certain time; in this case, there was a 5.5 per cent increase in turnover year on year

Profit earned from the business's core operations after expenses have been taken off, but before taxes have been deducted; it does not include money made on investments

Profit before tax after all income and expenses have been taken into account, excluding extraordinary payments

Level of profit that can be paid out in dividends to the company's shareholders

TYPICAL EXPENSES

Payroll
Salaries and wages paid to staff, temporary contractors, and indirect labour

Utilities
Water, electricity, and gas; postal services; transport

Insurance
Insurance on fixed assets and personal liability insurance for employees

Phone/internet bills
Cost of telephone, internet broadband, and mobile devices used by employees

Advertising
Sales and marketing of the company and its products

IT and office supplies
IT equipment and software used by employees; stationery, printer supplies, furniture, lighting

Legal fees and professional services
Accounting and legal fees, payable to accountants, auditors, and legal advisers

Interest on loans
Interest paid on money borrowed, which counts as a business expense

Tax
Varying among jurisdictions, this may include payroll tax and corporation tax

Entertainment
Legitimate costs of business entertaining

Case study: operating costs

This table breaks down the utility company's operating costs in more detail. It is important to read any notes regarding depreciation, and ordinary and extraordinary costs and gains.

Employee costs including basic pay, pensions, social security contributions, and directors' remuneration

Gradual decline in an asset's value, caused by factors such as wear and tear and market conditions.

Decrease in value over time of intangible assets or loans

Profit or loss on the sale of fixed assets

Leasing costs for buildings and equipment

Research and development carried out to improve the reliability and effectiveness of services

Funds spent by the company to create capital assets that have a life greater than one year

	Year 2021 £m	Year 2020 £m
Employee costs	133.3	125.5
Utility costs	36.3	35.1
Raw materials and consumables	17.1	16.1
Insurance	25.5	26.1
Depreciation	117.9	116.9
Amortization of intangible assets	8.1	5.1
Loss/(gain) on disposals of fixed assets	-0.3	-4.9
Operating leases for plant and machinery	5.3	4.8
Research and development	1.9	0.3
Other operating costs	142.0	132.0
Own work capitalized	-111.2	-100.1
	375.9	356.9
Fees paid to the auditor	0.3	0.3

Balance sheet

A balance sheet is a financial statement that shows what a business is worth at a specific point in time. Its primary purpose is to show assets, liabilities, and equity (capital), rather than financial results.

How it works

The balance sheet essentially shows what the company owns, what it owes, and how much is invested in it. It is based on the accounting formula, sometimes called the balance-sheet equation, which is the basis of double-entry book-keeping. This shows the relationship between assets, liabilities, and the business's capital – what the company owns (assets) is purchased either through debt (liability) or investment (capital). The equation always balances, as everything a company owns has to have been bought with the business's funds or through borrowing.

The balance-sheet equation

As the name suggests, the balance sheet must always balance. This is because everything the business owns (its assets) must be offset against the equivalent capital (or equity) and liabilities (debt).

Company has no liabilities

For example, a young business may have assets of **£1,000**. It currently has no liabilities so its capital is equal to its assets – that is, it is the amount of equity the owners or shareholders have invested in the business. Using the accounting formula, the equation would look like this:

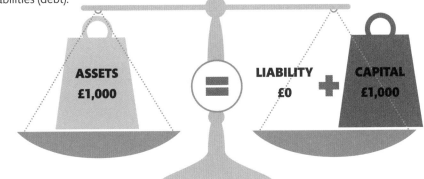

ASSETS £1,000 = LIABILITY £0 + CAPITAL £1,000

Company incurs £400 in liabilities

After spending **£400** on, for example, an illuminated sign for the shop front, the owner incurs **£400** in liabilities and so the formula changes. However, as the sign is worth **£400**, and the owner has **£600** remaining, the equation remains balanced – as it always does.

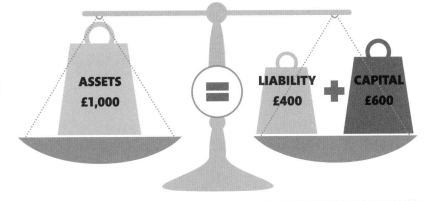

ASSETS £1,000 = LIABILITY £400 + CAPITAL £600

Case study: balance sheet

This example from a fictional transport infrastructure company shows how a balance sheet works in practice.

Fixed assets (or non-current assets) are not easily converted into cash and usually last longer than one year. They are either tangible, such as land, or intangible, such as logos

Current assets are assets that last one year or less, and can be easily converted into cash. Cash, cash equivalents, and inventory are the most common current assets

Current liabilities are the amounts that the company owes to individuals or organizations. Here, the money must be repaid in the current financial year

Net current assets equal current assets after current liabilities have been deducted

Total assets less current liabilities is the sum of fixed and net current assets minus liabilities due within the current financial year

Liabilities due in more than one year are amounts due to creditors, deducted from total fixed and net current assets.

Net assets are what is left once liabilities have been deducted from the company's fixed and net current assets to give the overall net assets

Shareholders' funds, or owner's equity, is the remaining capital; this money can be reinvested into the business or paid out as an annual dividend

ASSETS, LIABILITIES, AND CAPITAL	Year 2021 £m	Year 2020 £m
Fixed assets		
Tangible assets	**3,872.4**	**3,699.5**
Intangible assets	**60.1**	**44.6**
Investments	–	–
	3,932.5	3,744.1
Current assets		
Inventories	4.2	6.1
Trade and other receivables	185.1	189.6
Cash and cash equivalents	46.5	-22.4
	235.8	173.3
Current liabilities – amounts falling due within one year	-182.2	-274.4
Net current assets	**53.6**	**-101.1**
Total assets less current liabilities	**3,986.1**	**3,643**
Non-current liabilities – amounts falling due after more than one year		
Other interest-bearing loans and borrowings	-2,226.6	-2000.4
Contract liabilities	-6.9	-6.9
Employee benefits	-89.9	-121.1
Deferred grants and contributions	-299.2	-265.6
Provisions	-0.5	-0.9
Deferred tax liabilities	-444.3	-355.5
	-3,067.4	-2,750.4
Net assets	**918.7**	**892.6**
Equity		
Share capital	10	10
Retained earnings	908.7	882.6
Shareholders' funds	**918.7**	**892.6**

SYMBOLS FOR DEBITS AND CREDITS
Accountants use a number of different terms and symbols to indicate debits and credits. Some use "Dr" for debits and "Cr" for credits, others use brackets to show credits (negative numbers).

Understanding the notes

The balance sheet is a useful indication of the health of a business and it is important that investors know how to analyse it. It can be read in two ways – "at a glance", as on the previous page, where general information is summarized, or in depth, with more detailed information about each element. Provided after the summary, the detailed notes to the balance sheet explain the specific financial workings of the business. They show exactly where money has been gained or lost, in figures, and often include a written commentary about potential developments that may affect the company, such as court cases, staffing, or availability of resources.

Balance-sheet notes

Investors may want to know more about the figures in the summary section, so additional notes and tables give detailed breakdowns of the figures.

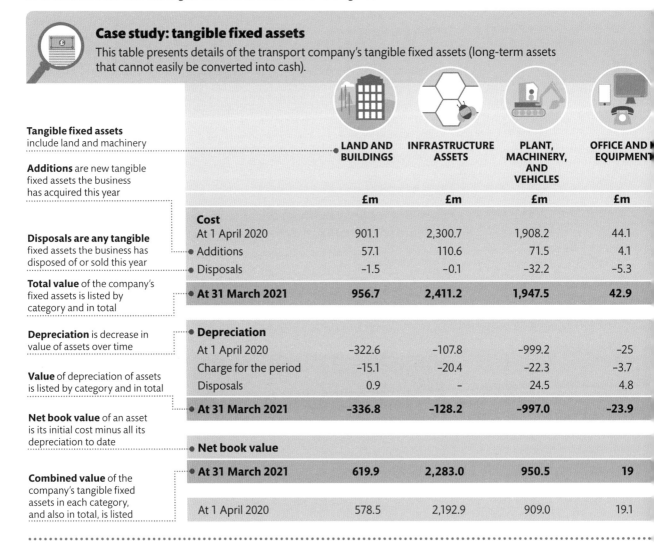

Case study: tangible fixed assets

This table presents details of the transport company's tangible fixed assets (long-term assets that cannot easily be converted into cash).

Tangible fixed assets include land and machinery

Additions are new tangible fixed assets the business has acquired this year

Disposals are any tangible fixed assets the business has disposed of or sold this year

Total value of the company's fixed assets is listed by category and in total

Depreciation is decrease in value of assets over time

Value of depreciation of assets is listed by category and in total

Net book value of an asset is its initial cost minus all its depreciation to date

Combined value of the company's tangible fixed assets in each category, and also in total, is listed

	LAND AND BUILDINGS	INFRASTRUCTURE ASSETS	PLANT, MACHINERY, AND VEHICLES	OFFICE AND EQUIPMENT
	£m	£m	£m	£m
Cost				
At 1 April 2020	901.1	2,300.7	1,908.2	44.1
Additions	57.1	110.6	71.5	4.1
Disposals	–1.5	–0.1	–32.2	–5.3
At 31 March 2021	**956.7**	**2,411.2**	**1,947.5**	**42.9**
Depreciation				
At 1 April 2020	–322.6	–107.8	–999.2	–25
Charge for the period	–15.1	–20.4	–22.3	–3.7
Disposals	0.9	–	24.5	4.8
At 31 March 2021	**–336.8**	**–128.2**	**–997.0**	**–23.9**
Net book value				
At 31 March 2021	**619.9**	**2,283.0**	**950.5**	**19**
At 1 April 2020	578.5	2,192.9	909.0	19.1

Case study: debtors

Debtors are individuals or entities that owe the business money. The transport company has various categories of debtor.

	2021 £m	2020 £m
Amounts receivable from customers	123.0	134.2
Owed by immediate holding company	22.1	23.2
Owed by fellow subsidiary companies	20.1	20.6
Owed by other group companies	0.2	–
Owed by associate companies	1.8	1.6
Prepayments	6.1	3.9
Contract assets	2.1	–
Other debtors	9.7	6.1
	185.1	**189.6**

Prepayments for services that will be received in the future, which the business has already been paid for

TOTAL

£m
5,154.1
243.3
–39.1
5,358.3
–1,454.6
–61.5
30.2
–1,485.9
3,872.4
3,699.5

Case study: creditors

Creditors are individuals or entities that the business owes money to. They are in credit to the transport company.

Individuals or entities that are owed money for supplying raw materials or components

Money owed to related companies that are owned by the same group

Payment to shareholders

Tax and employee benefit payments

	2021 £m	2020 £m
Trade creditors	12.0	19.1
Amounts owed to subsidiary company	20.4	18.3
Amounts owed to other group companies	0.5	0.5
Dividend	24.0	24.0
Other creditors	4.2	3.2
Corporation tax	2.6	99
Tax and social security	2.9	2.7
Accrued expenses	55.1	49.1
Contract liabilities	60.5	58.5
	182.2	**274.4**

Cash-flow statement

The cash-flow statement shows the movement of cash during the last accounting period. It is important because it reveals a company's liquidity – whether or not it has more money coming in than going out.

How to read a cash-flow statement

The statement of cash flows, to give it its official title, answers the key question of whether a business is making enough money to sustain itself and provide surplus capital to grow in the future, pay any debts, and give out dividends. Figures in brackets are negative numbers.

Case study: cash-flow statement

By analysing this fictional manufacturing company's statements, which includes a comparison to the previous year, decision-makers can base future plans on past cash flows.

	Year to 31 March 2021 £m	Year to 31 March 2020 £m
Net cash inflow from operating activities	340.7	349.4
Net cash from investing activities	–255.3	–245.6
Taxation paid	–28.4	–23.7
Net cash flow before financing activities	57	80.1
Net cash flow from financing activities	12	–141.8
Increase/decrease in cash and cash equivalents	69	–61.7
Opening cash and cash equivalents	–22.4	39.3
Closing cash and cash equivalents	46.6	–22.4
Increase/decrease in cash and cash equivalents	**69**	**–61.7**

Using profit before tax as a starting point, non-cash income and expenses are deducted to reach net cash inflow from operating activities

Returns on investment in this case is total interest received minus total interest paid, as well as interest paid on finance lease rentals

Taxation is the sum of all taxes paid and tax credits received

This is the sum of the figures above

Includes changes in borrowings and loans, and dividends paid

This is the change in cash flow, calculated by adding the two figures above – net cash flow before financing activities and net cash flow from financing activities – and must equal the difference between opening and closing cash flow for the year

This is the change in cash flow over the year, calculated from the closing cash position minus the opening cash position

How it works

The cash-flow statement is often more useful for investors assessing a business's health than other key statements, because it shows how the core activities are performing. The profit and loss statement, for example, obscures this by adding in non-cash factors such as depreciation. Similarly, the balance sheet is more concerned with assets than liquidity.

Three types of cash flow

Cash refers to actual money as well as cash equivalents including cash at the bank, bank overdrafts, and short-term, highly liquid investments for which there is little risk of a change in value. Cash does not include interest, depreciation, or bad debts (debts written off).

Cash flow from operating activities

The bulk of cash flow usually comes from operations, and is worked out with a formula. The change in working capital (current assets minus current liabilities) can be a negative figure.

$$\left(\begin{array}{c} \text{REVENUE} - \\ \text{COST OF} \\ \text{SALES} \end{array} \right) - \left(\text{TAXES} + \begin{array}{c} \text{REPAIR} \\ \text{COSTS} \end{array} + \begin{array}{c} \text{ANY CHANGE} \\ \text{IN WORKING} \\ \text{CAPITAL} \end{array} \right) = \begin{array}{c} \text{CASH FLOW} \\ \text{FROM OPERATING} \\ \text{ACTIVITIES} \end{array}$$

Cash flow from operating activities in practice

In this example, a juice company sells £100 worth of orange juice after spending £20 on oranges. It pays 25 per cent of its £80 earnings in tax. Its juicing machine incurs a repair expense of £20 over the period which is another cash outlay. There is no change in working capital (short-term assets to cover short-term debt).

A JUICE COMPANY SELLS **£100** WORTH OF ORANGE JUICE

-

AND SPENDS **£20** ON ORANGES

IT PAYS **25%** OF ITS EARNINGS IN TAX

+

ITS JUICING MACHINE INCURS A REPAIR EXPENSE OF **£20** OVER THE PERIOD

+

NO CHANGE IN WORKING CAPITAL **£0**

=£80 CASH FLOW FROM OPERATING ACTIVITIES

Cash flow from investing activities

Buying or selling assets or investments is in this category. This figure is usually a cash outflow (negative figure) due to buying more than selling, but can be positive if there are significant sales.

Cash flow from financing activities

This includes buying or selling stock and paying out debt or dividends. Money made from selling something is called cash inflow; money lost through paying out is cash outflow.

Total cash flow

Adding all three cash flows gives the total. Separating out the three types shows decision-makers the health of core activities as opposed to financing and investing, which bear little relation to day-to-day operations.

Environmental accounting

Environment regulations force companies to consider the impact of their activities and to adopt corporate social responsibility (CSR) as they grapple with legislation, climate change, and public opinion.

How it works

Globally, there are reams of different environment acts spread across multiple jurisdictions that affect the companies operating within their borders in different ways. Areas protected by environment acts include the atmosphere, fresh water, the marine environment, nature conservation, nuclear safety, and noise pollution. International acts are usually ratified by each country individually before taking effect there. An example of a common global means of reducing greenhouse gas emissions is emissions trading ("cap and trade"), by which companies must buy a permit for each tonne of CO_2 they emit over a certain level. Those emitting under the agreed level can sell their permits to other companies.

Environmental credentials

Most companies include a section on environmental accounting in their financial statement. Some details are required by law, but the statement also gives an opportunity to showcase environmental credentials to stakeholders.

Society

❯ **Programmes and practices** that assess and manage the impact of operations on communities

❯ **Fines and sanctions** for non-compliance with regulations

Product responsibility

❯ **Life-cycle stages** in which the health-and-safety impact of products and services are assessed for improvement

❯ **Adherence to laws**, standards, and voluntary codes relating to marketing communications

🔍 CASE STUDY

The Tata Group

The Indian multinational conglomerate prides itself as a values-driven organization and seeks to protect the environment through the efforts of its various businesses, and the support of environmental NGOs via its philanthropic Tata Trusts. Projects include:

❯ Tata Chemicals has established a 150-acre botanical reserve on the site of a factory in Mithapur, Gujarat, protecting indigenous and other plant species.

❯ Tata Motors has created 245 acres of urban wetlands within its plant in Pune, western India, attracting 150 bird species and 60 types of butterfly.

❯ In the last 30 years, Tata Power has planted more than 18 million trees around the Walwan Dam and its hydroelectric facilities in Maharashtra state.

❯ Other initiatives include efforts to protect turtles and whale sharks, as well as flood relief in Kerala.

GREENHOUSE GAS EMISSIONS

In some countries, companies are legally obliged to provide details of their greenhouse gas emissions. This is usually presented as a table within the environmental accounting section of the company's annual review. It includes direct and indirect emissions – by the company itself and by third parties – of gas, diesel, and other fuels; sulphur oxides and nitrous oxides; methane; and other ozone-depleting substances. In this table, from a fictional utility company, emissions are shown as $ktCO_2$ equivalents.

Appointed business	Direct fuel use	Grid electricity	Third parties	Total 2020–21	Total 2019–20
Gas, diesel, other fuels	7	0	2	9	7
Grid electricity	0	120	0	120	115
Transport	11	0	2	13	12
Methane	20	0	3	23	23
Nitrous oxide	12	0	5	17	18
Exported renewable	0	-6	0	-6	-5
TOTAL (net emissions)	50	114	12	176	170

Economic

> **Financial implications**, risks, and opportunities for the organization's activities due to climate change

> **Financial assistance** received from the government

Human rights

> **Investment agreements** that include human-rights clauses or that have undergone human-rights screening

> **Suppliers and contractors** that have undergone screening on human rights; actions taken to address any issues

Labour practices

> **Workforce** by employment type, contract, and region

> **Average hours of training** per year, per employee by employee category

> **Ratio of basic salary** of men to women by employment category

Environmental

> **Direct and indirect** energy consumption

> **Waste by type** and disposal method

> **Water withdrawal** by source; discharge by destination and quality

> **Fines and sanctions** for non-compliance with regulations

Depreciation

When a company buys an asset, its cost can be deducted from income for accounting and tax purposes. Depreciation allows the company to spread the cost, by calculating the asset's decline in value over time.

How it works

If a business buys a long-lived asset, such as a vehicle, machinery, or factory equipment to help it earn income, this expenditure can be offset as a cost against income earned. However, not all this income will be generated in the year of purchase and, over time, the asset will age and become less beneficial to the business, until it becomes outdated or unusable.

Accountants do two things to turn the declining value into a tax advantage. Firstly, they work out how much the asset's value decreases over a period of time –

typically a year. Secondly, they match that loss in value to the amount of income earned in that period, so depreciation becomes a deduction from taxable income.

There are many different ways to calculate depreciation. The method a company uses may depend on the kind of business, the type of asset, tax rules, or personal preference. In the US, companies must use MACRS (Modified Accelerated Cost Recovery System), a combination of straight-line and double declining balance methods, while the UK tax authorities set a system of capital allowances for different asset types.

Calculating depreciation

The straight-line method is the simplest way of working out depreciation and can be applied to most assets. Depreciation is calculated along a timeline, with value loss spread evenly over the asset's economic life. Scrap value is deducted from purchase value and the remainder is split into equal portions over time.

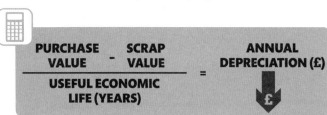

$$\frac{\text{PURCHASE VALUE} - \text{SCRAP VALUE}}{\text{USEFUL ECONOMIC LIFE (YEARS)}} = \text{ANNUAL DEPRECIATION (£)}$$

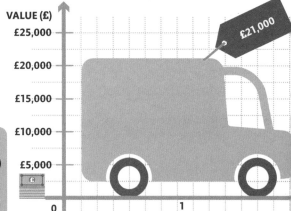

VALUE (£)
£25,000
£20,000
£15,000
£10,000
£5,000

£21,000

0   1

Example

A garden business buys a new van for £25,000. The tax office sets its scrap value at £5,000 after five years of use.

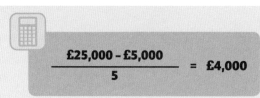

$$\frac{£25,000 - £5,000}{5} = £4,000$$

Year 1 After a year, the van's value has depreciated by £4,000 (its purchase value minus its scrap value, divided by its useful economic life). Its value is now £21,000.

TYPICAL LIFE OF FIXED ASSETS

Tax authorities often specify the typical useful (economic) life of a particular asset. This helps to standardize depreciation, and to eliminate uncertainty about value and the number of years over which an asset can be depreciated.

RACEHORSES
3 years

OFFICE FURNITURE
7 years

FENCES
15 years

Time (years)

IT EQUIPMENT
5 years

FRUIT-BEARING TREES
10 years

OFFICE BUILDINGS
39 years

60%
the value the average car loses after three years

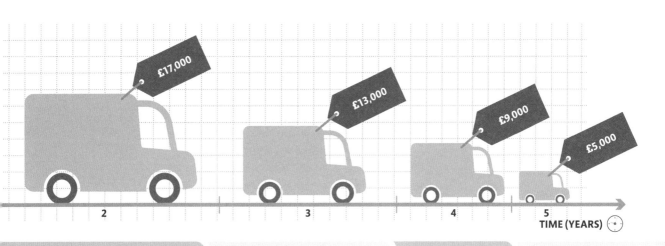

Year 2 After the second year, the value has depreciated by a further £4,000. The van will lose an equal amount of value each year for the next three years of its useful economic life.

Year 3 At the end of the third year, the van has depreciated by another £4,000, and its book value is £13,000, although its actual value may be more or less.

Year 4 The van has depreciated by a further £4,000, to £9,000, at the end of four years of life.

Year 5 By the end of year five, the van is valued at only £5,000 – its scrap value.

Applying depreciation

When calculating depreciation, there are a number of different factors to consider. For instance, a business needs to be able to predict the number of years an asset will last. Helpfully, tax authorities in most countries issue guidelines to accountants and businesses with estimates of the useful economic life of many common business assets.

Finance staff are trained to choose between the many methods of calculating depreciation to use for a given asset. Each method reflects a different pattern of depreciation, with some being more suitable for particular categories of assets. For example, the "accelerated" methods that chart rapid depreciation at the beginning of an asset's life are more suitable for technology, while the "activity" methods that link depreciation to actual hours of use or number of units produced are best suited to transport and production lines.

Again, tax authorities in most countries offer guidelines on which method to use. Although it is technically possible for a company to use two different methods for their own accounting and for tax purposes, this is best avoided.

⚠ WARNING

Misusing depreciation

❯ **The wrong method** A company has to use a method that is permissible for an asset type

❯ **Frontloading** Opting for an accelerated method can result in a taxable gain if an asset is sold early, for more than its book value

❯ **Claiming beyond useful life** Depreciation cannot be claimed after an asset's useful life

❯ **Ignoring depreciation** If a company fails to claim depreciation, it has to report a gain from the sale, despite the loss on deductions

---

Other depreciation methods

There are many different methods of calculating depreciation. Some are favoured by particular tax regimes, while others are specifically applicable to certain industries and types of asset, and their patterns of value loss.

Double declining balance method

This method is used to claim more depreciation in the first years after purchase, which is useful for assets that lose most of their value early on. It reduces a company's net income in the early years of an asset's life, but generates initial tax savings.

$$\left(\frac{\text{PURCHASE VALUE – SCRAP VALUE}}{\text{USEFUL ECONOMIC LIFE (YEARS)}} \right) \times 2 = \text{ANNUAL DEPRECIATION (\%)}$$

When to use it This accelerated method can be used for assets that lose most value early on, such as computers or a delivery vehicle.

Sum of the years' digits method (SYD)

Depreciation is calculated by dividing each year of the asset's life by the sum of the total years to give a percentage of the depreciable value. If the asset's useful life is 5 years, then the sum of the years as digits is 15 (5 + 4 + 3 + 2 + 1). In year 1, it loses 33 per cent (5 ÷ 15), in year 2, 27 per cent (4 ÷ 15), and so on.

$$\text{(PURCHASE VALUE – SCRAP VALUE)} \times \left(\frac{\text{REMAINING USEFUL LIFE}}{\text{SUM OF THE YEARS' DIGITS}} \right) = \text{ANNUAL DEPRECIATION (\%)}$$

When to use it This is another accelerated method, which can also be used for vehicles that lose most of their value early on.

DEPRECIATION ON THE BALANCE SHEET

A company's accounts have to list all assets held by the company, including all fixed assets such as property and equipment. The accumulated depreciation of these fixed assets over the year is deducted from their value at the start of the year to give the end-of-year total. Without a depreciation figure, the accounts would give a false reflection of the finances of the business. The assets would appear as their original cost value and that might well exceed their current value.

Fixed assets are shown distinct from current assets

Depreciation of fixed assets is deducted

Total assets are calculated after depreciation has been deducted

Previous year's total assets can be compared

COMPANY NAME		BALANCE SHEET
Assets	£	£
Current assets:	**2020**	**2021**
Cash	17,467.00	8,023.00
Investments	4,853.00	3,367.00
Inventories	1,056.00	2,138.00
Accounts receivable	2,165.00	3,600.00
Pre-paid expenses	3,000.00	3,000.00
Other	860.00	976.00
Total current assets	**29,401.00**	**21,104.00**
Fixed assets:	**2020**	**2021**
Property and equipment	64,553.00	58,219.00
Leasehold improvements	4,780.00	2,679.00
Equity and other investments	3,789.00	4,587.00
Less accumulated depreciation	5,625.00	4,171.00
Total fixed assets	**67,497.00**	**61,314.00**
Other assets:	**2020**	**2021**
Goodwill	1,577.00	1,650.00
Total other assets	**1,577.00**	**1,650.00**
Total assets	**£98,475.00**	**£84,068.00**

Units of production method

When a company uses an asset to produce quantifiable units, such as pages printed by a photocopier, it can claim depreciation with this method, which calculates depreciation according to the number of units an asset produces in a year.

$$\text{(PURCHASE VALUE – SCRAP VALUE)} \times \left(\frac{\text{UNITS PRODUCED PER YEAR}}{\text{LIFETIME PRODUCTION}} \right) = \text{DEPRECIATION (PER UNIT)}$$

When to use it This method is typically used by factories to calculate depreciation on machines that produce units of goods.

Hours of service method

In this method, the asset's decline in value is measured according to the number of actual hours it is in use. To calculate depreciation using this method, the company measures the hours of use per year as a percentage of the estimated total lifetime hours. It is particularly useful for transport industries.

$$\text{(PURCHASE VALUE – SCRAP VALUE)} \times \left(\frac{\text{HOURS USED PER YEAR}}{\text{LIFETIME HOURS}} \right) = \text{DEPRECIATION (PER HOUR)}$$

When to use it This method may be used to match an aeroplane's flying hours with the revenue generated from those hours.

Amortization and depletion

Similar concepts to depreciation, amortization and depletion are used by accountants to show how intangible assets and natural resources respectively are used up.

How it works

Amortization is how the cost of purchasing an intangible asset, such as copyright of an artwork, is spread over a period of time, usually its useful lifetime. It is shown as a reduction in the value of the intangible asset on the balance sheet and an expense on the income statement. In lending, amortization can also mean the paying off of debts over time. Depletion shows the exhaustion of natural resources such as coal mines, forests, or natural gas.

How to calculate amortization

There are two types of amortization, one for spreading the cost of an intangible asset, the other for loan repayment. Both are calculated in similar ways, but loan repayments are worked out as a percentage.

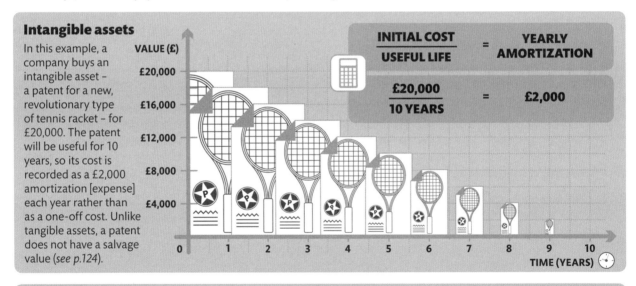

Intangible assets

In this example, a company buys an intangible asset – a patent for a new, revolutionary type of tennis racket – for £20,000. The patent will be useful for 10 years, so its cost is recorded as a £2,000 amortization [expense] each year rather than as a one-off cost. Unlike tangible assets, a patent does not have a salvage value (*see p.124*).

$$\frac{\textbf{INITIAL COST}}{\textbf{USEFUL LIFE}} = \textbf{YEARLY AMORTIZATION}$$

$$\frac{\textbf{£20,000}}{\textbf{10 YEARS}} = \textbf{£2,000}$$

VALUE (£): £20,000, £16,000, £12,000, £8,000, £4,000

TIME (YEARS): 0, 1, 2, 3, 4, 5, 6, 7, 8, 9, 10

Loan percentage

If a company has a loan outstanding worth £150,000, and pays off £3,000 of this loan each year, then £3,000 of the loan has been amortized. It can also be said that two per cent of the loan has been amortized, as it will take 50 years to repay the loan at this rate.

$$\frac{\textbf{COST OF LOAN}}{\textbf{YEARLY REPAYMENT}} = \frac{\textbf{YEARS TO REPAY}}{\textbf{100}} = \%$$

$$\frac{\textbf{150,000}}{\textbf{3,000}} = \frac{\textbf{50}}{\textbf{100}} = \textbf{2\%}$$

GOODWILL

In business, goodwill describes an intangible asset based on a company's reputation, including loyal customers and suppliers, brand name, and public profile. Goodwill arises when one company buys another for more than the fair market value of its net assets (total assets minus total liabilities). For example, if Company A buys Company B for £10 million but the total sum of its assets and liabilities is £9 million, the goodwill is worth £1 million. According to International Financial Reporting Standards since 2001, goodwill does not amortize, so it does not appear as amortization in financial statements. However, if the value of goodwill falls (through negative publicity, for example) it can be recorded as an impairment.

✓ NEED TO KNOW

> **Intangible assets** Non-physical assets, such as patents, trademarks, brand recognition, and copyright; their valuation is sometimes subjective

> **Patent** A licence granted by a government or authority giving the owner exclusive rights for making or owning an invention

How to calculate depletion

Like amortization, depletion is calculated using the straight-line method (*see pp.124–125*) unless there is a particular reason to use another method.

In this example, a logging company buys a forest with an estimated 60,000 trees for £10 million. The original salvage value is £1.5 million, but the company spends £500,000 on building log transport roads in the forest, bringing it down to £1 million. The company cuts down 6,000 trees during each accounting period.

$$\frac{\text{COST – SALVAGE VALUE}}{\text{TOTAL UNITS}} \times \frac{\text{UNITS}}{\text{EXTRACTED}} = \frac{\text{DEPLETION}}{\text{EXPENSE}}$$

$$\frac{10{,}000{,}000 - 1{,}000{,}000}{60{,}000} \times 6{,}000 = £900{,}000$$

NUMBER OF TREES — £10 MILLION, £9.1 MILLION, £8.2 MILLION, £7.3 MILLION, £6.4 MILLION, £5.5 MILLION, £4.6 MILLION, £3.7 MILLION, £2.8 MILLION, £1.9 MILLION, £1 MILLION

60,000 — 50,000 — 40,000 — 30,000 — 20,000 — 10,000 — 0

TIME (YEARS) 1 2 3 4 5 6 7 8 9 10

Management accounting

For a company's management to anticipate profit and loss, plan cash flow, and set effective goals for the business, the coming year's incomings and outgoings need to be set out in detail. Unlike financial accounting, which is primarily for external users such as investors, lenders, or regulators, management or cost accounting takes place within a business to project expected sales revenue and expenses, so that the business can decide how to best use its available resources.

Management accounting process

Planning is done for the financial (fiscal) year that lies ahead – this is also called the accounting year and is made up of 12 consecutive months. Start and end dates differ from country to country.

Department budgets

Managers estimate what funds will be needed for expected outgoings. See pp.136–137.

Purchase orders (POs)

POs tell the finance department exactly how much money to reserve for payment.

Timesheets

Staff employed on an hourly or daily basis fill in timesheets; these help managers calculate overall staff costs. See pp.140–141.

Invoices

Invoices submitted by contractors and suppliers have to be matched against purchase orders and paid out. See pp.134–135.

Goods received

Employees log receipt of merchandise, describing what the goods or services are and the quantity received.

Management

Managers create budgets and document business costs to monitor business performance, and plan for the short and medium term. The information they collate sheds light on the financial implications of ongoing projects.

Information is passed to finance department.

US$**157** billion

combined revenue of the Big Four accounting firms* in 2020

* Deloitte, PwC, Ernst & Young, and KPMG

COST ACCOUNTING PRINCIPLES

The Chartered Institute of Management Accounting (CIMA) in the UK and the American Institute of Certified Public Accountants (AICPA), with members in 177 countries, have established Global Management Accounting Principles (GMAP).

❯ **Communication provides insight that is influential** Facilitate good decision-making through discussion.

❯ **Information is relevant** Source best material.

❯ **Stewardship builds trust** Protect financial and non-financial assets, reputation, and value of organization.

❯ **Impact on value is analysed** Develop models to demonstrate outcomes in different scenarios.

Cost of production report (CPR)

CPR shows all of the costs that can be charged to a particular department. *See pp.140–143.*

Budget reports

Reports help management to determine the accuracy of budgets and analyse business performance. *See pp.136–137.*

Cash-flow statement

This shows how well the business will be able to meet its financial obligations and generate cash in the future. *See pp.120–121.*

Balance sheet

The balance sheet estimates the value of assets and inventory held, so that management can reduce it if necessary. *See pp.116–117.*

Profit and loss statement

Also called an income statement, the P&L statement tells management how much money the business made or lost over a particular time period. *See pp.114–115.*

Financial analysis is passed to managers.

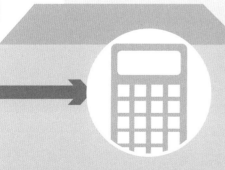

Finance department

Accountants in the finance department (or contracted from outside the business) receive information about the costs from managers. They then use these to generate reports and statements for the managers, who use this information to make decisions for the next financial year.

Cash flow

The money coming in and going out of a business is its cash flow. Inflows arise from financing, operations, and investment, while outflows are expenses, purchases of inventory, and capital costs.

Sales revenue

Cash for goods and services sold

❯ Revenue generated by core operations

❯ Basis of profit – does not have to be repaid, unlike loans or capital

❯ Company must be able to turn revenue into cash (get paid) to maintain cash flow

❯ Also known as cash flow from operating activities

Capital

Investment and lump sums

❯ Main source of cash inflow for start-ups

❯ Additional cash injection after initial start-up or at key stages in a company's growth

❯ Revenue from flotation of private companies (going public) and shares issued by public companies

❯ Also known as cash flow from investing activities

CASH IN

CASH IN

CASH IN

Cash in hand

CASH OUT

"The three most dreaded words in the English language are 'negative cash flow'."

David Tang, entrepreneur, 2011

Salaries and wages

Payments to employees

❯ Money paid to employees who are directly involved in the creation of goods or provision of services

❯ Salaries paid to staff as a fixed amount monthly or weekly (based on an annual rate)

❯ Wages paid to contractors for hours, days, or weeks worked

Overheads

Payment of bills

❯ Day-to-day running costs

❯ Rental cost of commercial property; utility bills – water, electricity, gas, telephone, and internet; office supplies and stationery

❯ Salaries and wages of employees not directly involved in creating goods and services (known as indirect labour)

Loan repayments

Debt servicing and shareholder profit

❯ Interest on long-term loans for asset purchases and on short-term loans for working capital

❯ Repayments on capital loans

❯ Commission paid to factoring companies

❯ Cash distribution to shareholders via share repurchases and dividend payments

How it works

Cash flow is the movement of cash in and out of a business over a set period of time. Cash flows in from sales of goods and services, from loans, capital investment, and other sources. Cash drains out to pay employees, rent and utilities, suppliers, and interest on loans. Timing is key – having enough cash coming in to pay bills on time keeps the company solvent.

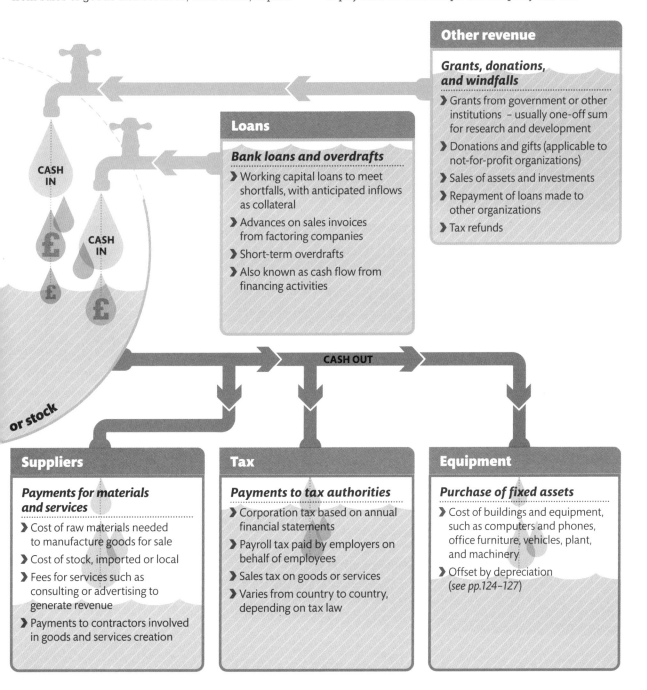

Other revenue

Grants, donations, and windfalls

> Grants from government or other institutions – usually one-off sum for research and development
> Donations and gifts (applicable to not-for-profit organizations)
> Sales of assets and investments
> Repayment of loans made to other organizations
> Tax refunds

Loans

Bank loans and overdrafts

> Working capital loans to meet shortfalls, with anticipated inflows as collateral
> Advances on sales invoices from factoring companies
> Short-term overdrafts
> Also known as cash flow from financing activities

CASH IN

CASH IN

or stock

CASH OUT

Suppliers

Payments for materials and services

> Cost of raw materials needed to manufacture goods for sale
> Cost of stock, imported or local
> Fees for services such as consulting or advertising to generate revenue
> Payments to contractors involved in goods and services creation

Tax

Payments to tax authorities

> Corporation tax based on annual financial statements
> Payroll tax paid by employers on behalf of employees
> Sales tax on goods or services
> Varies from country to country, depending on tax law

Equipment

Purchase of fixed assets

> Cost of buildings and equipment, such as computers and phones, office furniture, vehicles, plant, and machinery
> Offset by depreciation (see pp.124–127)

Cash-flow management

The handling of the cash flow determines the survival of any business. Equally important is a company's ability to convert its earnings into cash, which is known as liquidity. No matter how profitable a business is, it may become insolvent if it cannot pay its bills on time. New businesses may become victims of their own success and fail through "insolvency by overtrading" if, for example, they spend too much on expansion before payments start coming in and run out of cash to pay debts and liabilities. In order to manage cash flow, it is essential for companies to forecast cash inflows and outflows. Sales predictions and cash conversion rates are important. A schedule of when payments are due from customers, and when a business has to pay its own wages, bills, suppliers, debts, and other costs, can help to predict shortfalls. If cash flow is mismanaged, a business may have to pay out before receiving payment, leading to cash shortages. Smart businesses, such as supermarkets, receive stock on credit but they are paid in cash – generating a cash surplus.

⚠ WARNING

Top five cash-flow problems

> **Slow payment** of invoices
> **Credit terms** on sales invoices set at 60 or 120 days, while credit terms on outgoings are 30 days
> **Decline in sales** due to change in economic climate or competition, or product becoming outmoded
> **Underpriced product**, especially in start-ups trying to compete
> **Excessive outlay** on payroll and overheads; buying rather than hiring assets

Positive and negative cash flow

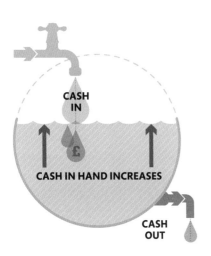

CASH IN

CASH IN HAND INCREASES

CASH OUT

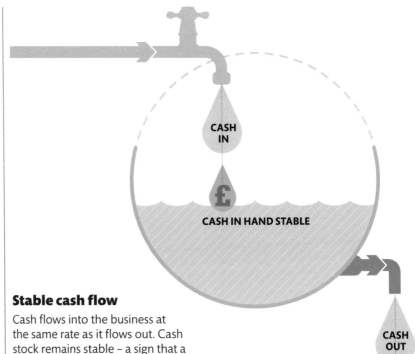

CASH IN

CASH IN HAND STABLE

CASH OUT

Positive cash flow

Cash flowing into the business is greater than cash flowing out. Cash in the tank – stock – increases. A business in this position is thriving.

Stable cash flow

Cash flows into the business at the same rate as it flows out. Cash stock remains stable – a sign that a business is healthy.

NEED TO KNOW

> **Factoring** Transaction in which a business passes its invoices to a third party (factor), which collects payment from the customer for a commission

> **Accounts payable** Payments a business has to make to others

> **Accounts receivable** Payments a business is due to receive

> **Ageing schedule** A table charting accounts payable and accounts receivable according to their dates

> **Cash flow gap** Interval between payments made and received

Cash conversion

Successful businesses convert their product or service into cash inflows before their bills are due. To make the conversion process more efficient, a business may speed up:

> Customer purchase ordering

> Order fulfilment and shipping

> Customer invoicing

> Accounts receivable collection period

> Payment and deposit

76%
of global small business owners are concerned about cash flow impacting on their growth

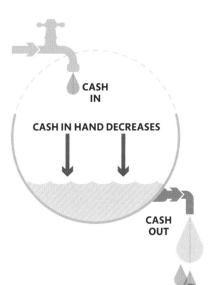

Negative cash flow

Less cash is flowing into the business than is flowing out. Over time, the stock of cash will decrease and the business will face difficulties.

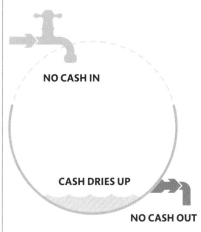

Bankruptcy

If cash flowing out continues to exceed cash flowing in, cash stock levels will drop so low that the business becomes insolvent.

HANDLING THE FLOW

Managing a surplus

> **Move excess cash** into a deposit account where it will earn interest, or make profitable investments.

> **Use cash** to upgrade equipment to improve production efficiency.

> **Expand the business** by taking on new staff, developing products, or buying other companies.

> **Pay creditors** early to improve credit credentials, or pay down debt before it is due.

Managing a shortage

> **Increase sales** by lowering prices, or increase profit by raising them.

> **Issue invoices** promptly and chase payment when it is due.

> **Ask suppliers** to extend credit.

> **Offer discounts** on sales invoices in return for quicker payment.

> **Use an overdraft** or short-term loan to pay off pressing expenses.

> **Continue to forecast** cash flow and plan to avert future problems.

Budgets

Setting the budget for a business involves planning the income and expenditure for the accounting year. This is usually broken down into months so that planned budget and actual figures can be compared.

How it works

Every business needs to budget for anticipated revenue and operating costs within the financial year. Unlike capital budgeting, in which senior management allocate what will be spent on specific projects or assets, revenue budgeting focuses on the overall projections for money coming in and money going out for each month of the coming financial, or accounting, year. Accountants compile operating budgets from each manager in the business, along with expected cash-flow projections for the business, to create a master budget. The master budget can also include figures for any financing that the company is expected to need over the coming year. As the year progresses, the projected budget and the actual money coming in and going out are monitored on a daily, weekly, or monthly basis, so that any deviations from the original budget can be identified, and, if necessary, remedied.

Setting and controlling budgets

Budget-setting is a process that takes place between the department managers, senior management, and finance department in a company to establish and control the cost of each department or project.

46%
of global firms say their revenue forecasts are accurate to within 5%

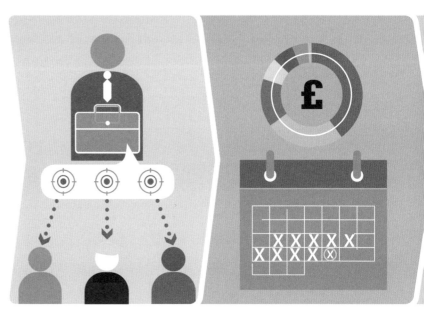

Consultation

Senior management set out the objectives of the company to the department managers. Each manager is then responsible for working out the budget required by their individual department, in order to meet those objectives for the coming year.

Prepare the budget

The budget is usually based on the accounting year, but broken down into shorter periods. Department managers submit their budgets to senior management for approval. These may cover areas such as operating costs (salaries and supplies) and administration (office expenses).

INCREMENTAL AND ZERO-BASED

There are two main approaches to setting budgets:

Incremental budget The budget for the year ahead is based on the previous year's budget. This budget takes into account any changes, such as inflation, which could have an impact on the new calculations. The downside is that previous inaccuracies may be carried forward.

Zero-base budget The coming year's budget starts afresh, with no reference to previous years. This means that each item that is entered into the budget is carefully scrutinized and has to be justified by the department managers. This method makes it easier to see the full cost of all planned changes.

✓ NEED TO KNOW

❯ **Planning, programming, and budgeting systems (PPBS)** A budgeting system used in public service organizations such as town councils and hospitals

❯ **Virement** An amount saved under one cost heading in a budget is transferred to another cost heading to compensate for overspend

❯ **Budget slack** Deliberately under-estimating sales or over-estimating expenses in a budget

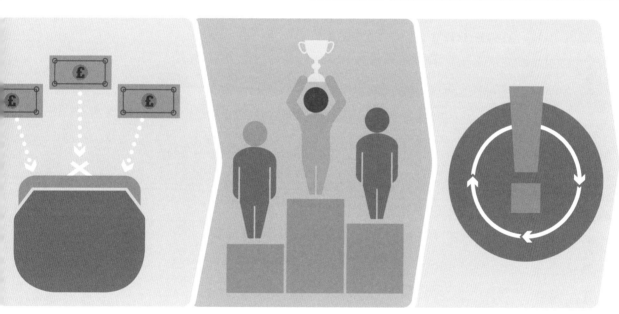

Master budget

Once approved, the budgets from each department are combined into a master budget for the year, which includes: a budgeted profit and loss account, a projected balance sheet, and a budgeted cash-flow statement, which typically shows a month-by-month breakdown.

Measure performance

After each month (or equivalent time period set in the budget), the actual figures realized by the company are compared with the original budget projections. Variations are examined closely to work out whether they are significantly different from the figure in the original budget.

Take action

If necessary, the budget is revised to take into account any unforeseen and continued expenditure, or any saving that was not anticipated. If income is less than expected, action may be taken to alter departmental processes or campaigns in order to reach the targets set in the budget.

Assets and inventory

A company's possessions, or assets, are divided into two categories: fixed (or long-term) assets and current (or short-term) assets. Current assets consist of cash in the bank and inventory.

How it works

Fixed assets are items that enable a business to operate. They tend to be long-term holdings and cannot be easily converted into cash. Fixed assets can be categorized as either tangible or intangible: tangible assets are material objects, while intangible assets have no physical form.

Current assets are held for the short term and used mainly for trading. The most important category in terms of generating revenue is current assets. The key component of these is inventory. Inventory can be finished goods ready for sale, but it can also be the raw materials that will be used for producing the goods.

Assets and inventory in practice

The partial balance sheets below show the current assets of a branch of Super Sports Ltd, a fictional sportswear and sports accessory company. These assets include cash in the bank and inventory held by the company. The inventory in this case consists of all the items in the shop that are ready for sale.

Super Sports Ltd
31 May

Assets	£
Cash at bank	12,000
Inventories	22,000
Total assets	**34,000**

Balance sheet as at 31 May

The "Assets" section of the balance sheet shows that the company holds £22,000 worth of inventory (or goods) at this point in time, as well as £12,000 cash in the bank.

Super Sports Ltd
15 June

Assets	£
Cash at bank	54,000
Inventories	0
Total assets	**54,000**

Balance sheet as at 15 June

Two weeks later, the company sells all of its inventory for £42,000 and receives payment for this sale on the same day. This means that total assets have risen by £20,000 – the profit made on the sale of the inventory – and increases the amount of cash in the bank by £42,000.

TYPES OF INVENTORY

Inventory can include three types of stock, depending on the kind of business being carried out: raw materials, unfinished goods, and finished goods. *See pp.316–317.*

Raw materials

Materials and components scheduled for use in making a product. For example, a chocolate factory will have:

> **Ingredients** in the form of sugar, cocoa mass, cocoa butter, additives, flavourings, and maybe milk or nuts.

> **Foil, plastic, and paper** for the wrappers and packaging

Work in progress

Materials and components that have begun their transformation into finished goods; these may be referred to as "unfinished goods". For instance, a graphic designer will have:

> **Layouts and designs** that are being developed and are awaiting client approval

Finished goods

The stock of completed products, or goods ready for sale to customers. A bookshop, for example, will have:

> **Hardback and paperback books** of various genres and formats supplied by publishing houses

> **Gift items** such as greeting cards and notebooks

Types of fixed asset

Super Sports Ltd owns a range of tangible and intangible fixed assets. As compared to tangible fixed assets, the worth of intangible fixed assets can sometimes be harder to evaluate.

Tangible fixed assets

LAND AND PROPERTY	FURNITURE	IT EQUIPMENT	VEHICLES	TOOLS AND MACHINERY
Retail outlets plus company headquarters	Shop displays and back office furniture	Computers and other IT devices and components	Trucks and branded company cars	Warehouse and distribution equipment

Intangible fixed assets

INTELLECTUAL PROPERTY	TRADEMARKS	BRANDS	COMPUTER SOFTWARE	COPYRIGHT AND ROYALTIES
Brands and designs, creative innovation	Legally protected words and symbols	Own-brands, including value and luxury ranges	Internet portal for online sales	Licensing revenue streams

Costs

Costs are the direct or indirect expenses that a business incurs in order to carry out activities that earn revenue, such as manufacturing goods or providing a service.

How it works

There are two main ways of classifying costs: variable costs, which increase as output increases, and fixed costs, which remain constant; direct and indirect costs, which contribute directly or indirectly to the overall running of the business, and can either vary with the level of production or stay fixed. There are three main costs that businesses need to account for. The first is labour – wages paid to employees to carry out a particular task. Labour can be regarded as a direct cost or overhead, or as variable or fixed. The second is the raw materials used in production and other materials used in service industries – these costs are variable. The third is expenses, which are other costs incurred by the business's activities.

Variable costs

The head chef orders the ingredients that will be required each day. For peak evenings the cost of the food order is higher; for quieter nights, the food order is lower.

LARGE FOOD ORDER

Fixed and variable costs

One way of looking at costs is to split them into two categories: fixed costs, which do not change with the level of business activity, and variable costs, which do change with the level of business activity. This helps accountants to determine how changes in business activity (for example, cutting or increasing production) will affect costs. In reality, some fixed costs will increase once business activity reaches a certain level – these are called stepped fixed costs.

Fixed costs

RENT AND INSURANCE COSTS

LAUNDRY SERVICES

STAFF SALARIES

CLEANING BILL

A restaurant rents premises to cater for 40 diners. The fixed costs are the same whether the restaurant serves 30 or 40 diners a night.

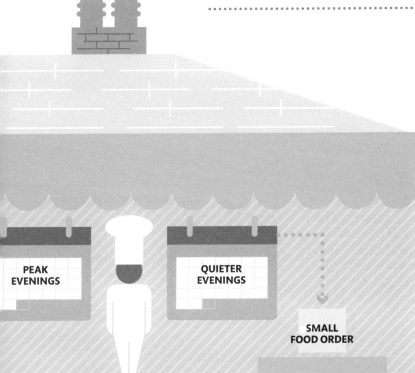

PEAK EVENINGS

QUIETER EVENINGS

SMALL FOOD ORDER

Stepped fixed costs

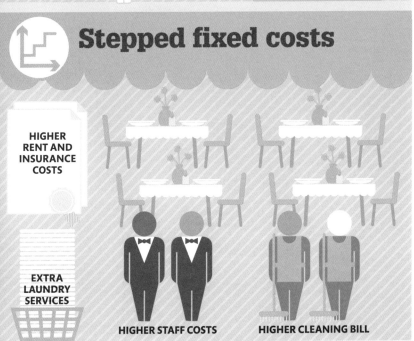

HIGHER RENT AND INSURANCE COSTS

EXTRA LAUNDRY SERVICES

HIGHER STAFF COSTS

HIGHER CLEANING BILL

€**28.5**
the average hourly labour cost in the EU in 2020

The restaurant becomes popular, so the owner rents the premises next door to serve an additional 40 diners a night. The costs that were fixed at a certain level have now doubled.

Product costing and pricing

Knowing the full cost of creating each product that a business sells is a vital piece of information, as it helps to price products accurately and assess the performance of the business.

How it works

Both direct and indirect costs contribute to the cost of a product, whether it is a manufactured good or a service being provided. In order to calculate the cost of a product, it is treated as one unit of production. The direct and indirect costs involved in creating that single unit are then assessed and added together to create the full cost.

25%

the average net profit margin in the banking sector. In food retail, the average is 2%

Full cost pricing

Direct costs can be measured in terms of how materials and labour are used to produce each unit. Indirect costs (overheads) are harder to assess but also need to be factored in so that the full cost of each product can be calculated. Managers and accountants must apportion indirect costs to reflect their contribution to the cost of creating a single product. Once this is ascertained, the full cost of that product can be determined. In general terms, the price is worked out by adding the direct and indirect costs of production with a profit margin that gives an appropriate selling price.

Direct costs
❭ Materials
❭ Direct labour
❭ Direct expenses
❭ All used exclusively to create a product or service for sale

Share of indirect cost
❭ Production and service overheads
❭ Administrative and management overheads
❭ Sales and distribution overheads

OTHER COSTING METHODS

There are several different approaches to costing and pricing depending on the industry, the type and size of the business, and the method of production.

JOB COSTING
Used for a customized order made to a client's specifications – for example, a printing company that prints brochures for a client

BATCH COSTING
Used when a batch of identical products is made – for example, an electrical goods company manufacturing television sets

CONTRACT COSTING
Used for a large one-off job, often the result of a tender process (when a company bids for work) and carried out at the client's site – for example, a construction company erecting houses on a new residential development

PROCESS COSTING
Used for an ongoing and continuous job, which often involves several manufacturing processes, making it difficult to isolate individual unit costs – for example, an oil refinery that processes crude into diesel oil

SERVICE COSTING
Used when the product being sold is a standard service offered to customers – for example, a nail salon offering an express manicure and pedicure within a set period of time and for a fixed price

 Profit margin
❯ Must be able to generate profit for the company
❯ Must be in line with how the product has been marketed
❯ Must be pitched realistically so that customers will buy

LUXURY HOUSE FOR SALE

Selling price
❯ Low: in order to gain market share, or to match competitors
❯ Cost-based: recover direct and indirect costs and profit margin that the market will accept
❯ Service-based: flexible since no manufacturing or distribution cost

Measuring performance

There are two main ways of measuring a company's performance: financial and non-financial. To assess financial performance, a company calculates financial ratios. To assess other areas of the business, a company examines its key performance indicators (KPIs), which help management and staff evaluate performance and how it can improve. KPIs also enable interested outsiders, such as investors, lenders, or analysts, to decide whether to invest in the business.

Financial and non-financial categories

Any company that publishes a financial report will be obliged to set out key figures on the revenue generated and the expenses incurred during the course of its activities. These figures can be compared using mathematical calculations called financial ratios. However, financial ratios alone may not give an accurate vision of the company's future prospects. Non-financial ratios, or key performance indicators, do not measure financial performance, but they do reveal other important characteristics of a company that will ultimately affect its profitability, such as customer loyalty and research and development (R and D) productivity.

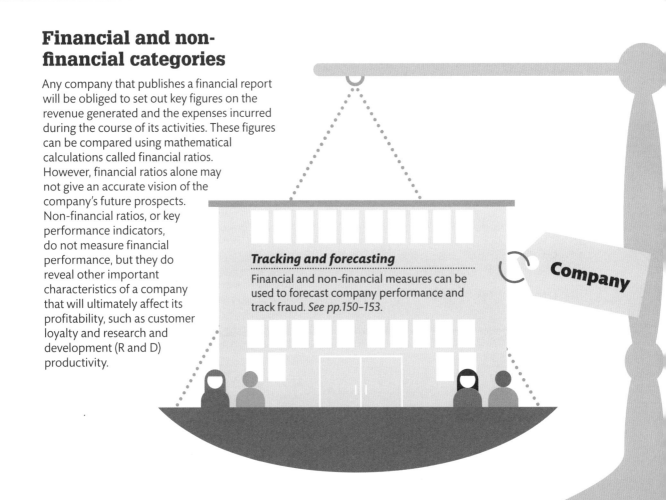

Tracking and forecasting

Financial and non-financial measures can be used to forecast company performance and track fraud. *See pp.150–153.*

Company

TREND ANALYSIS USING PERFORMANCE MEASUREMENTS

A comparison of either financial ratios or KPIs between companies in the same industry and across time is often used to track a company's performance. Current ratios are calculated by dividing current assets by current liabilities: the higher the ratio, the more liquidity a company has.

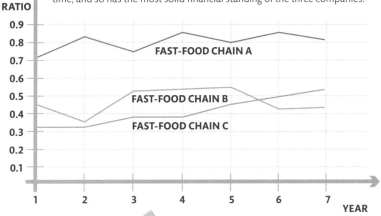

CURRENT RATIO COMPARISON OVER TIME
Fast-food chain A is shown to be a consistently better performer over time, and so has the most solid financial standing of the three companies.

CURRENT RATIO

0.9
0.8
0.7
0.6
0.5
0.4
0.3
0.2
0.1

FAST-FOOD CHAIN A

FAST-FOOD CHAIN B

FAST-FOOD CHAIN C

1   2   3   4   5   6   7   YEAR

Financial measures £

Non-financial measures

THE BIGGER PICTURE

Some professional bodies and services companies, such as the UK's CBI and multinational PwC, undertake regular surveys, interviewing senior executives to find out how optimistic they are about their sector and the wider economy. Such surveys help companies measure their own performance objectively.

Financial ratios

❯ Used by investors and lenders to gauge financial health of an organization: if it's likely to survive economic slump, and what prospects it has for future growth

❯ Standard set of ratios used by the financial industry

❯ Calculated based on figures provided in financial reports

See pp.148–149.

Key performance indicators

❯ Used internally and by investors, as they appear in financial statement

❯ May be calculated daily or even more frequently for internal use

❯ Companies can set diverse KPIs to reflect future goals

❯ Unique to each company

See pp.146–147.

4–10
KPIs are likely to be **crucial** for most companies

Key performance indicators (KPIs)

Key performance indicators (KPIs), or key success indicators (KSIs), are based on a company's goals and vary depending on the company and industry. KPIs are usually stated in a company's annual report.

How it works

KPIs are the non-financial measures of a company's performance – they do not have a monetary value but they do contribute to the company's profitability. Any company department can adopt KPIs to gauge its performance. A KPI for an accounts department might be the percentage of overdue invoices, as this will help determine the department's efficiency. This is an example of a lagging indicator – it is an outcome and therefore easy to measure, but not straightforward to influence. Companies also look for leading indicators, which are focused on inputs and easier to change. A leading KPI for the accounts department might be the percentage of purchase orders raised in advance.

Corporate KPIs

KPIs can be set up as dashboards on computers so that they can be checked frequently. These dashboards show examples of KPIs specific to departments in a company. Having set their KPIs, the departments are subject to managerial review, which could result in action if KPIs are sub-standard.

Accounts

Number of retrospectively raised purchase orders; finance report error rate (measures the quality of report); average cycle time of workflow; number of duplicate payments

Sales and marketing

Net promoter score (NPS – how many customers would recommend company); customer retention rate; customer lifetime value (total amount of money generated by one customer)

Customer services

Number of customer complaints; customer satisfaction (measured over time); average email response time; number of products sold compared to total sales calls made

93%
of companies say their Balanced Scorecard is extremely or very helpful

BALANCED SCORECARD SYSTEM

This strategic system offers a different way of monitoring a company's performance, presenting a more balanced view rather than one solely focused on financial results. It was proposed by Robert Kaplan and David Norton at the Harvard Business School in the 1990s, and over 50 per cent of large companies in the US, Europe, and Asia now use the approach. The Balanced Scorecard consists of four ways to view an organization's performance:

> **Learning and growth**
Employee training and corporate culture

> **Business processes**
Includes specific measurements for monitoring daily performance

> **Customer perspective**
Customer satisfaction

> **Financial perspective**
Traditional financial data

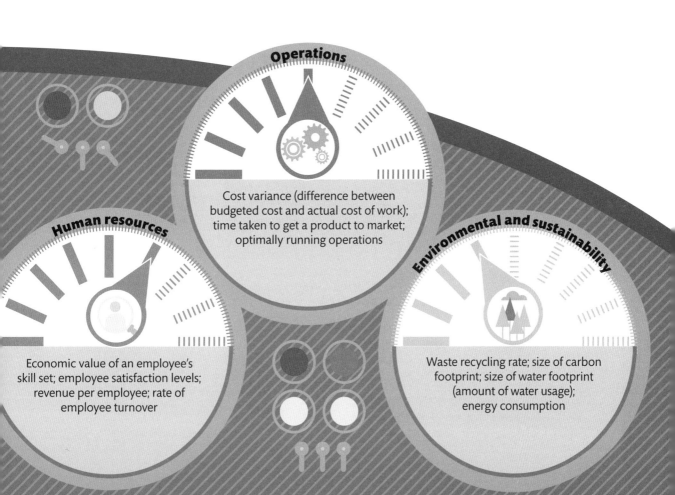

Operations
Cost variance (difference between budgeted cost and actual cost of work); time taken to get a product to market; optimally running operations

Human resources
Economic value of an employee's skill set; employee satisfaction levels; revenue per employee; rate of employee turnover

Environmental and sustainability
Waste recycling rate; size of carbon footprint; size of water footprint (amount of water usage); energy consumption

Financial ratios

Lenders, investors, analysts, internal management, and other interested parties calculate financial ratios to decipher what financial statements are really saying about the state of a business.

How it works

Financial ratios are used to assess the financial standing of a business and identify any problem areas that might affect its future prospects. The process involves comparing two related items in the financial statement, such as net sales to net worth or net income to net sales, and using those ratios to measure the relative performance of the company. There are many different ratios to choose from, depending on the purpose – for example, whether the purpose is to measure the company's ability to provide a good return to shareholders, its capacity to handle debt, or the efficiency with which it operates. The ratios can also be used to compare a business with its competitors or in comparison to specific benchmarks within the company to determine how consistent its financial results are.

Top financial ratios

These are some of the ratios most commonly used by people involved with assessing businesses. They are best considered comparatively and in the context of the economic climate. The ratios are for analysing established companies, usually public ones with shares traded on the stock exchange – start-ups and small-to-medium enterprises generally do not have a full enough range of figures to provide any kind of reliable guide.

Profitability ratios

These are used to see how effective a company is at generating profit; profitability ratios may mirror investment valuation ratios. One example is the operating profit margin ratio. A high ratio is good, as it indicates that a high proportion of revenue (gross income) converted into operating income (profit minus costs).

$$\text{OPERATING PROFIT MARGIN} = \frac{\text{OPERATING INCOME}}{\text{REVENUE}}$$

Other profitability ratios

❯ **Return on equity (ROE) ratio** is measured as net income after tax / shareholders' equity. The higher the ratio, the greater the profitability, but not if a company relies on borrowing.

❯ **EBITDA to sales ratio** is measured as EBITDA (earnings before interest, taxes, depreciation, and amortization) / revenue. It gauges the profitability of core business operations. The higher the margin, the greater the profits.

Efficiency ratios

These show how efficiently the company uses its assets and resources to maximize profits. An example is the sales revenue to capital employed ratio, which indicates a company's ability to generate sales revenue by utilizing its assets. Similar ratios can examine how quickly the company settles its bills and invoices.

$$\text{SALES REVENUE TO CAPITAL EMPLOYED RATIO} = \frac{\text{NET SALES}}{\text{CAPITAL EMPLOYED}}$$

Other efficiency ratios

❯ **Accounts receivable turnover ratio** is measured as net credit sales / average accounts receivable. It shows how efficiently a company turns sales into cash. The higher the ratio, the more frequently money is collected.

❯ **Inventory turnover ratio** is measured as the cost of goods sold / average inventory. It shows how efficiently a company manages its inventory level. A low ratio usually equates to poor sales.

WARNING

Investors beware

Ratio analysis must be used over time – at least four years – to understand how a company has reached its current position, not just what the position is. For instance, if debt has suddenly gone up it could be because the company is branching out into new areas of potential profit or to limit the damage of a poor past decision.

10-14%

the minimum return on investment (ROI) needed to fund a company's future growth

Liquidity ratios

This group of ratios reveals whether or not a company has enough cash or equivalent assets to meet its debt repayments. An example is the working capital ratio (also a measure of efficiency), which indicates whether a company has enough short-term assets to cover its short-term debt.

$$\text{WORKING CAPITAL} = \frac{\text{CURRENT ASSETS}}{\text{CURRENT LIABILITIES}}$$

Other liquidity ratios

❯ **Cash ratio** is measured as total cash (and equivalents) / current liabilities. It shows whether a company's short-term assets could repay its debts. A high ratio is seen as favourable.

❯ **Quick ratio (acid-test ratio)** is measured as current assets minus inventories / current liabilities. It shows how easily a company can repay short-term debt from cash. The higher the ratio, the more easily it can pay.

Solvency ratios

While liquidity ratios look at a company's short-term ability to meet loan repayments, solvency ratios indicate the likelihood of a company being able to continue indefinitely with enough cash or current assets to pay its debts in the long run. An example is the debt to equity ratio.

$$\text{DEBT TO EQUITY RATIO} = \frac{\text{TOTAL LIABILITIES}}{\text{SHAREHOLDERS' EQUITY}}$$

Other solvency ratios

❯ **Equity ratio** is measured as shareholders' funds / total assets. It indicates the company's long-term or prospective solvency position. A high ratio is favourable; a low ratio can signal high risk for creditors.

❯ **Debt ratio** is measured as total liabilities / total assets. It indicates the percentage of the company's assets that are financed by debt. A low ratio is considered favourable.

Investment valuation ratios

These ratios are typically used by investors to gauge the returns they are likely to get if they buy shares in a company. An example is the dividend payout ratio. It indicates how well earnings support the dividend payments — more mature companies tend to have a higher payout ratio.

$$\text{DIVIDEND PAYOUT RATIO} = \frac{\text{YEARLY DIVIDEND PER SHARE}}{\text{EARNINGS PER SHARE}}$$

Other investment valuation ratios

❯ **Net profit margin ratio** is measured as profit after tax / revenue. Another measure of a company's profitability, it is also useful for comparing a company with competitors. The higher the ratio, the more profitable the company.

❯ **Price to earnings ratio** is measured as market value per share / earnings per share. It indicates the value of the company's shares. A high ratio demonstrates good growth potential.

Forecasting

Predicting future business performance is necessary to estimate probable sales, income, costs, and profitability, and so gain investment and maintain confidence in the company.

How it works

Forecasting success or failure relies on historical data – financial statements, financial ratios, and key performance indicators – that reflect business operation and can be tracked over time. The tracked and monitored data can provide an early warning system for potential problems. For small businesses and start-ups, accurate forecasts provide a basis for

Forecasting with Z-score models

Realizing that traditional financial ratios, such as the ratio of costs to revenue, created only a partial picture of a business's financial performance, Altman devised a set formula that combined four or five key ratios to give a Z score. The model has proven 90 per cent accurate in predicting business failure over one year, and 80 per cent accurate over two years.

✓ **Working capital / total assets**
A measure of liquidity: the more working capital in a company, the more it is able to pay its bills.

✓ **Market value of equity / book value of total liabilities**
A measure of the market confidence in the company: a ratio of less than one means the firm is worth less than it owes – it is insolvent.

✓ **Retained earnings / total assets**
A measure of leverage: a high ratio indicates profits are funding growth; a low ratio indicates growth is financed by debt.

✓ **Earnings before interest and taxes / total assets**
A measure of return on assets: it gauges operating income generated by assets.

✓ **Sales / total assets**
A measure of efficiency: the sales generated by the assets.

Corporate success
Efficiently run companies with a healthy balance between assets and liabilities, and profit and debt inspire confidence in investors.

HMS Success

Finding the Z score
Each of the above ratios is multiplied by a specific value, to give them weighting; results are added together to give Z score.

❯ A score of 0.2 or lower means the company is highly likely to fail.

❯ A score of 0.3 or higher means the company is unlikely to fail.

raising external finance, while for larger companies this information provides an indication of financial strength for investors and markets. There are many different prediction methods and models – which ones you choose will depend on exactly what you want to forecast. One of the most frequently used to predict the chances of a business going bankrupt is the Z-score model, devised by Edward Altman, a New York University finance professor, in 1968.

✓ NEED TO KNOW

❯ **Ohlson O score**
Alternative to Z score for predicting failure

❯ **Overtrading** When a company's sales grow faster than its finance

❯ **Undertrading** When a company trades at low levels compared to its finance levels

❯ **Zeta analysis** Second-generation Z-score model

Signs of corporate failure

There are many signs that a company is doing badly and perhaps sliding into insolvency. These signs make investors nervous, which is likely to lower share price if they start selling their shareholding. However, most companies that fail are in profit, but run out of cash.

59%
of organizations say they are now using advanced and predictive analytics

HMS Failure

❌ **Selling assets** to pay off debts

❌ **Cuts** to employee benefits

❌ **Repeated dividend cuts** to shareholders

Bankruptcy occurs if the company cannot pay its debts

❌ **Top management** resigning and taking jobs elsewhere

❌ **Low cash flow**, seen in continued pattern of decline in cash holdings in balance sheet over consecutive years

❌ **High borrowing**, high interest payments and dwindling revenue

❌ **Low profitability**, seen in consistent downslide in profit on profit-and-loss statements from consecutive years

Tracking fraud

For keen observers of financial statements, warning signs that indicate fraudulent business activities may be detected in overly optimistic statements and evasive attitudes of senior management.

How it works

Public companies are required to have their annual financial statements audited (checked) by an independent auditor. It is typically during this process that any financial shenanigans – creative accounting tricks used to manipulate the figures and improve the performance of a company in its financial statements – and outright fraudulent activity is uncovered. It is the auditor's job to ensure that business records and statements are accurate and have been honestly reported. Auditors carry out a systematic examination of the company's records and may identify any irregularities that may indicate fraud. If evidence of fraud is found, the next step is to involve forensic accountants and specialist criminal investigators, who may prosecute the perpetrators.

 NEED TO KNOW

❱ **Asset stripping** Selling off the assets of a company for a profit to raise funds, often resulting in the closure of the business

❱ **Tunnelling** A particular type of fraud in which assets and funds are illicitly transferred to management or shareholders

Red flags indicating fraud

Auditors may be alerted to fraud by a number of recognized warning signs, or "red flags" – these may be either directly to do with the behaviour of the CEO or other top executives, or in the form of irregularities within the financial statements.

6
the average number of fraud incidents reported per company in the last two years

Suspicious figures on financial statements

❱ Cash flows that are negative for three quarters, then suddenly and dramatically become positive

❱ Sudden increase in gross margin, at odds with industry average and company's previous performance pattern

❱ Large sales to companies with dubious track records

❱ Sales recorded before they have been made

❱ Made-up, non-existent sources of revenue

❱ Expenses moved from one company to another, or classified as assets

❱ Ongoing, long-term growth of earnings per share

❱ High payments to executives compared to base salary

How to detect fraud

Procedures should be in place to hold anyone who handles expenses accountable. When these fall short, internal and external auditors need to take more drastic measures.

Applying ratio analysis to reveal key long-term trends (*see* pp.148–149)

LINE-UP: TOP FIVE NOTORIOUS FRAUDS

Some of the worst frauds stem from the most prestigious companies. Enron was one of the top seven US companies, while JPMorgan Chase & Co was the largest American bank when measured by assets.

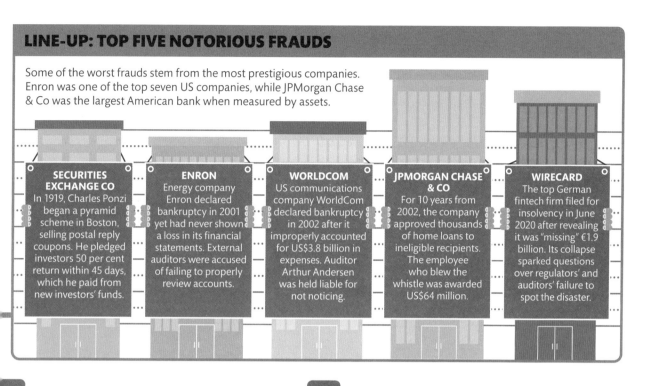

SECURITIES EXCHANGE CO
In 1919, Charles Ponzi began a pyramid scheme in Boston, selling postal reply coupons. He pledged investors 50 per cent return within 45 days, which he paid from new investors' funds.

ENRON
Energy company Enron declared bankruptcy in 2001 yet had never shown a loss in its financial statements. External auditors were accused of failing to properly review accounts.

WORLDCOM
US communications company WorldCom declared bankruptcy in 2002 after it improperly accounted for US$3.8 billion in expenses. Auditor Arthur Andersen was held liable for not noticing.

JPMORGAN CHASE & CO
For 10 years from 2002, the company approved thousands of home loans to ineligible recipients. The employee who blew the whistle was awarded US$64 million.

WIRECARD
The top German fintech firm filed for insolvency in June 2020 after revealing it was "missing" €1.9 billion. Its collapse sparked questions over regulators' and auditors' failure to spot the disaster.

CEO behaviour
> Evasive behaviour by executives over important financial details
> Attempts by CEO to steer auditors away from certain documents

Technicalities
> Late lodgement of sales or earnings adjustments
> Missing approvals or signatures

Setting up confidential hotline for current and past employees or others with knowledge of the company

Using the element of surprise, such as undertaking an aggressive internal audit without prior warning

Conducting a surprise cash count to determine whether current cash flow matches statements

Data mining with auditing software to detect any mismatch between past patterns and current statements

Raising finance and capital

When a company needs additional funds it can either use internal or external sources, or both, depending on whether it is looking for large amounts of funding for long-term growth, such as an expansion, or smaller amounts for short-term expenses, such as to cover operating costs. In addition, the number of external sources available depends on whether the business is well established or whether it is relatively new and does not have much of a track record.

Sources of finance and capital

When considering the prospect of raising finance, the finance directors will first evaluate the financial health of the company. They will then decide what proportion of the company will be funded by equity (the company's own reserves of cash and money raised from issuing shares) and what proportion will be funded by borrowing money from an outside source, such as a bank, so that the company takes on debt.

59% of US financial managers say financial flexibility is the most important factor in deciding how much debt the company takes on

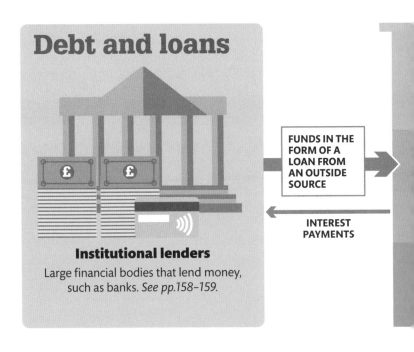

Debt and loans

Institutional lenders
Large financial bodies that lend money, such as banks. *See pp.158–159.*

FUNDS IN THE FORM OF A LOAN FROM AN OUTSIDE SOURCE

INTEREST PAYMENTS

EVALUATING CAPITAL STRUCTURE

When investors consider buying shares in a company, they look at its capital structure to assess the future prospects of the business. The capital structure refers to the percentage of a company's finances made up of funds from shares and earnings, called equity, and the percentage made up from borrowed funds, or debt. When evaluating capital structure, investors consider the following:

❯ As a general rule, companies with more equity than debt are considered less risky to invest in because their assets outweigh their liabilities. So a company with significantly more equity than debt has a low debt-to-equity ratio and is generally seen to be a low-risk investment.

❯ A company with significantly more debt than equity has a high debt-to-equity ratio and is more risky as an investment.

❯ Debt is not always bad. If interest rates are low, a company could take on more debt to fund expansion, as long as the revenue it makes from the borrowed funds is greater than the interest payable. So although this company may be more risky, it may also have greater potential for growth – this is known as "gearing". *See pp.174–175.*

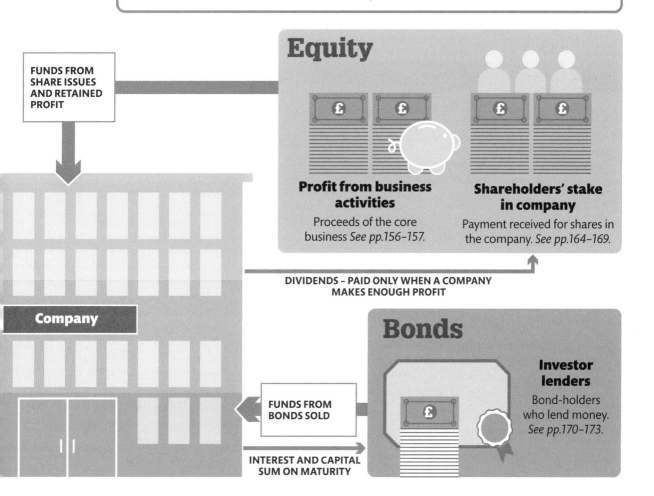

FUNDS FROM SHARE ISSUES AND RETAINED PROFIT

Equity

Profit from business activities
Proceeds of the core business *See pp.156–157.*

Shareholders' stake in company
Payment received for shares in the company. *See pp.164–169.*

DIVIDENDS – PAID ONLY WHEN A COMPANY MAKES ENOUGH PROFIT

Company

Bonds

Investor lenders
Bond-holders who lend money. *See pp.170–173.*

FUNDS FROM BONDS SOLD

INTEREST AND CAPITAL SUM ON MATURITY

Internal finance

Most companies prefer to secure funding from their own internal resources, rather than either take on debt through borrowing or give up a stake in the company by issuing shares, both of which cost more.

How it works

When a business needs funds, or capital, to pay for expansion or investment in order to maintain its current operations, it is faced with two choices: either find the money from external sources, or it must find the money from within the organization itself. Since there are costs attached to bringing in funds from outside sources, such as interest that has to be paid on a bank loan, the business managers must weigh up the opportunity cost of using its own funds – that is, the profit it could earn by investing those funds – against the cost of financing.

Raising internal finance

Whether a company's need for additional funds is long- or short-term, steps can be taken to increase the level of funds within the company.

Short-term finance

For businesses keen to raise funds without recour to external sources, there are three main strategie they can implement to maximize the amount of cash available for day-to-day operations and capital expenditure.

Tighten credit control

Strategies include chasing debtors so that invoices are paid on time; ensuring new customers are creditworthy by conducting strict credit checks; and setting a 30-day payment term.

Delay payment

Large suppliers may offer a discount for early payment, but they may also allow a company longer terms for payment, boosting cash levels in the short term.

THE RECENCY BIAS

When a company receives payment for its invoices on time this helps maintain its levels of funds. Interestingly, invoices issued straight after completion of work tend to get paid sooner than those invoices that are sent later. Recency Bias explains this phenomenon: the brain prioritizes recent events over those that occurred longer ago.

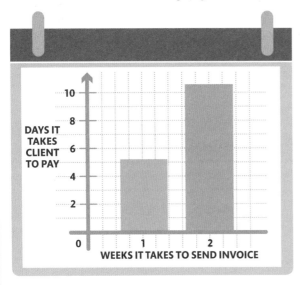

DAYS IT TAKES CLIENT TO PAY

WEEKS IT TAKES TO SEND INVOICE

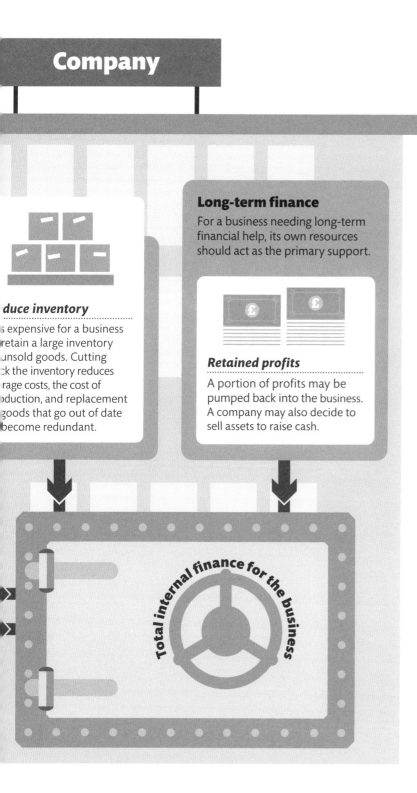

Company

Long-term finance

For a business needing long-term financial help, its own resources should act as the primary support.

Retained profits

A portion of profits may be pumped back into the business. A company may also decide to sell assets to raise cash.

duce inventory

s expensive for a business
retain a large inventory
unsold goods. Cutting
ck the inventory reduces
rage costs, the cost of
oduction, and replacement
goods that go out of date
become redundant.

Total internal finance for the business

USING PROFITS TO FUND EXPANSION

A company seeking to grow may choose to fund the expansion with its profits. This option offers both advantages and disadvantages.

Pros

〉 The use of profits means that no interest payment has to be made, unlike on money that is borrowed.

〉 Existing owners and directors are able to retain full control over the business, rather than sharing it with new investors.

〉 The company is able to keep a low debt profile, which will appeal to future investors and lenders.

Cons

〉 Profits can take time to build up sufficiently to fund expansion.

〉 Withholding dividends may upset some shareholders who prefer to receive the profit as dividends.

〉 Opportunity to earn funds from investing profit rather than spending it can be lost.

37

the average number of days **it takes a UK company to** pay a supplier invoice

External finance

When business growth or unforeseen expenses cannot be met using internal sources of finance, such as retained profit, organizations must rely on finding funds from lenders or investors.

How it works

External financial support comes in various forms, including bank loans and issuing shares. Yet the outside sources of finance available depend on the amount a company requires, and whether the money is needed to resolve a short-term issue, such as cash flow, or for the long-term growth of the business. While short-term finance is easier to secure, finding larger sums for an expansion is more challenging. A company that is either already listed on a stock exchange or is preparing to enlist will be able to raise the capital through the sale of shares. However, an unlisted company may struggle to raise a comparable amount. A company with a large amount of debt will also find it hard to raise funds, since lenders or investors may see the business as risky.

Raising external finance

Generating funds from external sources can be a challenge, especially when securing investors. However, the funds do not necessarily need to take the form of a loan. There are a number of strategies that can be implemented through working with external parties in order to provide a company with good working capital.

43%

of US small businesses applied for new financing in 2019

Short-term finance

A company can make a range of financial agreements with outside parties to raise cash in the short-term and help to provide the company with immediate funds.

Bank overdraft

Borrow from business current account up to an agreed limit, with interest typically charged at a high rate.

Asset financing

Borrow against assets owned by the business, including inventory, equipment, and property. These can be seized by lender if firm defaults.

Invoice discounting

Borrow money against sales invoices that customers are yet to pay (often at a disadvantageous rate).

DEBT FACTORING

Debt factoring is another means by which businesses can raise short-term cash. A company sells unpaid invoices (accounts receivable) to a third party, known as a "factor". The factor advances the company a major portion of the amount, retains the rest until the account is paid, then charges a fee.

Company negotiates
an agreement in which its unpaid receivables (invoices) are sold at a discount to a "factor".

Company sends out
invoices to customers, and copies these to the factor. Customer now owes payment to factor.

Factor pays company
an agreed percentage of the invoices (typically 80–90 per cent) within a few days of receipt.

Customer pays
factor the invoice amount after 30 days (or more if terms of payment are longer).

Factor pays remaining
invoice amount to company, minus a fee (usually 2–5 per cent of the invoice amount).

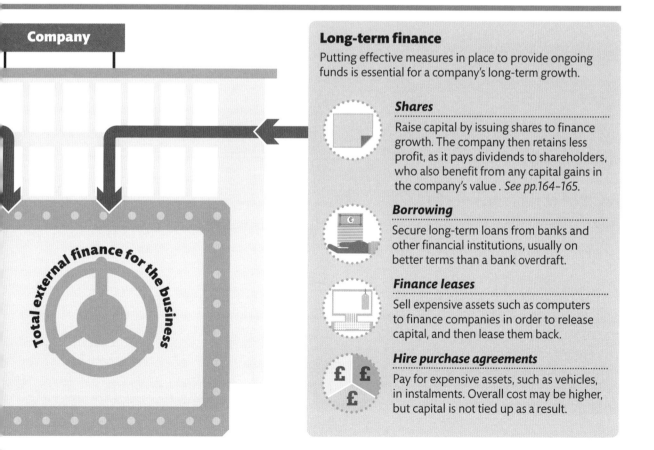

Company

Total external finance for the business

Long-term finance

Putting effective measures in place to provide ongoing funds is essential for a company's long-term growth.

Shares

Raise capital by issuing shares to finance growth. The company then retains less profit, as it pays dividends to shareholders, who also benefit from any capital gains in the company's value . See pp.164–165.

Borrowing

Secure long-term loans from banks and other financial institutions, usually on better terms than a bank overdraft.

Finance leases

Sell expensive assets such as computers to finance companies in order to release capital, and then lease them back.

Hire purchase agreements

Pay for expensive assets, such as vehicles, in instalments. Overall cost may be higher, but capital is not tied up as a result.

Flotation

When a company changes from private to public, it offers shares for sale to members of the public. This process is known as flotation and enables the company to raise money for growth.

How it works

The flotation of an organization (also known as going public) marks the beginning of its life as a public company, after which it is no longer privately owned by a small number of shareholders or company members. A company may choose to float when it needs capital to finance growth. The process usually happens over several months: the company puts legal and financial preparations in place before the final stage when it releases company shares for sale, either to selected investors, or to the general public, or to a combination of both. Each share represents a "stake" in the company, and the money that the company receives from the sale of shares becomes capital, or wealth, which it now owns.

WARNING

> **Underestimation** If the initial valuation of shares by the underwriters is too cautious, then the company will fail to realize the true value of its stock

> **Overestimation** If underwriters overestimate the value of shares newly on the market (new issue) it may flop due to lack of demand

> **Volatility** Share prices in the first few days of an IPO may fluctuate dramatically due to political or economic events

Ways to list on a stock exchange

There are three primary ways to float a company, each of which have different associated costs. The method of flotation that a company chooses will be determined by its size and how much capital it needs to raise.

Introduction

A company joins a new stock exchange without raising capital, but by trading its existing shares. To do this, a significant proportion of the shares must already be in public hands (on other stock exchanges) and no one shareholder can own a majority of shares.

Placing

Select groups of institutional investors are invited to buy shares. This involves fewer costs than undertaking a full public share offering (*see below*) but the amount of capital that can potentially be raised is limited since there are fewer shareholders.

Initial public offering (IPO)

Institutional and private investors are invited to subscribe to, or buy from, the first round of shares that the company issues. This is the most expensive way to go public, but allows for a company to raise large amounts of capital.

1,415

the number of IPOs that took place around the world in 2020

TEN LARGEST IPOS IN HISTORY

When a well-known private company undertakes an IPO there is fierce competition between investors to buy its shares, and record-breaking activity can ensue. This graph shows the largest IPOs to date until 2021.

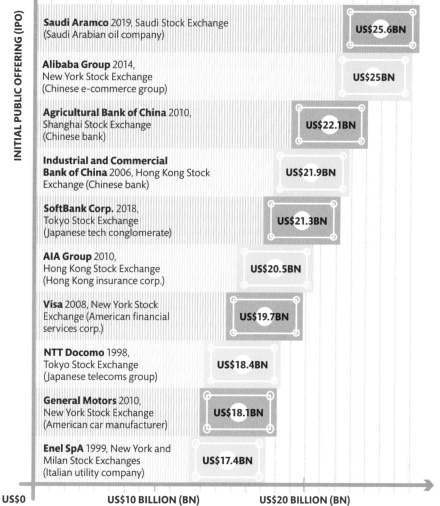

INITIAL PUBLIC OFFERING (IPO)

Saudi Aramco 2019, Saudi Stock Exchange
(Saudi Arabian oil company) — US$25.6BN

Alibaba Group 2014,
New York Stock Exchange
(Chinese e-commerce group) — US$25BN

Agricultural Bank of China 2010,
Shanghai Stock Exchange
(Chinese bank) — US$22.1BN

**Industrial and Commercial
Bank of China** 2006, Hong Kong Stock
Exchange (Chinese bank) — US$21.9BN

SoftBank Corp. 2018,
Tokyo Stock Exchange
(Japanese tech conglomerate) — US$21.3BN

AIA Group 2010,
Hong Kong Stock Exchange
(Hong Kong insurance corp.) — US$20.5BN

Visa 2008, New York Stock
Exchange (American financial
services corp.) — US$19.7BN

NTT Docomo 1998,
Tokyo Stock Exchange
(Japanese telecoms group) — US$18.4BN

General Motors 2010,
New York Stock Exchange
(American car manufacturer) — US$18.1BN

Enel SpA 1999, New York and
Milan Stock Exchanges
(Italian utility company) — US$17.4BN

US$0 | US$10 BILLION (BN) | US$20 BILLION (BN)

VALUE (USD)

Stock exchange

A financial market in which company securities (stocks and shares) are bought and sold according to current market rates. *See pp.170–171.*

A closer look at IPOs

An Initial Public Offering (IPO) is the first time that shares in the company are offered for public sale. It is the most common way for a private company to go public if it needs a large injection of capital to fund major expansion. There are other reasons for going public – for example if a government wants to privatize a state-owned company, such as a national railway, or if the members of a large family-owned enterprise want to sell their stake.

WORLD'S TOP 10 STOCK EXCHANGES

The largest exchanges manage shares belonging to some of the world's most lucrative businesses and, as a result, substantial sums of money flow through them. The following exchanges are listed in order of the size of market capitalization, in other words, by the total monetary value of shares issued by the companies listed on each exchange.

1. **New York Stock Exchange**
2. **NASDAQ OMX, New York**
3. **Hong Kong Stock Exchange**
4. **Shanghai Stock Exchange**
5. **Japan Exchange Group**
6. **Euronext (Pan-European)**
7. **Shenzhen Stock Exchange**
8. **London Stock Exchange**
9. **Bombay Stock Exchange**
10. **National Stock Exchange**

The IPO process

Before a company can issue shares, it has to be listed on a stock exchange where trading (the buying and selling of shares) can take place. The company must then fulfil the criteria necessary to secure investors. This process is lengthy, subject to strict financial regulations, and extremely expensive to undertake. Only once all stages of the process are complete can the share offering be officially declared on a stock exchange.

3

File a prospectus

This document contains information about the offering, the business, and its financial history, as well as proposed plans. Details are still subject to change.

1

Meet the qualifications

The specific requirements are set by the stock exchange where the company plans to list. Listing conditions vary between exchanges, but typically demand:

✓ Pre-tax earnings above a certain level

✓ Three years of audited financial statements

✓ Ability to pay the annual listing fee

2

Appoint underwriters

These financial professionals will be responsible for buying and selling the shares to the public.

US$**7.63** trillion

the total market capitalization **of** companies **listed on the** Shanghai Stock Exchange* * as of May 2021

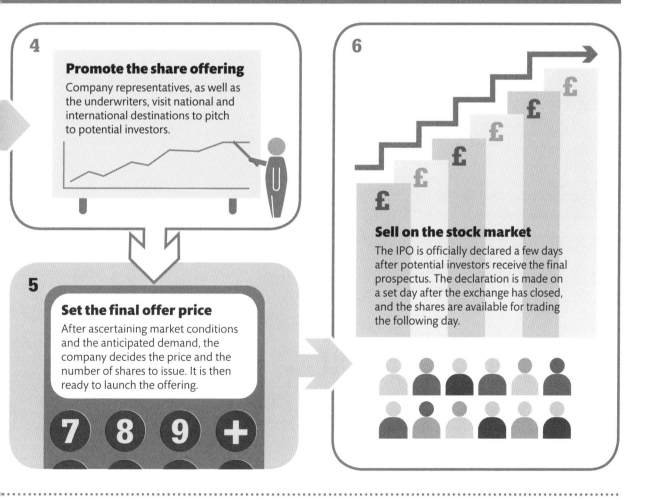

4

Promote the share offering

Company representatives, as well as the underwriters, visit national and international destinations to pitch to potential investors.

5

Set the final offer price

After ascertaining market conditions and the anticipated demand, the company decides the price and the number of shares to issue. It is then ready to launch the offering.

6

Sell on the stock market

The IPO is officially declared a few days after potential investors receive the final prospectus. The declaration is made on a set day after the exchange has closed, and the shares are available for trading the following day.

Shares and dividends

When a company goes public, it sells shares to investors who become part owners in return for capital investment. The number and type of shares bought by each investor determine the size of their ownership.

How it works

Before floating on a stock exchange, a company undergoes a valuation process to set the initial price of its shares. This process involves the directors, prospective investors, and an investment bank, which is appointed to assess the company's value. Together, they reach a decision on the most financially viable price for the shares that will be offered on the exchange. Upon flotation, a company issues ordinary shares to investors as the basic unit of ownership, commonly referred to as a stake in the business. A company may also issue shares privately, rather than publicly to investors via the stock exchange, to retain greater management control.

Company shares

Issued directly

A share of the pie

Ordinary shares, issued by all companies when they go public, are the most common type of shares. There are also other share types, which give the company more flexibility to control rights available to different shareholder groups. Most shares are sold on the stock exchange, but non-voting and management shares are issued directly to holders. Different types of shares entitle the holder to different rights.

Management shares

Issued (usually given not sold) to owners and members of company management, who have:

✓ Extra voting rights, so control of company stays in the same hands

Non-voting shares

Issued to employees, who:

✓ Receive a part of remuneration in the form of dividends

✗ Have no voting rights

✗ Receive no invitation to attend annual general meeting (AGM)

Ordinary shares

Shareholders:

✓ Share in the company dividends

✓ Share in the company's assets

✓ Have right to attend AGM

✓ Have right to vote on important company matters such as appointment of directors

✓ Receive the company's annual report and financial statements

Sold via stock exchange

Preference shares

Shareholders:

✓ Receive fixed dividend, paid ahead of any dividends paid out to ordinary shareholders

✓ Take priority in receiving a share of any assets left after debts are paid if company is insolvent

✗ Have fewer, if any, voting rights

Deferred ordinary shares

✓ Shareholders receive company dividends and share of assets, but only after other shareholders

✓ NEED TO KNOW

❯ **Stagging** Buying and quickly reselling IPOs for a large profit

❯ **Redeemable shares** Ordinary or preference shares that are later bought back by the issuing company for a cash sum

US$
67,564

what $100 invested in Apple's 1980 IPO was worth 40 years later

RAISING MORE SHARE CAPITAL

After the initial sale of shares, when a company goes from private to public, the business can raise additional funds by issuing more shares. There are three main ways to do this:

❯ **Rights issue** entitles existing shareholders to buy additional shares from the company within a set time frame, before they are offered to other buyers.

❯ **Public issue** is a process by which the company issues a new allotment of shares to sell to the public on the stock market.

❯ **Private placing** is a practice by which the company sells its shares (or other securities) directly to private investors, usually large institutions, bypassing the stock exchange all together.

Establishing share value

The forces of supply and demand set the price of shares. Companies issue only a limited number of shares to the public, which can then be bought and sold on the stock exchange. Demand for those shares is determined by whether investors think the company has good future economic prospects. If investors believe that the company is primed for substantial growth, they will want to buy shares in it, which consequently drives up the share price.

25%
the drop in share value over four days during the Wall Street Crash of 1929

SPLITTING SHARES

A company occasionally carries out a "share split" to its existing shares. This increases the total number of shares, although the combined value of shares stays the same. A share split allows a company to lower the price of its shares to bring them in line with the price of competitor shares. The share split is usually a two-for-one or three-for-one increase, whereby the shareholder sees the number of their shares double or treble.

Rising value of shares

Financial market observers believe that the emphasis on optimizing the value of shares for shareholders came in 1976, when the idea of maximizing profit for shareholders became a priority. Since then, the market has experienced a general upward trend with occasional deep dips. The graph tracks the average value of all shares on London's FTSE from 1964 to 2021.

✓ NEED TO KNOW

> **Bear market** Market that has seen decline of 20 per cent over a period of 2 months or more

> **Bull market** Market where share prices are rising and investor confidence is high

> **Market correction** Short-term decline in share prices to adjust for an overvaluation

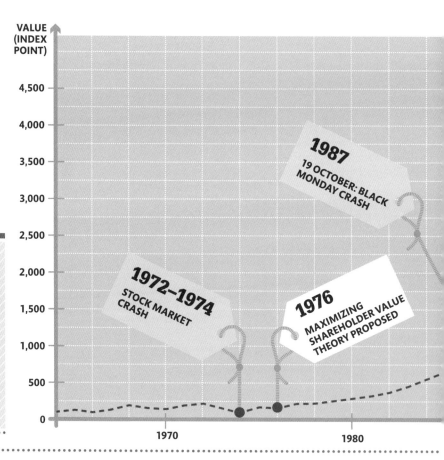

VALUE (INDEX POINT)

1972–1974 STOCK MARKET CRASH

1976 MAXIMIZING SHAREHOLDER VALUE THEORY PROPOSED

1987 19 OCTOBER: BLACK MONDAY CRASH

SHARE PRICE TOO HIGH
A company listed on the stock exchange has seen its share price increase so that its shares now cost more than its competitors'. The high price puts off investors.

SHARES SPLIT
The company decides on a share split. It halves the price of each existing $3 share, so each share is now worth $1.50.

SHARE CERTIFICATES ISSUED
It issues new share certificates to holders, doubling shares held: a shareholder with 1,000 shares at $3 each now has 2,000 at $1.50 each. Total worth is still $3,000.

SHARE VALUE ALIGNED
The value of shares is now similar to that of competitors. The price encourages new investors to make a purchase.

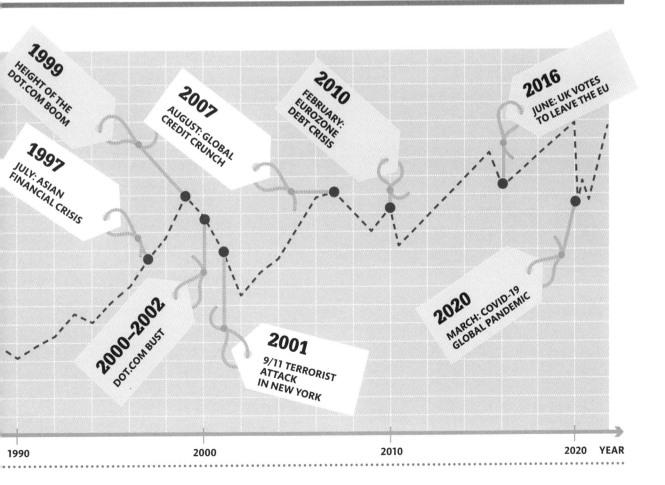

1999
HEIGHT OF THE DOT-COM BOOM

2007
AUGUST: GLOBAL CREDIT CRUNCH

2010
FEBRUARY: EUROZONE DEBT CRISIS

2016
JUNE: UK VOTES TO LEAVE THE EU

1997
JULY: ASIAN FINANCIAL CRISIS

2000–2002
DOT.COM BUST

2001
9/11 TERRORIST ATTACK IN NEW YORK

2020
MARCH: COVID-19 GLOBAL PANDEMIC

1990   2000   2010   2020   YEAR

What is a dividend?

Shareholders in a company are usually entitled to a payment of cash from its profits. The company pays a dividend sum on every share it has issued, but it is up to the company's board to decide how much profit to reinvest and pay out. Investors may look at a company's rate of dividend payout, along with its capital growth, to gauge its financial health and decide whether to invest in it. Investors who rely on shares for income are likely to invest in companies that reliably pay out dividends. In a good economic climate, they win twice over – the dividend provides income and the capital value of the shareholding increases. However, there is always a risk that the value of shares will go down, and companies only pay dividends if they have made a profit.

Paying dividends is a good way for a company to attract investors. It is essentially a reward for putting money into a company so that it can fund its existing output and develop and expand the business.

> **✓ NEED TO KNOW**
>
> ❯ **Dividend yield ratio** Measure of how much a company pays out in dividends relative to the price of each share
>
> ❯ **Dividend per share** Sum paid on each share after retained profits have been calculated
>
> ❯ **Dividend payout ratio** Percentage of a company's net income that is paid out in the form of dividends

How it works

Shareholders usually receive a dividend if the company in which they hold shares has retained enough profit in that financial year to make the payment. The decision to make a payment is taken by the board of directors. The dividend might be paid every quarter (four times a year), or in two parts – an interim dividend may be made part way through the year, with the final dividend paid just after the end of the financial year.

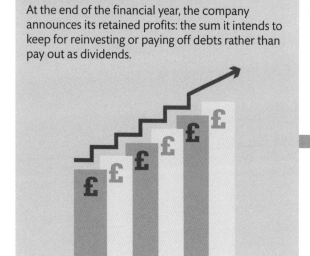

Announcing retained profits

At the end of the financial year, the company announces its retained profits: the sum it intends to keep for reinvesting or paying off debts rather than pay out as dividends.

Making the decision for dividends

The board of directors makes a decision on whether there is enough to warrant a dividend payment, and if so how much. It records details of each payment in dividend vouchers.

INTEREST RATES AND DIVIDENDS

When interest rates are low, shares with high dividend payouts become extremely attractive to investors because they provide a better return than investments that yield an interest payment. This economic climate encourages companies to pay out top-rate dividends and so attract as many investors as possible, which in turn increases the share value.

Conversely, when interest rates are rising, investors may prefer to put their money into fixed-income assets, which will pay high rates as a result of the hike without the risk attached to buying shares.

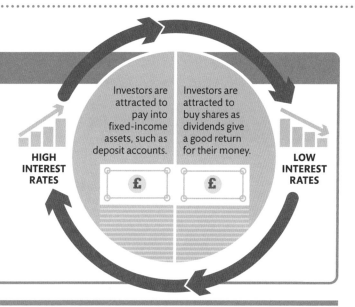

HIGH INTEREST RATES

Investors are attracted to pay into fixed-income assets, such as deposit accounts.

Investors are attracted to buy shares as dividends give a good return for their money.

LOW INTEREST RATES

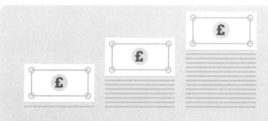

Keeping funds for growth

The company keeps some of its profit to put back into the business. It needs to strike a balance between pleasing investors and expanding its operation.

1602

the year the Dutch East India Company became the first business to issue stocks and bonds

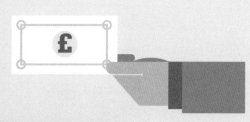

Making the payment

Most dividends are cash dividends. Sometimes companies distribute stock dividends, issuing more shares instead of cash to shareholders.

Paying tax

Shareholders must declare dividends on their tax return and pay tax on them.

The capital market

A global financial marketplace for trading long-term securities – bonds with a maturity of at least a year and shares – the capital market is where governments and businesses can raise funds and investors make money.

How it works

There are two types of product sold on the capital market: shares (equity) and bonds (debt investments). Shares and bonds are sold first on the primary market, where they are originally issued, and later traded on the secondary market. The capital market is crucial to a functioning economy, because it channels funds to users of capital, such as businesses and government, and capital is what enables goods and services to be produced. The original issuers of the shares and bonds do not gain from trading activity in the secondary market, which is purely for investors. However, share value and bond trading levels reflect confidence in a company or institution, reinforcing its financial position.

The structure

The capital market encompasses the debt capital market, where bonds are sold, and the stock exchange, where shares are sold. Both have a primary and a secondary market.

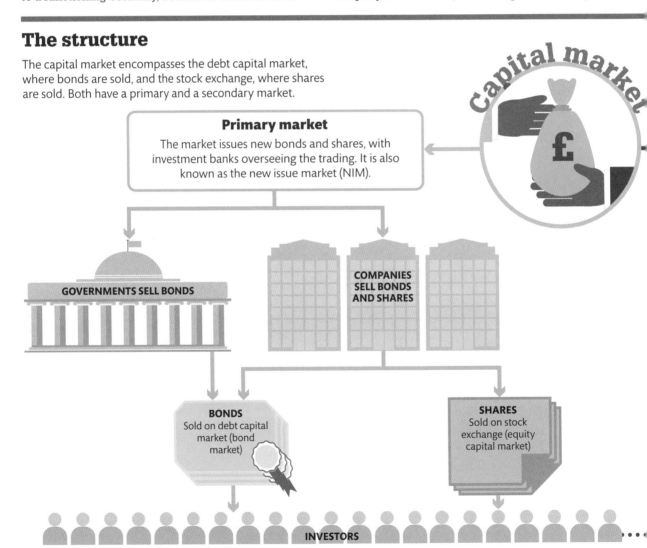

Capital market

Primary market
The market issues new bonds and shares, with investment banks overseeing the trading. It is also known as the new issue market (NIM).

GOVERNMENTS SELL BONDS

COMPANIES SELL BONDS AND SHARES

BONDS
Sold on debt capital market (bond market)

SHARES
Sold on stock exchange (equity capital market)

INVESTORS

WHAT IS A BOND?

A bond is a debt security that a company issues to investors. By buying bonds, an investor is effectively loaning money to the issuers, who in return agree to pay interest to the investor. A bond has a set term of maturity (a limited number of years of validity) and until that time the interest is paid to the investor annually. When the bond matures, the issuer repays the original sum of the loan to the investor. Companies or governments issue bonds to raise money that can then be put back into the business or pay off government debts.

US$**119** trillion

the estimated value of global bond markets

Bonds and shares: pros and cons

Bonds (debt investments)

✔Sellers are contractually obliged to pay interest

✔Bonds are less risky: debt capital markets are less volatile than stock exchanges; if the issuing company has trouble, bondholders are paid before other expenses and before compensation to shareholders

✘Buyers of bonds have no stake in the company

✘Buyers cannot access principal sum until bonds mature

Shares (equity)

✔Buyers of shares gain a stake in the company

✔Sellers of shares have to pay dividends, although these can be reduced or suspended if the company feels it is necessary

✘Shares are more risky: changes in company profit and in the economy as a whole can cause share prices to rise and fall; if the company fails, the shares become worthless

Secondary market

Investors buy bonds and shares from other investors, not from issuing companies. The cash proceeds go to an investor, not to the underlying company or entity.

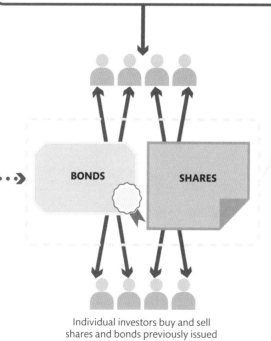

BONDS

SHARES

Individual investors buy and sell shares and bonds previously issued on the primary market

How do bonds work?

Bondholders effectively buy a slice of a larger loan with each bond, for which they receive interest, along with the original sum on maturity. Issuing, buying, and selling bonds takes place in the debt capital market. The marketplace has several functions: it offers bonds and other types of loan to investors; it operates as a fixed-income market, because the issuer is obliged to pay regular interest; and it enables companies and governments to raise long-term funds. Overall, the debt capital market is much larger than the stock exchange (equity capital market), where shares are bought and sold. It attracts investors because bonds provide more protection from risk than shares. There are various types of bond, some safer than others – the risk lies in whether the issuer will be able to pay the interest and repay the principal sum on maturity. A secured bond is backed by an asset, such as property; an unsecured bond is not and so carries more risk.

Bonds and shares are referred to as securities. The term describes the share or bond itself, and the certificate of ownership or creditorship that gives the holder the right to receive a dividend, in the case of shares, or interest payments, in the case of bonds.

✓ NEED TO KNOW

- **Debt instrument** Official term for bond or other long-term debt
- **Convertible bond** Bond that can be converted into shares of the issuing company, or cash
- **Warrant** Security that allows the holder to buy stock in a company at a fixed price
- **Redeemable bond** Bond that gives the issuer the right to redeem it before maturity
- **Irredeemable (perpetual) bond** Bond that has no maturity and cannot be redeemed or sold back to the issuer, but continues to provide interest

Investing in the debt capital market

A company wants to raise £100 million to finance growth but does not wish to issue further shares. Instead, it raises the money by issuing bonds on the debt capital market.

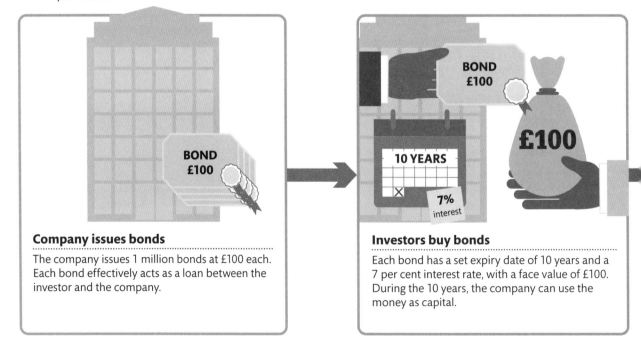

Company issues bonds

The company issues 1 million bonds at £100 each. Each bond effectively acts as a loan between the investor and the company.

Investors buy bonds

Each bond has a set expiry date of 10 years and a 7 per cent interest rate, with a face value of £100. During the 10 years, the company can use the money as capital.

TYPES OF BOND

Government bonds

GOVERNMENT BONDS

Secured

Government bonds are the safest type of bond since governments in developed capitalist economies are unlikely to default on interest payments on the loan or on the principal sum. These bonds are also known as "gilt-edged" because they used to be issued with gilded edges.

Corporate bonds

DEBENTURES

Secured

Debentures are secured on the assets of a company, making them a less risky investment than shares – if the company becomes bankrupt, these bonds will be paid out first.

SUBORDINATED DEBENTURES

Unsecured

Subordinated debentures are unsecured and a riskier investment – if the company fails, investors are paid only after secured bonds have been paid out. Because they are more risky, investors expect a higher return (interest) on their investment.

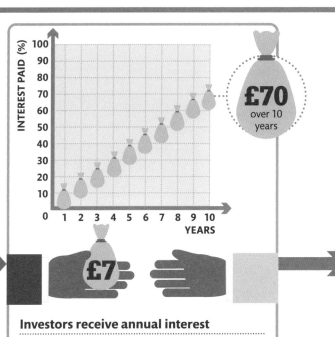

£70 over 10 years

Investors receive annual interest

Each year, the company pays an investor £7 (7 per cent of £100) for each bond bought, in return for using the principal sum as capital to fund its business. After 10 years, the investor has received a total of £70 interest per bond.

10 YEARS

£100

Mature bond is repaid

Once the bond reaches its date of maturity, in this case 10 years, the original sum of money, £100, is repaid to the investor. So the investor receives a total of £170, including interest, over the full term, in return for the original £100 investment.

Gearing ratio and financial risk

Capital gearing is the balance between the capital a company owns and its funding by short- or long-term loans. Investors and lenders use it to assess risk.

How it works

Most businesses operate on some form of capital gearing (also called financial leverage). They partly fund their operations by borrowing money, via loans and bonds, on the condition that they make regular repayments of a fixed amount to the lender. If the level of gearing is high (in other words, the business has taken on large debt), some investors will be concerned about its ability to repay and see this as an insolvency risk. However, if the amount of operating profit is more than enough to repay interest, high gearing can provide better returns to shareholders. The optimum level of gearing for a company also depends on how risky its business sector is, how heavily geared its competitors are, and what stage of its life cycle it is at.

Equity finance (shares)

Pros

❯ Does not have to be repaid

❯ Shareholders absorb loss

❯ Good for start-ups, which may take a while to become profitable

❯ Angel investors share expertise

❯ Low gearing seen as a measure of financial strength

❯ Low risk attracts more investors and boosts credit rating

Cons

❯ Shared ownership, so company has limited control of decisions

❯ Shared profit in return for investors risking their funds

❯ Legal obligation to act in the interests of shareholders

❯ Heavy administrative load

❯ Complex to set up

Low gearing

Company has less debt

Company has more equity

Low proportion of debt to equity, also described as a low degree of financial leverage. Equity comes from:

❯ Reserves (retained profits)

❯ Share capital

Gearing ratio calculation

Analysts and potential investors assess the financial risk of a company with this calculation, presented as a percentage.

$$\frac{\text{LONG-TERM DEBT}}{\left(\begin{array}{c}\text{SHARE CAPITAL +}\\\text{RESERVES +}\\\text{LONG-TERM DEBT}\end{array}\right)} \times 100$$

Low gearing

A software company is going public. Its ratio of 21.2 per cent tells investors that it has relatively low gearing and is well positioned to weather economic downturns.

$$\frac{£1.2\text{ MILLION}}{\left(\begin{array}{c}£2\text{ MILLION} + £2.455\text{ MILLION} +\\£1.2\text{ MILLION}\end{array}\right)} \times 100 = 21.2\%$$

High gearing

Company has more debt

High proportion of debt to equity, also described as a high degree of financial leverage. Typical examples of debt are:

> Loans
> Bonds

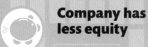

Company has less equity

Debt finance (loans)

Pros

> If the company makes a profit, it can reap a larger proportion
> Paying interest is tax deductible
> Does not dilute ownership
> Company retains control of decisions
> Repayment is a known amount that can be planned for
> Quicker and simpler to set up
> Small business loans at favourable rates may be available to start-ups

Cons

> Loan must be repaid
> Interest must be paid, even if operating profit shrinks
> Debt may be secured on fixed assets of company
> Unpaid lender can seize assets and force bankruptcy
> Lenders first to be paid in the event of insolvency
> High gearing considered a measure of financial weakness
> High risk may put off investors and adversely affect credit rating

✓ NEED TO KNOW

> **Interest cover ratio** An alternative method of calculating gearing – operating profit divided by interest payable
> **Overleveraged** A situation in which a business has too much debt to meet interest payments on loans
> **Deleverage** Immediate payment of any existing debt in order to reduce gearing

25%

the ratio at or below which a company is traditionally said to have low gearing

High gearing

A water company is the only water provider in the area, with several million customers. The ratio of 64 per cent is acceptable for a utility company with a regional monopoly and a good reputation.

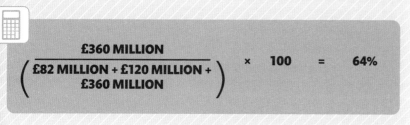

$$\left(\frac{\text{£360 MILLION}}{\text{£82 MILLION + £120 MILLION + £360 MILLION}} \right) \times 100 = 64\%$$

HOW
SALES AND
MARKETING
WORK

Marketing mix ❯ Marketing approaches
Outbound marketing ❯ Inbound marketing
Business development ❯ Information management

Marketing mix

The successful marketing of a product or service depends on the consideration of four key elements – the product itself, its price, how it is promoted, and where it is sold. This combination is called the marketing mix, and it is used as a tool for planning product launches and campaigns. Before focusing on the marketing mix, marketers need to define the target market for their product by determining which groups of customers are most likely to purchase it.

The 4Ps and 4Cs of the marketing mix

The classic marketing mix tool contains the 4Ps: product, price, promotion, and place. These have now been recast as the 4Cs, which emphasize the customer-oriented dimension of the tool.

The 7Ps of the marketing mix

Some marketers use a more detailed model of the marketing mix, which has three additional elements.

❯ **Product** *See pp.180–183.*
❯ **Price** *See pp.186–187.*
❯ **Place** *See pp.188–189.*
❯ **Promotion** *See pp.190–191.*
❯ **People** Does the business employ the right people to deliver optimum service to customers?
❯ **Process** Are effective systems in place for handling orders and dealing with customer queries and complaints?
❯ **Physical environment** Does the design and layout of the business premises appeal to customers?

Commodity
❯ **Has the product been specifically engineered** and designed to meet and exceed customer expectations?

Product
❯ **Is the product the right design, size, and colour** to appeal to customers?
❯ **What are its unique features?** How does it compare with competitors?

Communication
❯ **What is the most meaningful way** to get marketing messages to customers and provide them with useful information?

Promotion
❯ **What combination** of marketing and media channels will be most effective?
❯ **When is the best time** to run promotions?

> "Product, promotion, and place create value. But price harvests value."

DEFINING THE MARKET

In order to establish a marketing strategy for the product they are introducing to the marketplace, businesses have to define the customers they aim to sell to by researching and segmenting the market.

Market research
See pp.192–193.

> Identifies gaps in the market for the launch of new products
> Measures customer reactions to new offers and campaign messages

Market segmentation
See pp.194–195.

> Breaks down the market into smaller customer groups with similar needs
> Allows more focused campaigns with a greater chance of success

Price
> **What is the value of the product** to prospective customers?
> **What is the usual price point** for this type of product?

Cost
> **How much will the product cost the customer**, and will it be seen to represent good value?

Place
> **Where should the product be sold** – shops, online, or catalogues?
> **Where do competitors sell**, and is there a way to stand out in the same place?

Convenience
> **How easy is it for busy customers to find** and buy the product?

The 7Cs of the marketing mix
This model offers a customer-focused variation of the 7Ps, adding three more elements to the 4Cs.

> **Commodity**
> **Cost**
> **Convenience (or Channel)**
> **Communication**
> **Corporation** How do company structure, stakeholders, and other competitors affect marketing?
> **Consumer** What are the customer's needs and wants? Is the product safe? What product information is available?
> **Circumstances** Can the business deal with external factors, such as laws, weather, economy, culture?

Product

The goods and services a company sells are its product. A product can be defined in terms of features, design, size, packaging, service type, return policies, and warranties, all of which aim to meet the customer's needs.

How it works

Consumers can be said to buy benefits rather than products. For the marketer, the product itself is that benefit, as packaged and presented to the consumer.

Marketers identify the goods and services they sell in three or five product levels, with the benefit at the core. The marketer's job is to translate and communicate each product level as an offer to the consumer.

Total product concept: three product levels

From a marketer's perspective, a product is more than the end commodity bought by a customer. It is a total product concept with several layers of benefit, and these must be conveyed to the consumer.

Core product
Product's basic function and its core benefit to consumer

Actual product
Packaging, brand name, quality level, design, and additional features that set it apart from rival products

Augmented product
Additional benefits, such as delivery and credit, warranty, after-sales service

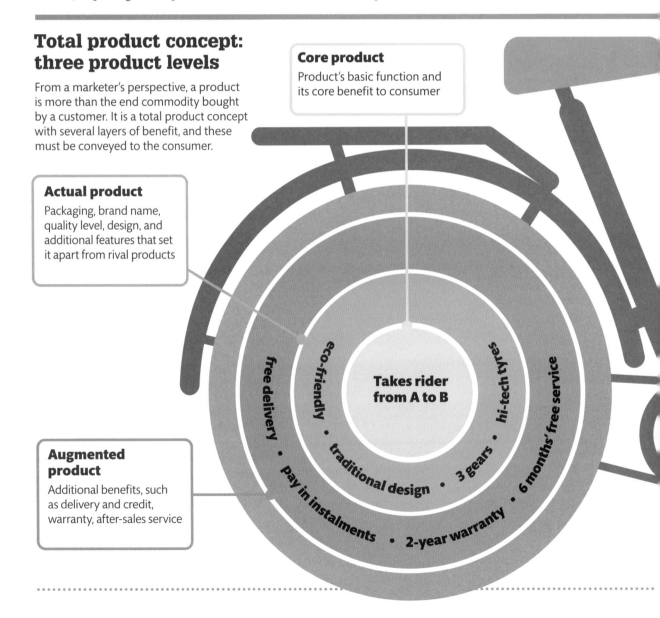

free delivery • eco-friendly • hi-tech tyres

pay in instalments • traditional design • 3 gears • 6 months' free service

Takes rider from A to B

2-year warranty

40%
of new products are still on the shelves three years later

Variation: five product levels

This variation on the total product concept is more detailed. It introduces two more levels by breaking down the actual product level into a generic and an expected product, and also includes an extra level of benefit — the potential product.

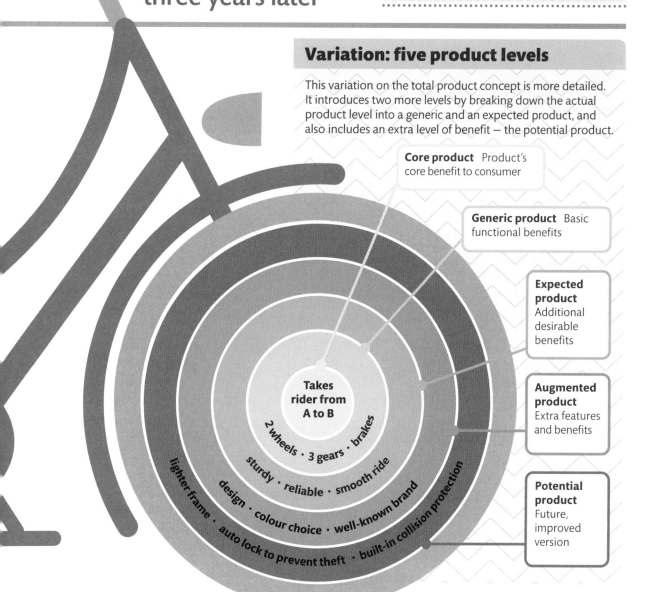

Core product Product's core benefit to consumer

Generic product Basic functional benefits

Expected product Additional desirable benefits

Augmented product Extra features and benefits

Potential product Future, improved version

Takes rider from A to B

2 wheels · 3 gears · brakes

sturdy · reliable · smooth ride

design · colour choice · well-known brand

lighter frame · auto lock to prevent theft · built-in collision protection

Product positioning

A vital step in the process of deciding how to market a product is defining how it is distinct from the competition – what is unique about it and what are the qualities that make it better than rival products.

How it works

Before a company launches a product, the marketing department has to decide how best to position it in the marketplace compared to its competitors. To determine this, marketers must define the most important features and values of the product or brand, and clarify how it is different from similar types of products offered by competitors. They also need to identify those criteria that customers are most likely to use when choosing a particular product or brand. With this information the marketers can then create a product positioning matrix or map.

Product positioning maps

Marketers commonly create a perceptual "map", using a product's two most important attributes, presented as variables on an x and y axis, to work out where to position it. Attributes may include price, quality, status, features, safety, and reliability. Once the map is labelled, existing products are placed on it, which indicate the best position or gap for the proposed launch.

FOUR POSITIONING STRATEGIES

> **Value positioning** A product plotted on the map so that it can offer best value for money, and deliver good functional qualities.

> **Quality positioning** A product that is located on the map on the basis of its perceived quality or superiority.

> **Demographic positioning** A product mapped according to its appeal to a specific population segment, such as consumers with a particular occupation.

> **Competitive positioning** A product that is very similar to those of competitors, relying on correct pricing to find a viable position in the marketplace.

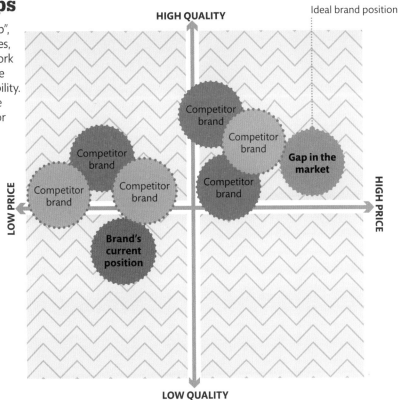

Product positioning template

The map shows how marketers position competing products in the marketplace according to the price/quality variables (the most commonly used) to identify a gap for the new product.

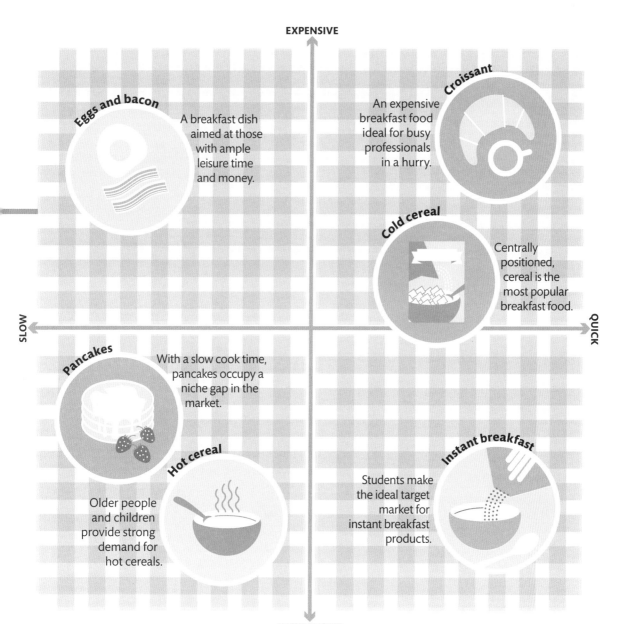

EXPENSIVE

Eggs and bacon
A breakfast dish aimed at those with ample leisure time and money.

Croissant
An expensive breakfast food ideal for busy professionals in a hurry.

Cold cereal
Centrally positioned, cereal is the most popular breakfast food.

SLOW ← → **QUICK**

Pancakes
With a slow cook time, pancakes occupy a niche gap in the market.

Hot cereal
Older people and children provide strong demand for hot cereals.

Instant breakfast
Students make the ideal target market for instant breakfast products.

INEXPENSIVE

Breakfast positioning map

The positioning of the various breakfast foods has been determined by the speed at which the food is prepared, measured from slowest to fastest, and the price of each food type, from the least expensive to the most expensive.

"**Positioning** is not what you do to a product. (It) is what you do to the mind of the prospect."

Al Ries and Jack Trout, *marketing strategists*

Product life cycle

Every successful product launched on the market experiences growth followed by decline. To maximize profitability, business managers must recognize and manage each stage of the product's lifespan.

How it works

There are typically six identifiable stages in a product life cycle, with the product's rate of growth measured by time and revenue. Most businesses have more than one product on the market at any time, and strategic manipulation of the portfolio of products at their different stages in the cycle is crucial to maintaining business growth. The life of older products may be prolonged by extension strategies, but if they are no longer grabbing new market share, the business must consider launching new products in order to continue generating revenue.

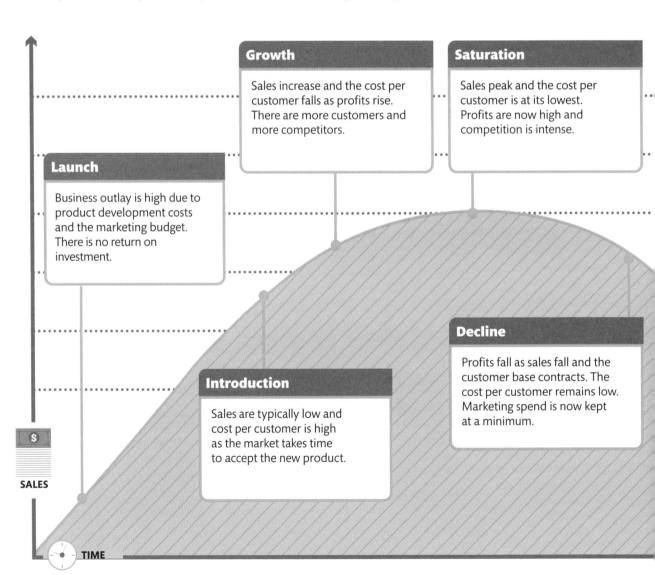

Growth

Sales increase and the cost per customer falls as profits rise. There are more customers and more competitors.

Saturation

Sales peak and the cost per customer is at its lowest. Profits are now high and competition is intense.

Launch

Business outlay is high due to product development costs and the marketing budget. There is no return on investment.

Decline

Profits fall as sales fall and the customer base contracts. The cost per customer remains low. Marketing spend is now kept at a minimum.

Introduction

Sales are typically low and cost per customer is high as the market takes time to accept the new product.

SALES

TIME

6 months

the length of time a product can be labelled as "new"

Withdrawal

The product is phased out as sales stall or continue to fall. The business introduces a replacement product before the old one is withdrawn.

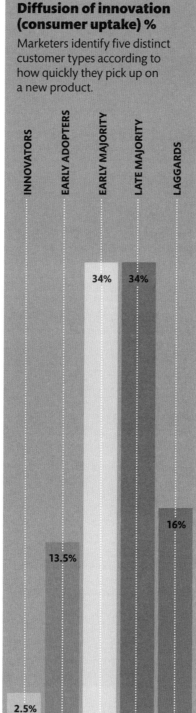

Diffusion of innovation (consumer uptake) %

Marketers identify five distinct customer types according to how quickly they pick up on a new product.

- INNOVATORS — 2.5%
- EARLY ADOPTERS — 13.5%
- EARLY MAJORITY — 34%
- LATE MAJORITY — 34%
- LAGGARDS — 16%

NEED TO KNOW

> **Extension strategy** Revival of a product by rebranding, repackaging, or repricing it, or by finding new markets

> **Portfolio analysis** Process of measuring a company's products by growth rate and market share to determine marketing spend

> **Product life cycle management (PLM)** Management of a product from inception to withdrawal

PORTFOLIO ANALYSIS

Rising stars
Products with a high market share in a high-growth market; they require a big marketing spend to keep them growing.

Cash cows
Products with a high market share in a low-growth market; they generate money to support rising stars.

Problem children
Products with a low market share in a high-growth market; they need a big marketing spend.

Dogs
Products with low market share and low growth; they may stay in portfolio to keep customers happy.

Price

Price is a crucial variable of the marketing mix as it generates revenue while product, promotion, and place yield costs. Pricing may also be the marketer's most potent tool because even minor tweaks affect returns.

How it works

To set the price of a product, marketers adopt a pricing strategy that is based not only on the actual cost of production but also on the perceived attractiveness of the product to consumers. If consumers think a product has a high value, they will be prepared to pay more for it, but if they believe the value of the product is low they will look for the cheapest price among competing products.

A business must also take into account the price charged by any rival organizations, particularly in competitive markets. Setting a price above that charged by competitors can only work if its product is superior to others.

Pricing strategies

A number of different strategies can be used to determine the price of a product. Cost-plus pricing is a retail mark-up used by many companies to ensure a profit is made. For example, adding a mark-up of 50 per cent to a product that costs £2 to make means that every unit will sell for £3, generating a £1 profit.

Pricing matrix: price vs quality

A product's quality affects its price tag – the higher the quality, the more money consumers will pay for it – but marketers use strategies that play on the interaction between price and perceived quality.

> "Price is what you pay. Value is what you get."
> Warren Buffett, *investor*

Low price · **High price**

Low quality

Economy

> **High prevalence** Manufacture a product that is very similar to others in the same category.
> **Low price** Undercut competitors' pricing and gain a larger share of the market.
> **Minimal marketing** Keep the marketing and branding spend as low as possible.

Skimming

> **High launch price** Charge more than usual in the short term while a product is seen as unique.
> **Correct timing** Set a higher price when the business has a temporary advantage within the marketplace, before competing products appear.
> **Price adjustment** Reduce the price once competitors enter the market, or to draw more customers.

PRICING MARK-UP COMPARISON

Different industries adopt different approaches to mark-ups. A mark-up of between two and five times the cost is typically applied to drinks served in bars and restaurants. The highest mark-up is usually applied to the second cheapest bottle of wine on the wine list, as people tend to avoid the cheapest item.

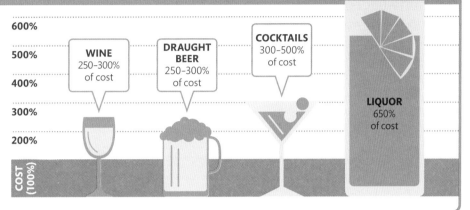

600%
500%
400%
300%
200%

COST (100%)

WINE
250–300%
of cost

DRAUGHT BEER
250–300%
of cost

COCKTAILS
300–500%
of cost

LIQUOR
650%
of cost

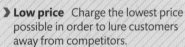
High quality

Market penetration

> **Low price** Charge the lowest price possible in order to lure customers away from competitors.
> **Price adjustment** Increase the price to a normal level as soon as the product has a loyal following.
> **Pricing flexibility** Reassess pricing; initial high-volume sales lower cost of production, allowing price tweaks.

Premium

> **High price** Charge as much as the market will pay for an item.
> **Unique value** Apply premium prices to products that have no comparable substitute, such as famous brand-name goods.
> **High production cost** Charge a premium price because a product is customized and so offers no savings on volume manufactured.

Other pricing strategies

Psychological pricing
Manipulate a customer's emotions, appealing to their thrifty side or desire for prestige.

Bundle pricing
Offer several products for an overall price, providing better value than buying separately.

Geographic pricing
Charge different prices for the same product in different locations.

Non-pricing strategies
Avoid adjusting the price to attract sales, promoting superiority of product instead.

Place

Knowing where customers shop, where a product is sold, and how efficiently goods can be delivered to the consumer – called "place" in marketing terms – are essential to sales success.

How it works

Whether a company sells goods or services, customers must be able to find and buy those products as easily as possible. Businesses have to decide on the best sales outlet and sales channel to get their products to customers in a way that benefits both parties.

A sales outlet is the place where a product or service is sold, such as physical outlets or e-commerce websites. Sales channels are the merchants, agents, distributors, and platforms that take a product from the seller and bring it to the consumer, such as Amazon or TV shopping channels like QVC.

38% revenue growth globally **at online retailer** Amazon **in 2020**

Main distribution channels

A product reaches the marketplace through one of four main types of distribution channel. The most suitable distribution channel is usually dictated by where customers prefer to buy the product.

Producer
A producer chooses the distribution channel, or a combination of channels, that will maximize the number of customers it can reach while keeping costs as low as possible.

Selling direct to consumers
Product is sold directly by the producer, usually online, and delivered to customer without intermediary.

Selling through retailers
Goods are delivered by producer directly to retail outlets; retailer adds a mark-up on to the price it pays producer.

Selling through wholesalers and retailers
Products are distributed in two stages: by producer to wholesaler and then to retailer.

Selling through an agent
Products are distributed in three stages: from producer to agent, from agent to wholesaler, and then on to retailer.

PROS AND CONS OF USING INTERMEDIARIES

Pros

> Enables wider market coverage so producer can reach more customers, especially those in distant areas.

> Minimizes distribution cost for producer as intermediaries are responsible for this service.

> Provides producer with specialist knowledge of customer-buying habits, as well as delivery logistics.

Cons

> Raises difficulty of making direct communication with customers to learn about their preferences.

> Increases the risk of slow, inefficient delivery, especially if several intermediaries are involved.

> Takes away control over how products are handled and displayed at point of sale.

✓ NEED TO KNOW

> **Channel margin** Cost that an intermediary adds to producer's selling price, which is added to price paid by customer

> **Push strategy** Method in which producer promotes products to wholesalers, wholesalers to retailers, and retailers to customer

> **Pull strategy** Use of advertising and promotion to sell to customer

Example

E-commerce site selling vitamins; they are sent to customer by post or courier.

Consumer

Example

Electronics company distributes its television sets to a chain of retail stores.

Retailer

Consumer

Example

Farmer sells apples to wholesaler who sells them on to grocery shops and supermarkets.

Wholesaler

Retailer

Consumer

Example

Chocolatier in France uses import agent in Japan to sell its products to wholesalers and on to retailers.

Agent

Wholesaler

Retailer

Consumer

Promotion

Promotion is necessary for generating interest in and sales of a product or service. A complex and expensive part of the marketing mix, it involves communicating to customers and influencers, such as peer groups.

How it works

The primary purpose of promotion is to boost sales by attracting new customers, while enticing existing ones to try out something new. Most companies use a number of communication activities to inform and remind their target audience of a product's benefits (*see pp.196–231*).

One of the long-term benefits of communicating with customers is that it helps to build brand loyalty, but be aware that rules apply to the use of personal data.

✓ NEED TO KNOW

> **Integrated Marketing Communication (IMC)** Promotion of same brand message across all media channels

> **MarCom (Marketing Communication)** Full range of promotional activities used to reach out to the market

73%
of marketers say social media marketing has been effective for their business

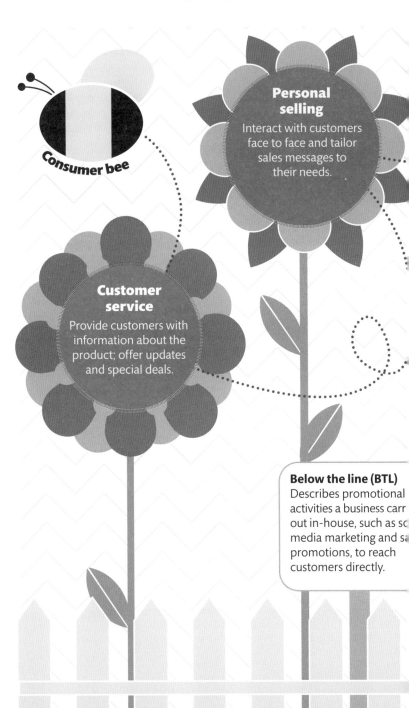

Consumer bee

Personal selling
Interact with customers face to face and tailor sales messages to their needs.

Customer service
Provide customers with information about the product; offer updates and special deals.

Below the line (BTL)
Describes promotional activities a business carr out in-house, such as sc media marketing and sa promotions, to reach customers directly.

Advertising
Run ad campaigns through media channels most likely to reach target market, and stick to budget appropriate for the product.

Direct marketing
Send product offers and information directly to the potential consumer via social media or email.

Interactive marketing
Build long-term relationships with customers using two-way communication, especially online.

Sales promotion
Entice customer with offers, free samples, gifts, competitions, packaging, and point-of-sale displays.

Public relations
Generate positive interest by pitching content to media, or getting endorsements from influencers.

Above the line (ATL)
Refers to online/offline advertising a business pays for in order to target customers.

Market research

Asking customers what they think about a product or service is a vital part of the decision-making process for marketers. Research offers insight into how a product might sell and lowers the risk of marketing ventures.

How it works

Market research is used to make decisions throughout the entire business planning cycle, from generating ideas to evaluating solutions. Researchers use a variety of data sources, including internal business information, primary (new) research, and external sources, such as social media. Primary research is broken down into quantitative and qualitative. Quantitative is numbers-focused, and often involves asking fixed questions to large groups. Qualitative is more exploratory, and is about understanding topics in depth among smaller groups. Marketing departments use both types of research, depending on the specific business questions they want answering.

Primary data collection

New research to answer specific question

Observations

❯ Researchers may watch from a distance as customer interacts with product, or they may identify themselves and talk to customer.

❯ They observe customer using equipment such as eye-tracking analysis and checkout scanners.

❯ They study credit-card records or computer history to observe past consumer behaviour.

Quantitative surveys

❯ Researchers question many people for a broad view, generating numerical data.

❯ They carry out surveys, usually online, to obtain a quick result from a large sample.

Qualitative surveys

❯ Researchers probe small groups or individuals for their in-depth view.

❯ They conduct focus groups and other types of interpersonal discussions.

Marketer has a question

Marketer reaches a decision

DATA REQUESTED

DATA RETURNED

 CASE STUDY

Helping Hummel

When Danish sportswear brand Hummel wanted to expand into leisurewear, it turned to market research firm Ipsos to help it better understand its consumers and market position. Ipsos conducted 16 qualitative focus group studies and 6,500 quantitative interviews in Denmark and Germany, enabling it to identify five unique market segments, and areas with development potential. It also created animations and infographics, and ran workshops to communicate the findings to Hummel staff. "This gives us a strong foundation for making both strategic and operational decisions," said Lene Christensen Heinz, leader of Hummel's business intelligence team.

Secondary data collection
Published material on a subject

Agency
Organization that carries out original research and organizes research data into meaningful results

US$ 73.4 billion
the value of the global market **research sector**

Internal sources
> Web usage data (for example browser logs and online sales records)
> Customer profiles with buying history and demographic data
> Accounting records, such as financial statements
> Original data from past market-research reports

External sources
> Industry reports by trade bodies, institutions, and private research companies
> Reports by broadcast, print, and internet media
> Academic papers, university thinktank reports, and research library holdings
> Government surveys, reports, and statistics
> Social media and search-engine data

Market segmentation

In order to make decisions about who to sell their product to, marketers try to identify distinct groups of consumers with similar wants and habits – who together form a "segment" of the market.

How it works

Marketing departments use a strategy of market segmentation to find potential customers who are most likely to buy a particular product, thereby increasing the chances of a successful product launch. They divide a broad group of consumers into sub-groups based on many factors including age, lifestyle preferences, location, family structure, household income, and job. This process narrows down a potentially huge market into segments, which allows marketers to identify the ones more inclined to buy the product on offer. For example, after applying this strategy, a company trying to launch premium-price organic baby food realizes that instead of marketing to all women who have young children, it should aim its product at working mothers with children under six months, above-average incomes, and an interest in healthy eating.

 NEED TO KNOW

> **Silver surfers** Pensioners who regularly use the internet, especially for online shopping, searches, and social media

> **Generation X** People born between 1960 and the early 1980s

> **Millennials/Generation Y** People born between the early 1980s and mid-1990s

> **Generation Z** People born between the mid-1990s and the early 2010s

Defining market groups

To establish different consumer groups, marketers create five segments and focus on each individually. Besides identifying groups by geography and demographics, marketers also explore psychology, to ascertain how consumers behave so that they gain a better idea of which products might appeal to which consumer groups. *See also pp.258–261.*

Behavioural

Focuses on behavioural patterns when it comes shopping. Understanding this helps marketers adapt campaigns to target specific groups. Potential focus areas include:

> Brand loyalty
> Regularity of purchase
> Credit-card usage
> Typical expenditure
> On- or offline shopping
> Heavy product user

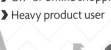

"Market segmentation is a natural result of the vast differences among people."

Don Norman, *cognitive science researcher and professor*

Sociographic

Identifies individuals' connections on social media, or membership of political and other groups, helping marketers learn about consumers' passions and interests. Potential focus areas include:

> Group memberships
> Number of friends on social media

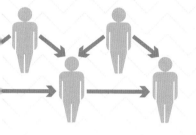

Psychographic

Focuses on a consumer's interests, values, and opinions, which can help marketers develop relevant messages and find the right media channels to target a segment. Potential focus areas include:

> Risk-taking behaviour
> Charitable giving
> High achieving
> A tendency towards expensive tastes
> A preference for email contact

Geographic

Concentrates on a customer's place of residence, so that any product launched is made relevant to their environment. Potential focus areas include:

> Post code
> Continent
> City
> Neighbourhood
> Population density
> Climate

Demographic

Uses basic consumer data, such as age or gender, as a means of categorizing needs and targeting products appropriately. Potential focus areas include:

> Income
> Nationality
> Family size and age
> Ethnic background
> Occupation
> Religion

Marketing approaches

Every product launch requires strategic planning to make sure messages about a new product reach the right types of consumer, are communicated through the most effective combination of channels, and have the most relevant content and style. Once marketers have researched the market and defined their target audience, they face several key decisions on how to make their approach.

Types of approach

Whom to target and how to go about it are crucial to success. Marketers may use several complementary approaches to different groups of potential consumers.

Rather than sending the same message via different media, they usually mould the tone and style of the marketing pitch to suit the channel as well as the target consumer.

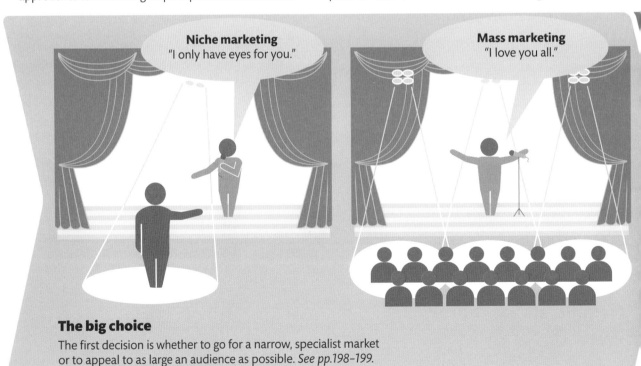

Niche marketing
"I only have eyes for you."

Mass marketing
"I love you all."

The big choice
The first decision is whether to go for a narrow, specialist market or to appeal to as large an audience as possible. *See pp.198–199.*

89% of women worldwide say they control or share the shopping for daily needs

Engagement marketing
"Come and dance with me." It entices the customer to collude in product sales. *See pp.204–205.*

Sensory marketing
"Wake up and smell the roses." It seduces the customer with sights, sounds, and smells. *See pp.206–207.*

Traditional channel allied with a dominating style. "Let me tell you," it blares. *See pp.200–201.*

Digital channel allied with a softly, softly approach. "Let me woo you," it gently whispers. *See pp.202–203.*

Relationship marketing
"Let's be friends." It builds a rapport with its audience of consumers. *See pp.208–209.*

How to tell the customer
Marketers often get the best of both worlds by using traditional and online channels in varying styles.

Making a move
Turning the buying transaction into an experience the consumer enjoys can help sell a product.

Niche vs mass marketing

Two fundamental choices traditionally face marketers: whether to try to sell a product with broad appeal to as many people as possible, or to focus on selling a tailored product to a defined group.

How it works

Both niche and mass marketing strategies offer businesses the potential to make a high return on investment. A niche approach generally works on the basis of low-volume sales at a premium price to a specific group of consumers, while a mass approach tends to use heavy promotion to a wider audience and aims to achieve high-volume sales.

In reality, businesses tend to mix up both approaches, launching a niche product and then expanding it to a mass market. Marketers also use internet channels to promote the same product to different groups of customer within a mass audience.

20%
of sales can make up to 80% of profit

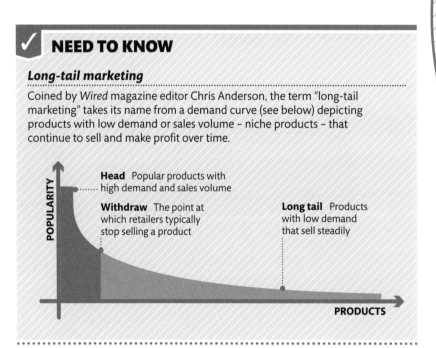

✓ NEED TO KNOW

Long-tail marketing

Coined by *Wired* magazine editor Chris Anderson, the term "long-tail marketing" takes its name from a demand curve (see below) depicting products with low demand or sales volume – niche products – that continue to sell and make profit over time.

POPULARITY

Head Popular products with high demand and sales volume

Withdraw The point at which retailers typically stop selling a product

Long tail Products with low demand that sell steadily

PRODUCTS

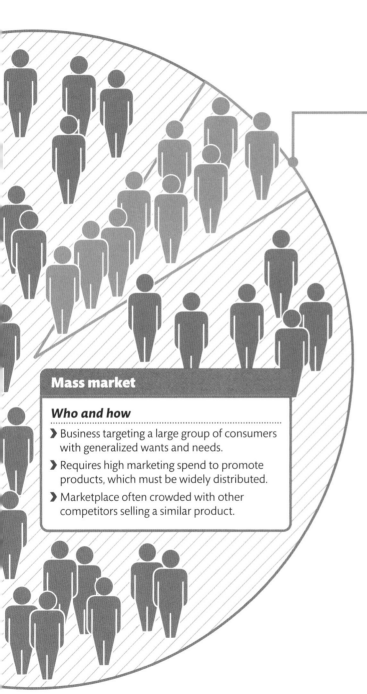

Niche market

Who and how

> Business targets a select group of consumers with specific needs and wants.

> Customers often prepared to pay a premium price for an uncommon product.

> Sales volume of niche product low, so does not benefit from production economies of scale (manufacturing of large quantity that reduces the unit cost of production).

Mass market

Who and how

> Business targeting a large group of consumers with generalized wants and needs.

> Requires high marketing spend to promote products, which must be widely distributed.

> Marketplace often crowded with other competitors selling a similar product.

HYBRID APPROACHES

Using social media to identify and reach more than one target market, marketers have developed hybrid approaches that are more flexible than conventional niche or mass-market positioning of products.

Mass market

An unfocused strategy that aims at the broadest customer base.

Large segment

Channels marketing resources to one large segment of the mass market.

Adjacent segment

Once large segment is fully penetrated, product expands into related segment.

Multi segment

Markets to several segments at once, with a customized strategy for each.

Small segment

Markets to a small segment with few competitors, if resources are limited.

Niche segment

Focuses marketing resources on a specific group of customers.

Mass customization

Customizes a strategy for each sub-segment within the mass market.

Traditional marketing

Before the digital age, marketers relied exclusively on non-digital channels, such as TV, radio, and print media, as well as direct mail, events, and cold-calling, to convey their message to the consumer.

How it works

Traditional marketing encompasses a number of tried-and-tested ways of building a brand and pushing a product to sell more. It remains a key facet of marketing. Nowadays, however, most businesses use a mix of traditional and digital marketing methods. One of the advantages of traditional marketing is that companies have face-to-face contact with customers through person-to-person selling, special events, and event sponsorship.

Events
Staging sports activities, themed displays, parades, or exhibits to promote a product, cause, or brand.

TV
Promoting sales through TV ads, programme sponsorship, or product placement.

Traditional marketing process
Small and large businesses use a range of conventional marketing channels, and often integrate them with digital marketing strategies.

Direct mail
Mailing catalogues or circulars to targeted consumers, often promoting offers (in compliance with data protection rules).

Face-to-face
Approaching customers directly to create brand awareness or persuade them to buy a product.

Telemarketing
Phoning potential customers who have an identifiable need for a product to give a sales pitch (in compliance with cold-calling rules).

Product samples

Offering free samples of a product to customers, giving them the opportunity to try it before making a purchase – an effective way to launch new products and build customer base.

Billboards

Renting large outdoor advertising spaces to market products. Hiring cost dependent upon the size of space, its visibility, and the amount of traffic that passes the location.

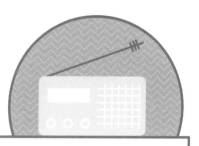

Radio

Using commercial slots on radio to promote the products either locally or nationally, depending on the station's reach.

Newspapers and magazines

Hiring space in print media to run advertisements, or creating advertorials to market products or services.

25%

Traditional marketing
Digital marketing

75%

Brochures and flyers

Promoting through mailing or hand-distributing pamphlets locally to promote businesses.

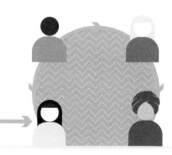

Networking

Interacting with other people at specialist events to develop professional contacts.

70%
higher brand recall by people exposed to direct mail ads rather than digital ones

Digital marketing

By using the internet, marketers can connect directly and instantly with current and potential customers to build brand recognition, collect data, and encourage word-of-mouth recommendations.

How it works

Unlike traditional offline marketing, digital marketing gives a business direct, two-way communication with customers. Digital marketing employs some conventional approaches, such as "pop-up" or "banner" ads on web pages, but it also relies heavily on the power of social media for raising awareness of a product or brand. This makes it harder to measure return on investment. Digital marketing is often used in conjunction with traditional marketing techniques, a hybrid known as "tradigital" marketing.

Tradigital in practice

A new health club is launched using a tradigital approach to marketing. TV adverts are aired with a call to action to visit the gym's website and schedule a free workout with a fitness trainer. Print ads feature a voucher or a Quick Response (QR) code to scan and present at the health club for a free trial. At the club, members get free Wi-Fi access. The Wi-Fi landing page has a link to download the gym's free app. The club may also use pop-up ads, podcasts, email, and texting to attract or retain members.

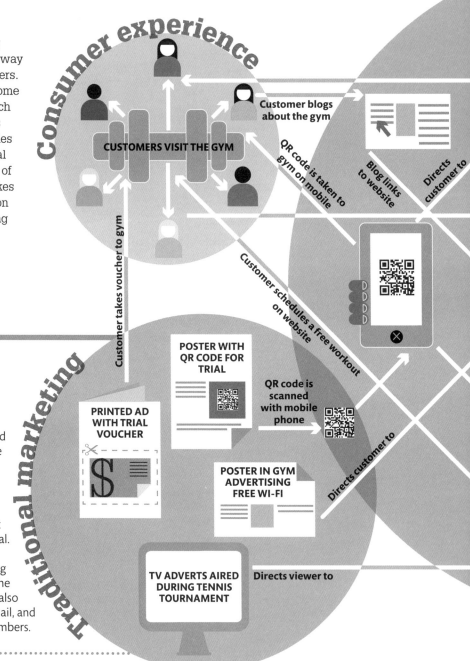

Consumer experience

CUSTOMERS VISIT THE GYM

Customer blogs about the gym

QR code is taken to gym on mobile

Blog links to website

Directs customer to

Customer takes voucher to gym

Customer schedules a free workout on website

Traditional marketing

PRINTED AD WITH TRIAL VOUCHER

POSTER WITH QR CODE FOR TRIAL

QR code is scanned with mobile phone

POSTER IN GYM ADVERTISING FREE WI-FI

Directs customer to

TV ADVERTS AIRED DURING TENNIS TOURNAMENT

Directs viewer to

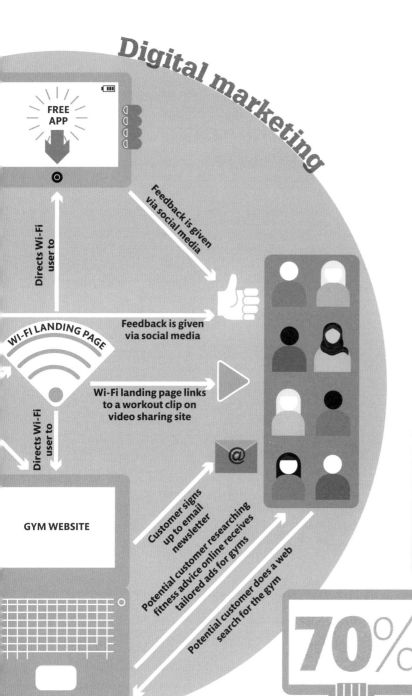

Digital marketing

FREE APP

Directs Wi-Fi user to

Feedback is given via social media

WI-FI LANDING PAGE

Feedback is given via social media

Directs Wi-Fi user to

Wi-Fi landing page links to a workout clip on video sharing site

GYM WEBSITE

Customer signs up to email newsletter

Potential customer researching fitness advice online receives tailored ads for gyms

Potential customer does a web search for the gym

70% of advertising spending in China is set to go on digital ads in 2021

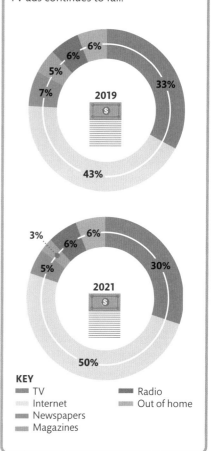

% SHARE OF GLOBAL AD SPEND BY MEDIUM

The internet is expected to account for more than half of global ad spending in 2021 as the expenditure on print and TV ads continues to fall.

2019
33%
6%
6%
5%
7%
43%

2021
3%
6%
6%
5%
30%
50%

KEY
- TV
- Internet
- Newspapers
- Magazines
- Radio
- Out of home

Engagement marketing

By involving customers directly in the development of a brand, marketers hope to build a strong two-way relationship with customers and win long-term loyalty.

How it works

Engagement marketing harnesses several online and offline strategies to draw a customer's interest and get them talking about products and services on offer. This contrasts with the more traditional style of marketing in which a brand concept and product proposal are presented to the customer as fixed, to be either accepted or rejected. Engagement marketing, on the other hand, encourages customer input so that they feel closer to the brand. The aim is to lure potential customers to the website with an initial experience, and then work hard to keep them there.

Start with a "wow" experience

Provide interesting, informative, or entertaining content to draw potential customers to a web page.

End with a sale

Follow up purchase with after-sale call, full of feel-good reinforcement.

PURCHASE

New prospects

Offer incentives to existing customers for recommending product or sharing content.

 NEED TO KNOW

> **"Sticky" customers** Consumers who are loyal to a company and return to make more purchases

> **Decision simplicity** Ease with which consumers can find trustworthy information about a product

> **Churn rate** Percentage of customers who cut ties with the company in any given time period

> **WOM** Word-of-mouth marketing, which relies on satisfied customers who recommend product to others

COMMENTS AND SHARES

Social visibility

Post interesting and relevant content on social media, and encourage dialogue.

72% of people are more likely to be loyal to a brand if it offers a personalized experience

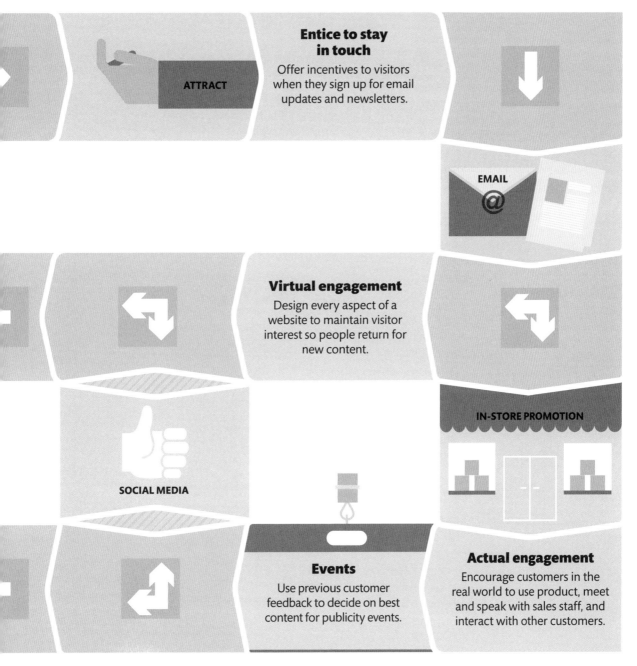

ATTRACT

Entice to stay in touch
Offer incentives to visitors when they sign up for email updates and newsletters.

EMAIL
@

Virtual engagement
Design every aspect of a website to maintain visitor interest so people return for new content.

SOCIAL MEDIA

IN-STORE PROMOTION

Events
Use previous customer feedback to decide on best content for publicity events.

Actual engagement
Encourage customers in the real world to use product, meet and speak with sales staff, and interact with other customers.

Sensory marketing

Sensory marketing targets multiple senses to sway purchasing decisions. Based on research showing how the brain responds to sensory input, this type of marketing acts covertly on the customer.

How it works

Sensory marketing is most obviously used by the food and drinks industries, but its use extends to diverse products and services: computers designed with tactile materials, hotels scented to relax customers, and even firework displays featuring edible confetti.

Typical channels for sensory marketing include field marketing, such as in-store events, samples, and person-to-person sales, direct mail, and product delivery. For online businesses, however, finding a way to use it remains a challenge.

Sight
Technology is making advances with this, the most stimulated sense in marketing, by using optical illusions, digital effects, 3-D, and 360-degree photography.

Touch
Marketers use 2-D and 3-D textural print techniques for promotional materials and packaging, as well as to sell products with tactile appeal.

Smell
Customers are willing to pay more for a product sold in an environment that is scented appealingly.

72%
of consumers born from 1980 to 1996 value experiences over material items

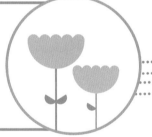

Taste
Taste sensations can be enhanced or subtly altered by combining them with touch, sight, and especially the closely linked sense of smell.

Attitude, memory, behaviour, and mood

The sensory input results in a short- or long-term effect on attitude, memory, behaviour, and mood. This can be influenced by the intensity of sensory data and by using it to stimulate more than one sense at the same time.

Perception

The brain receives stimuli from one or more senses.

Emotion

Sensory stimuli taps into the store of emotional memories, as both are processed by same area of the brain.

Cognition

After processing sensory stimuli, brain embeds memory, regulates emotion, and makes decision.

Hearing

Sound is more effective than sight in triggering the brain areas that process emotions.

Relationship marketing

The strategy of relationship marketing is to develop and manage a trusting, long-term association with customers and other stakeholders that have links with the company.

How it works

Relationship marketing aims to replicate the type of interaction old-fashioned village shops have with their customers, offering a high level of personalized service to win them over for a lifetime. While small, local businesses naturally work this way, large corporations have now changed their focus from making the sale to relationships; from short-term reward to long-term gain. The marketer can extend the network beyond the engaged customer to include employees, suppliers, and others.

Supplier markets
Building a relationship of collaboration with suppliers makes good commercial sense.

Six markets model

Using relationship marketing, experts have established a strategy for communicating with the customer. This strategy defines six markets – not just traditional ones – where companies should direct their marketing efforts.

CASE STUDY

Starbucks

The strategy of coffee-shop chain Starbucks exemplifies effective relationship marketing. Centred on core customer and internal markets, it also involves suppliers, referrals, and recruitment (employee) markets.

Marketing to customers
> Social media
> Business crowdsourcing
> Familiarity with customers
> Loyalty programme
> Reward card app
> Mobile payment

Marketing internally
> Barista training
> Tech development opportunities

Marketing via referrals
> Word of mouth
> Social media shares

Marketing to employees
> Stock options
> Medical insurance
> Partnership

Marketing to suppliers
> Fairtrade programmes
> Quality control

Influence markets
To maintain good PR, the company works closely with regulators and consumer or environmental groups.

Referral markets

Customers can be word-of-mouth advocates for a company. Related businesses may also refer trade.

> "Advertising brings in customers, but word of mouth brings in the best customers."
>
> Jonah Berger, *marketing professor*

Customer markets

The main marketing focus is on customers, but activities are based more on building long-term customer relationships than on acquiring new customers.

Internal markets

A company's employees are its internal customers, working together to represent its goals, mission, and strategy.

Recruitment markets

To attract the best employees, a company may market itself by offering incentives to staff.

 NEED TO KNOW

> **Key account management (KAM)**
> Marketing strategy that coordinates all departments in a business-to-business (B2B) firm to build relationships with major clients

> **Frequency marketing** Promotion aimed at increasing repeat sales by rewarding customers for repeat purchases

> **Direct response (DR)** Marketing that invites consumers to respond directly to advertiser by telephone or email

> **Transaction marketing** Strategy that aims to persuade customers to make additional one-off purchases at the point of sale

Outbound marketing

Also called interruption marketing, outbound marketing involves a marketer pushing a message to consumers. With this type of marketing, businesses typically reach out to a wide audience by paying for advertisements to feature on various media channels. Although the audience may have no interest in the advertisement, outbound strategy relies on delivering a high-impact message and generating a response by creating familiarity through repetition.

Outbound marketing process

Outbound marketing takes a traditional approach to grabbing consumers' attention, but may use both non-digital and digital media platforms. There are two stages to the outbound process. First, the company communicates a message to an audience and tries to convert them into customers; second, it analyses the results to identify the channels and campaigns that have generated the most sales.

Broadcast

Marketers select a media channel with proven reach to the target audience, then communicate the message about brand or product to that audience.

Communication channels

> **Ads on prime-time TV** slots to find widest possible audience – ideal for raising brand awareness.

> **Presence at trade events** for increasing corporate visibility and to reach a business audience.

> **Banner ads and pop-up ads** on relevant internet sites, or attached to blogs that link to the company's website.

> **YouTube video ads** stay in the viewer's mind longer than static ads, so can be effective.

> **Sponsorship** of sporting or cultural events puts a name or brand in front of a large audience.

Convert

Marketers link offline outbound campaigns with digital channels as part of an overall strategy to persuade potential customers to respond.

Means of conversion

> **Radio advertisement** that repeats easy-to-recall phone number to elicit immediate action.

> **Online advertisement** that has prominent position on web page and clear click-through point that invites customers to click, find out more about product, and buy it.

> **Flyer** distributed door to door that includes an appealing introductory offer on the product for a limited period of time.

> **Direct mail** that makes high-impact call for customer response or delivers strong novelty value; includes prepaid postal reply form and customer service contacts.

86%
of businesses use video as a marketing tool

Analyse

Marketers monitor the progress of outbound campaign and adjust the mix of media or other paid-for channels, then measure campaign results.

Actions

❯ **Run control and test streams** to compare the success of different media or campaign strategies.

❯ **Examine click-through-rate** analytics, which look at how many customers have clicked through to find out about or buy product, to determine online ad success.

❯ **Analyse sales by outbound spend** to establish which channels offer the best return on marketing investment (ROMI).

❯ **Measure direct mail response rates**, including breakdown of different mailing lists or target demographics.

TYPES OF OUTBOUND MARKETING

Offline

❯ **Cold calling** Campaign can be more effective if conducted at the right time of day to suit target audience; message should be scripted carefully and delivered in a genuine tone. Be aware of rules governing its use. *See pp.218–219.*

❯ **TV commercials** Although many consumers now switch off TV advertisements, they are familiar with and open to this type of media, and repetition gets the message across. *See pp.212–213.*

❯ **Radio** This medium is the world's most popular mass communication channel with a global reach, and is ideal for outbound messages aimed at an international market. *See pp.212–213.*

❯ **Guerrilla marketing** The use of a creative and unconventional approach in high-traffic public places can be a cost-effective way to raise brand awareness. This is a form of engagement marketing. *See pp.204–205.*

Online

❯ **Social media** The types of advertising on social media sites are increasing and include sponsored posts, promoted pins, and direct forms, such as banner ads and video ads. *See pp.228–229.*

❯ **Mobile technology** Advertising that is tailored for mobile devices takes the form of text and images, or both, to offer special deals to users; promotions are also made via apps. *See pp.214–215.*

❯ **Social lead targeting** This strategy taps into individual profiles from social media and tailors messages, which are sent via online networks, such as Twitter and LinkedIn.

❯ **Search engine optimization (SEO) keywords** Paying for popular SEO keywords relevant to a brand can improve exposure by raising them in the internet search engine listings page. *See pp.230–231.*

Traditional offline advertising

Offline advertising uses traditional media channels, such as magazines, TV, radio, and billboards, to market a product or service. Online advertising has grown fast to rival offline as the predominant form of advertising globally.

How it works

The common criteria for both online and offline advertising is that businesses pay for ads that are intended to catch a consumer's attention with a brand or product message.

Businesses calculate the success of their advertisement by looking at the return on investment (ROI) for every ad "dollar" spent. To maximize the ROI, they must ensure they choose the right channel for their target audience.

Marketers choose different channels according to the target market defined for the product or service being advertised. The choice may also be based on the ROI that a company has previously experienced for that channel. However, tracking the response rate of offline advertising is more difficult and less accurate than that of online advertising (*see pp.214–215*).

71% of advertising in India in 2021 was offline – but digital is catching up, growing 9% since 2019

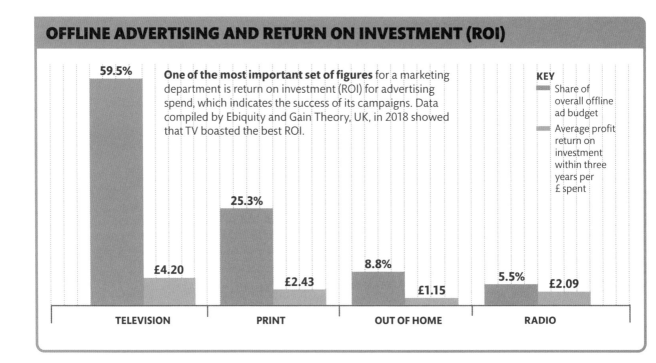

OFFLINE ADVERTISING AND RETURN ON INVESTMENT (ROI)

One of the most important set of figures for a marketing department is return on investment (ROI) for advertising spend, which indicates the success of its campaigns. Data compiled by Ebiquity and Gain Theory, UK, in 2018 showed that TV boasted the best ROI.

KEY
- Share of overall offline ad budget
- Average profit return on investment within three years per £ spent

TELEVISION: 59.5% — £4.20
PRINT: 25.3% — £2.43
OUT OF HOME: 8.8% — £1.15
RADIO: 5.5% — £2.09

Offline advertising channels

	Pros	Cons
Televison	Offers local, national, and global reach; mix of sound and vision creates high-impact message	Expensive; ad repetition may cause viewer fatigue; viewers likely to skip ads on pre-recorded shows
Radio	Inexpensive; quick and easy production process; most stations play to specific demographic	Competition for prime "commute" slots; radio on as background noise renders ad ineffective
Newspapers	Fast publication process; themed newspaper sections allow for more targeted advertising	Ads compete for attention with other material on page; usually black and white, and text only; readership has declined
Magazines	May remain in circulation for months; niche trade and special-interest titles allow focused advertising	Real circulation figures hard to source; securing ad slot requires planning months in advance
Direct mail	Cost-effective; delivered straight to people's homes and offices; targets specific markets; can stand out more	May be perceived as junk mail and instantly thrown away; response rate usually low; rules limit who you can target
Billboards	High reach makes channel cost-effective; advertiser's message visible 24 hours a day	Heavy competition for prime sites; format limits message length and complexity
Cinema	Potential to impress with sophisticated, creative production; it has captive audience members	Audience numbers limited; members may choose to enter cinema after ads are shown

✓ NEED TO KNOW

> **Television rating point (TVR)** Indicates percentage of target viewers in programme audience

> **Cost per thousand (CPT)** Figure used to measure outlay to reach a thousand people via any channel

> **Advertising to sales ratio (A/S)** Method of measuring money spent on advertising and sales generated

> **Share of voice** Percentage of total activity claimed by one advertiser for product sector

70%

of Europe's population watches television on a daily basis, averaging three hours and 39 minutes a day

Online advertising

Marketers are increasingly advertising online to push marketing messages to consumers. Online channels include display and mobile technologies, email, search engine, and social media marketing.

How it works

When marketers advertise on the internet, they must choose both the form of the ad and a location that has an audience matching their target market. There are several advertising channels, but the two most often used are display advertising and search advertising.

Display advertising includes banners with text and images, which appear on websites known to be used by target consumers, such as news, social media, or video content sites. Online ad tracking aims to target ads more precisely, delivering more relevant content based on a consumer's web activity.

Search advertising places ads in the web pages showing search engine results. While display ads are likely to get more views overall, search ads have a better chance of reaching the target audience.

Other forms of digital advertising include mobile advertising, which embeds ads in mobile content viewed on smartphones and tablets, or sends text messages; email, which delivers ad copy directly to an email address; and social media advertising, which a company uses to promote products via its social media profile. A major advantage of online advertising is that response rates can be tracked effectively.

94%
of all Facebook's ad revenue comes from mobile advertising

MOST EFFECTIVE ONLINE MARKETING CHANNELS

Which digital marketing method is best for generating sales? In a 2021 global survey by AWeber, marketers placed email at the top, thanks to its potential for personalization and greater engagement.

1.7%
16.3%
7.5%
8.3%
11.2%
18.9%
36.1%

KEY
- Email marketing
- Social media marketing
- Landing pages
- Advertising
- Content marketing
- Web push notifications
- Other / not applicable

Which digital marketing channel is best at driving traffic to your website?

0.8%
13.5%
27.2%
10%
10.6%
10.9%
27%

KEY
- Social media marketing
- Email marketing
- Advertising
- Landing pages
- Content marketing
- Web push notifications
- Other / not applicable

Online advertising channels

	Pros	Cons
Display advertising	Attention-grabbing; if ad is clicked on, success can be tracked with pay-per-click system	Internet users suffer ad fatigue and ignore advertisements
Search advertising	Good for targeting consumer, as search user keywords are matched to advertiser keywords (see pp.230–231)	Potentially expensive if using premium keywords; can take time to see results
Mobile	Cheaper to develop content for mobiles than for computers; easy to track ad effectiveness	Different screen sizes and systems can distort ad layout; user may feel annoyed by interruption
Email	Offers means to reach millions of potential customers (see pp.216–217)	Recipient may delete email without reading it, and is more likely to do so if they feel bombarded; consent normally needed
Social media	Easy to target specific audience; offers chance of ad going viral and achieving many views (see pp.228–229)	Continual posts and updates can easily distract user's attention away from placed ad

✓ NEED TO KNOW

> **Clickstream** User activity profile that summarizes what an individual has clicked on

> **Behavioural targeting** Process whereby websites capture data from landing page visitors and use it to improve ad effectiveness

> **Interstitials** Ads that precede the content page a user expects to land on, or appear right after it

🔍 CASE STUDY

Click fraud and botnets

With pay-per-click (PPC) advertising, a business pays a website for every click made on one of its ads, but click fraud has become a serious issue. Fraudsters set up a website and sell PPC advertising, then infiltrate the computers of unsuspecting users with a computer virus known as a "botnet" to generate fake traffic to the website. Advertisers on the site end up paying the fraudsters for the large number of clicks received. In 2018, the FBI, Google, and other agencies took down the "3ve botnet", which had grown to infect an estimated 1.7 million computers and span 10,000 fake websites. The network stole around US$30 million in ad revenue over five years.

19%
of marketing emails are opened on Fridays – the highest "open rate" of the week

Direct mail

By targeting a large number of potential customers via post or email, marketers hope to convert some into actual customers. This is achieved through the timing, design, and wording of the message.

How it works

Direct mail works on the basis of sending a product offer to a large, but targeted, group of potential consumers in the knowledge that at least some of them will take it up. The more targeted this group can be (perhaps by job title, location, previous purchase, or enquiry), the better the response rate is likely to be.

Direct mail relies on lists of names and addresses, which could be the company's existing clients or people who have previously made enquiries, or a list managed by a specialist agency. It is important to comply with data protection laws governing the use of personal data. In the UK, there are slightly different rules governing text messages, email, and post, with rules for postal marketing slightly less restrictive. However, you may not send personally addressed letters to anyone who is on the Mail Preference Register or who has asked you not to contact them. The most up-to-date rules can be found on the website of the Information Commissioner's Office.

Marketers are allowed to send direct mail to businesses, though they are advised to keep a list of any that opt out. The percentage of people who respond to direct mail, take up the offer, and become customers, a category known as the conversion rate, is extremely low, but nevertheless proves to be profitable.

Direct mail and email – A/B testing

A/B testing compares the effectiveness of two versions of a marketing email or direct mail copy. The two versions are sent to different groups of potential customers, and the response to each is measured.

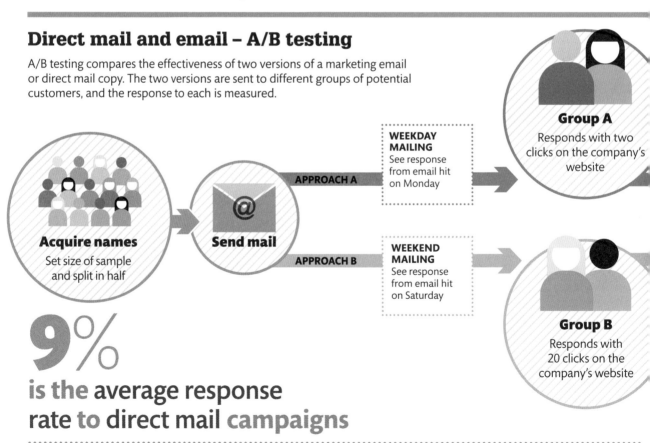

Acquire names
Set size of sample and split in half

Send mail

APPROACH A

APPROACH B

WEEKDAY MAILING
See response from email hit on Monday

WEEKEND MAILING
See response from email hit on Saturday

Group A
Responds with two clicks on the company's website

Group B
Responds with 20 clicks on the company's website

9%
is the average response rate to direct mail campaigns

HOW TO SEND DIRECT MAIL

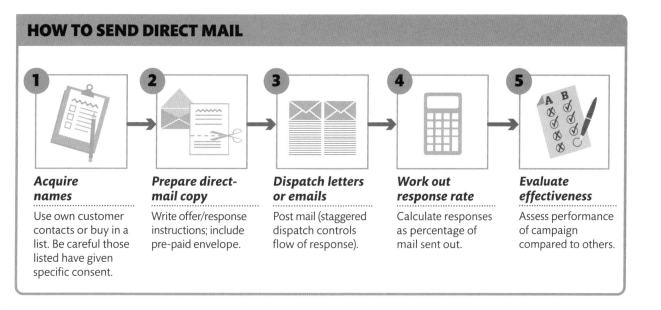

1 Acquire names
Use own customer contacts or buy in a list. Be careful those listed have given specific consent.

2 Prepare direct-mail copy
Write offer/response instructions; include pre-paid envelope.

3 Dispatch letters or emails
Post mail (staggered dispatch controls flow of response).

4 Work out response rate
Calculate responses as percentage of mail sent out.

5 Evaluate effectiveness
Assess performance of campaign compared to others.

Campaign B

Send emails to remainder of the group on Saturday

Data analysis
Result comparison shows that Saturday time slot is more effective

Evaluate effectiveness
Full email blast reveals that approach B yields the best response

✓ NEED TO KNOW

❯ **Cleaning** Correcting name and address details on traditional mailing lists and email lists to ensure they remain current and effective

❯ **Lettershop** Company that specializes in printing and mailing out letters and catalogues on behalf of a client.

Merge/purge Software system that pulls together different mailing lists, searches for any duplicates, and makes corrections

Telemarketing

Businesses use telemarketing to initiate direct contact with existing and potential customers. Customers can also contact the company directly. Telemarketing offers businesses a way to retain and acquire customers.

How it works

Telemarketing works in two directions: inbound and outbound. A customer making a call to a business (with a question or complaint, for example) is referred to as an inbound call. It gives the business a chance to retain a customer who may be dissatisfied with a product or service, or to win over a new customer contacting it for the first time. When a business makes an outbound call, it is either to sell additional products or services to an existing customer, or to entice a new customer to make a purchase. Telemarketing sales can be monitored in orders per hour – for example, agent A may make 140 calls per hour and generate £400.

A more effective measure is revenue per call – if agent B makes 60 calls per hour but £450 worth of sales, the conversion rate per call is higher for agent B than agent A.

Companies using telemarketing must comply with data protection and other laws. In the UK, telemarketers cannot call any individual or organization listed on the Telephone Preference Service (TPS) or Corporate TPS – registers of everyone who has opted out of receiving marketing calls. Neither can they call those who have objected to receiving their calls in the past, or if they are selling certain products, including pensions and personal legal services.

Outbound and inbound telemarketing process

Telemarketers usually refer to a list of telephone numbers retrieved from a database to contact new or existing customers. Call-centre agents have access to product information to help them deal with queries and complaints.

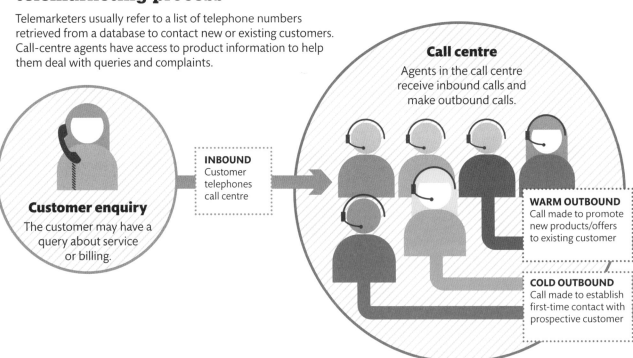

Customer enquiry
The customer may have a query about service or billing.

INBOUND
Customer telephones call centre

Call centre
Agents in the call centre receive inbound calls and make outbound calls.

WARM OUTBOUND
Call made to promote new products/offers to existing customer

COLD OUTBOUND
Call made to establish first-time contact with prospective customer

MAJOR CALL-CENTRE LOCATIONS

The Philippines is one of the top call-centre locations for US firms. This is because of the high number of Filipinos who have a US education and knowledge of American culture.

Ireland ● ● Poland
● China
India ● ● Philippines

✓ NEED TO KNOW

❯ **After-call work (ACW)** Tasks agents have to complete after making a call, such as processing sales forms

❯ **Average handling time (AHT)** Typical length of calls made to customers

❯ **Automatic call distributor (ACD)** Computerized telephone system that connects each customer's call to correct agent

❯ **Average speed of answer (ASA)** Measure of time it takes to answer inbound calls

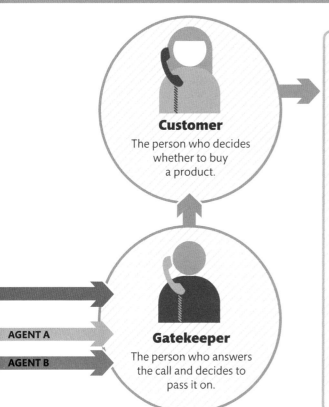

Customer
The person who decides whether to buy a product.

Gatekeeper
The person who answers the call and decides to pass it on.

AGENT A
AGENT B

Evaluate effectiveness
Telemarketers constantly evaluate the effectiveness of calls.

Agent A
May adopt a particular sales strategy or have a personal approach.

Agent B
May use a different communication or selling technique.

Outcome
At the conclusion of a marketing drive, telemarketers appraise strategies and styles to help them decide on future campaigns.

Inbound marketing

Inbound marketing lures customers by offering them appealing content, and engaging with them. The approach pulls customers into a relationship with a brand rather than "pushing" them into making a purchase, which is how advertising works. Inbound marketing is also known as permission marketing as potential customers are giving a business permission to communicate with them. In other words, they are actively interacting with the company or brand.

Inbound marketing process

Content forms the core element of inbound marketing. This includes text, images, and video that consumers seek out online, especially on social media sites, or in person at events, such as trade fairs, and share with their network of friends, family, and colleagues. Potential customers respond to inbound marketing because the business or brand is offering interesting and relevant information, entertainment, or content with emotional value. Businesses expect this interaction to culminate in a sale, or create brand recognition that leads to a sale.

Top types of content marketing

1. Blog
2. How-to guides
3. Images
4. Infographics
5. Video
6. Testimonials/reviews
7. Case studies
8. Internet memes
9. Email newsletter
10. Ebooks
11. Podcasts
12. Twitter chat
13. Newsjacking (giving content to news media)

Exploration
Publish and actively promote content; use search engine optimization (SEO) to attract consumers online

Decision-making
Ensure content captivates potential customers or solves problems for them; encourage two-way communication

Purchase
Entice interested site visitors to become customers; make shopping online an easy and positive experience

Advocacy
Provide excellent customer service; spur customers to make recommendations and share on social media

---

✓ **NEED TO KNOW**

> **Top of funnel marketing (TOFU)** Offers content to grab the initial attention of potential customer

> **Middle of funnel marketing (MOFU)** Offers more detail and encourages participation

> **Bottom of funnel marketing (BOFU)** Attempts to win a sale with low pricing, offers, or via customer recommendations

82%

of marketers surveyed
in 2021 say they actively
use content marketing,
up from 70% the
year before

Search engines, social media networks,
web publishers, and third-party blogs

Company website, blog, podcast,
community, and interactive tools

E-commerce process, product,
price, discount, and promotion

Customer championing
of product or service

INBOUND MARKETING STRATEGIES

Offline

❭ **Optimize retail space**
Provide a well-designed physical
environment that will both draw
customers in and encourage them
to come back.

❭ **Engage media**   Generate press
releases to gain media coverage.
Focus on topics of real interest,
especially ones that can be backed
up by stats and research.

❭ **Interact face to face**
Conduct events in-store that
provide a new experience/benefit
to customers; hire a stand at a trade
event and offer key information.

Online

❭ **Post blogs**   Update company blog
with appealing content to attract
visitors. *See pp.224–225.*

❭ **Create podcasts**   Ensure content
relevant to customers searching for
information; engage experts to add
value. *See pp.226–227.*

❭ **Produce other content**   Post
articles, photos, and videos
on social media sites; target
influencers to encourage
viral sharing. *See pp.228–229.*

❭ **Apply search engine optimization
(SEO)**   Fill search engine listings with
key phrases that answer specific
questions; add inbound links from
popular sites. *See pp.230–231.*

Outbound vs inbound marketing

Outbound marketing interrupts consumers to promote a product or brand, but inbound marketing needs consumers' permission – they have to seek information that leads to the marketing message.

How it works

Before the rise of the internet and the phenomenon of social media, most marketing strategies were outbound. In other words, marketers pushed messages onto consumers by interrupting them with advertisements or direct mail. The same principle applies to outbound marketing that appears on the internet, with pop-up ads interrupting the content the consumer wishes to access. However, as consumers from all over the world now use the internet to search for information and entertainment, marketers have adopted inbound strategies instead, providing content that draws the consumer to the brand or product, rather than pushing marketing messages onto them.

> ✓ **NEED TO KNOW**
>
> ❯ **Push or interruption-based**
> Alternative marketing terms used to describe outbound marketing
>
> ❯ **Pull or permission-based**
> Alternative marketing terms used to describe inbound marketing

Pros and cons

Marketers interrupt consumers with hundreds of outbound marketing messages every day, but they also use subtle inbound marketing tactics to attract consumers. Each strategy has its advantages and drawbacks.

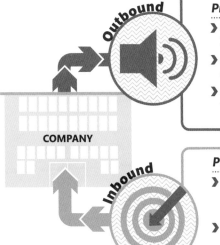

COMPANY

Outbound

Pros	Cons
❯ **Campaign results** can be forecast and measured	❯ **Customer conversion rates** are low
❯ **Marketing material** is easier to create	❯ **Marketing campaigns** are expensive to create
❯ **Campaigns** can be tightly controlled	❯ **Effects** of campaign are often short-lived

Inbound

Pros	Cons
❯ **More likely** to draw customers with long-term interest in the brand	❯ **Response** from market may take longer
❯ **Nonintrusive** approach welcomed by customers	❯ **New content** must be generated regularly to keep customer interested
❯ **Cost-effective** compared with outbound campaigns	❯ **Campaign results** can be difficult to measure

ADVERTISING

BLOGGING

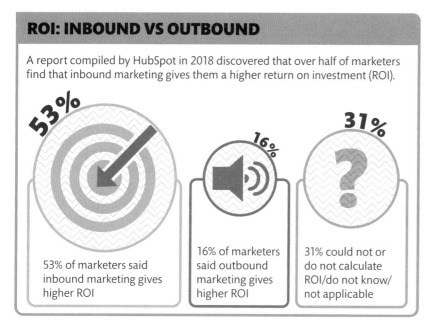

ROI: INBOUND VS OUTBOUND

A report compiled by HubSpot in 2018 discovered that over half of marketers find that inbound marketing gives them a higher return on investment (ROI).

53%
53% of marketers said inbound marketing gives higher ROI

16%
16% of marketers said outbound marketing gives higher ROI

31%
31% could not or do not calculate ROI/do not know/ not applicable

74%
of **marketers** say **their** organizations primarily conduct **inbound marketing**

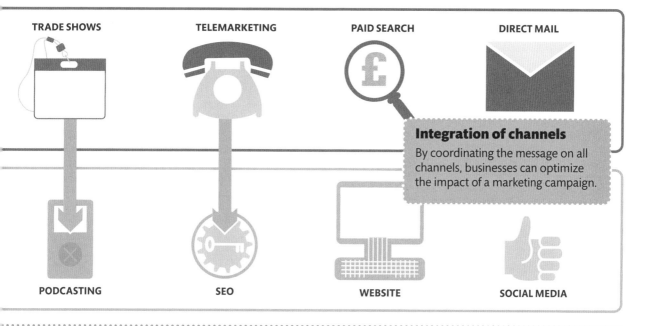

TRADE SHOWS

TELEMARKETING

PAID SEARCH

DIRECT MAIL

Integration of channels
By coordinating the message on all channels, businesses can optimize the impact of a marketing campaign.

PODCASTING

SEO

WEBSITE

SOCIAL MEDIA

Blogging

Businesses post information articles on web logs, or blogs, as a way to attract consumers to their websites. They may blog on their own website or rely on independent bloggers to achieve this aim.

How it works

Unlike a conventional website, a blog is a site that consists purely of informational posts or entries that appear in chronological order, starting with the most recent. Blogs first started appearing in the mid 1990s, when new web tools made it possible for non-experts to publish material online. This type of web content has since become one of the most common sources of information and opinion on the internet. Although it was once only individuals who published blogs, many are now commissioned or professionally edited and produced by the company's marketing department.

Blogging process

Marketers may use SEO tools (*see pp.230–231*) to gain insight into what's being talked about online, which helps them to determine the most suitable topics for blogs. Many companies have the in-house talent to create blog content.

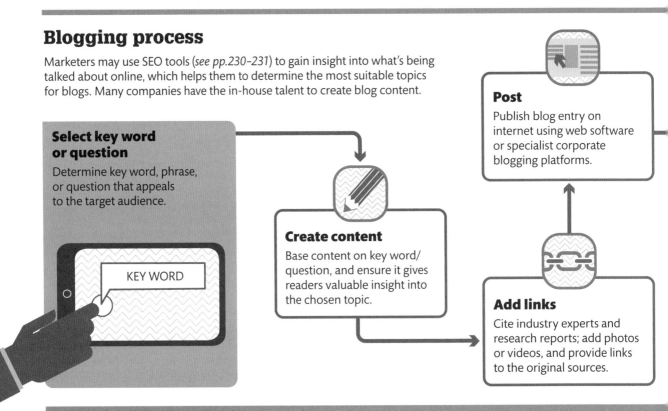

Select key word or question
Determine key word, phrase, or question that appeals to the target audience.

KEY WORD

Create content
Base content on key word/question, and ensure it gives readers valuable insight into the chosen topic.

Post
Publish blog entry on internet using web software or specialist corporate blogging platforms.

Add links
Cite industry experts and research reports; add photos or videos, and provide links to the original sources.

THE RISE OF BLOGGING

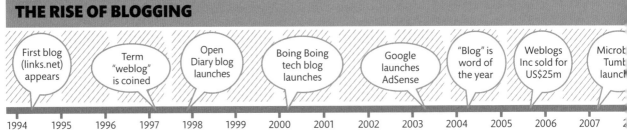

| First blog (links.net) appears | Term "weblog" is coined | Open Diary blog launches | Boing Boing tech blog launches | Google launches AdSense | "Blog" is word of the year | Weblogs Inc sold for US$25m | Microb Tumb launch |

| 1994 | 1995 | 1996 | 1997 | 1998 | 1999 | 2000 | 2001 | 2002 | 2003 | 2004 | 2005 | 2006 | 2007 | 2 |

40%
of all websites are powered by blogging tool WordPress

✓ NEED TO KNOW

> **Disclosure** Disclosure of whether blog is sponsored, or if reviewed products are given to blogger or were independently bought

> **Splog** Spam blog containing fake articles designed to increase search engine rankings of specific websites

Syndicate/share

Submit blog to syndication sites and share with social media networks, such as Facebook, Twitter, Instagram.

Track and measure

Monitor key blog statistics, such as the number of unique visitors and the number that sign up for RSS feed and email.

BLOGGING VITAL STATISTICS

Top five statistics to track

> **Number of visitors** Potential customers visiting blog and their route in – via links or direct entry

> **Bounce rate** Share of visitors who leave site after one page

> **Pages per visit** Number of pages viewed by visitor

> **Conversions** Proportion of visitors who subscribe to blog

> **Keywords** Common words visitors use to find blog site

Three blogging mistakes

> **Obsession with SEO** Although SEO is important, focus should be on publishing quality content

> **Omitting facts** Posts should offer factual information, not just opinion or repackaged content

> **Lack of legibility** Poorly designed blogs with unclear typography will discourage customers from reading content

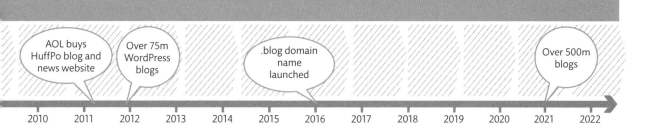

AOL buys HuffPo blog and news website

Over 75m WordPress blogs

.blog domain name launched

Over 500m blogs

2010 2011 2012 2013 2014 2015 2016 2017 2018 2019 2020 2021 2022

Podcasting/vlogging

Businesses may post audio or video files on the internet to attract and engage website users – the goal is to convert first-time users into subscribers. Once consumers engage with podcasts or vlogs, companies try to sell products either via advertising on the podcast or its download page, or by sponsoring the podcast or vlog to create brand reinforcement.

✓ NEED TO KNOW

> **Podcast** A series of audio or video files that you can download to a personal media player

> **Vlog** A blog in video format, usually recording a person's thoughts or experiences

> **Rich site summary (RSS)** Format used for frequently updating text, audio, and video content online

Podcasting/vlogging process

In order to get commercial results from a podcast or vlog, a company needs to create and publish interesting and informative content.

Capture content
Decide on topic, and create an outline, then record audio or video material.

Process content
Edit video footage or audio track to rid background noise, mistakes, and repetitions. Test and edit further, if necessary.

Select correct format
Save audio in MP3 or AAC format; save video in MP4 format; compress file size for optimal download speed.

Publish content
Upload file to hosting service, and embed on website. Generate feed address via host or app, and submit to podcast platforms.

Tracking
Count number of subscribers; use web feed services to access user location, level of interaction, and other statistics.

1 billion people listen to podcasts every week

BUSINESS BLOGGING AND PODCASTING ETHICS

Independent online reviewers often collaborate with businesses, which is beneficial to both. Bloggers are obliged by law to disclose payments or gifts they receive in exchange for creating promotional content, but ethical boundaries can still become blurred.

Blog /podcast reviews include products such as fashion, hotels and restaurants, and technology.

NO

YES

Other content

Business gives free sample of product or service to blogger/podcaster for testing and reviewing.

NO

YES

Business provides support to reviewer through paid content and advertisements.

Business provides support to reviewer by offering further free products and services.

NO

YES

YES

NO

Reviewer writes consumer report.

Possible conflict of interest

Possible conflict of interest

Reviewer tries to be neutral.

Blog/podcast helps generate revenue for both parties.

NO

YES

Reviewer site builds own reputation and has its own agenda.

Reviewer site depends on revenue that business provides.

KEY

Business potentially influences blogger

Blog generates revenue for blogger/business

Blogger operates independently of business

Social media marketing

By posting content on social media, marketers try to attract website traffic and draw attention to their products and services. Occasionally, interest in the posted content can multiply rapidly across these channels.

How it works

Social media marketers are responsible for generating engaging content. Typically, the content provides entertainment or offers useful information that social media users actively look out for. If the content is compelling enough it will attract followers, who will share it with their audiences. As the content continues to be shared, liked, and commented upon, it gets picked up by Google and other search engines, helping to generate more interest.

Social media marketing in practice

The makers of a new health supplement for repairing sun-damaged skin generate video content showing the dramatic results of the product, and launch it across two social media channels. Video footage, an image, or a story that is spread quickly and widely via the internet is said to have gone viral.

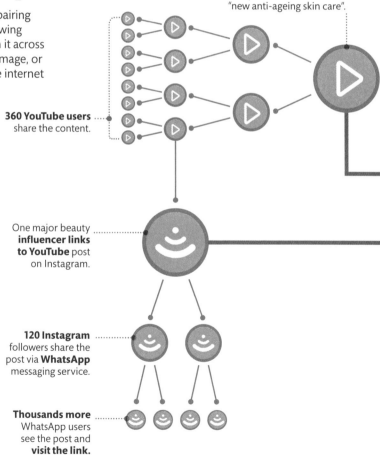

Content is posted on **YouTube** as "new anti-ageing skin care".

360 YouTube users share the content.

One major beauty **influencer links to YouTube** post on Instagram.

120 Instagram followers share the post via **WhatsApp** messaging service.

Thousands more WhatsApp users see the post and **visit the link.**

FROM SEARCHERS TO SUBSCRIBERS

One key aim of content marketers is to convert people who have arrived on a website, blog, or social media page into engaged consumers, who subscribe and allow two-way communication.

Stage 1 Marketers post content, such as a video, article, or special offer, to draw in consumers.

Stage 2 They rely on social media users to share content with their friends, and spread their post to a wider audience.

Stage 3 They monitor response rates from consumers and audit their posts.

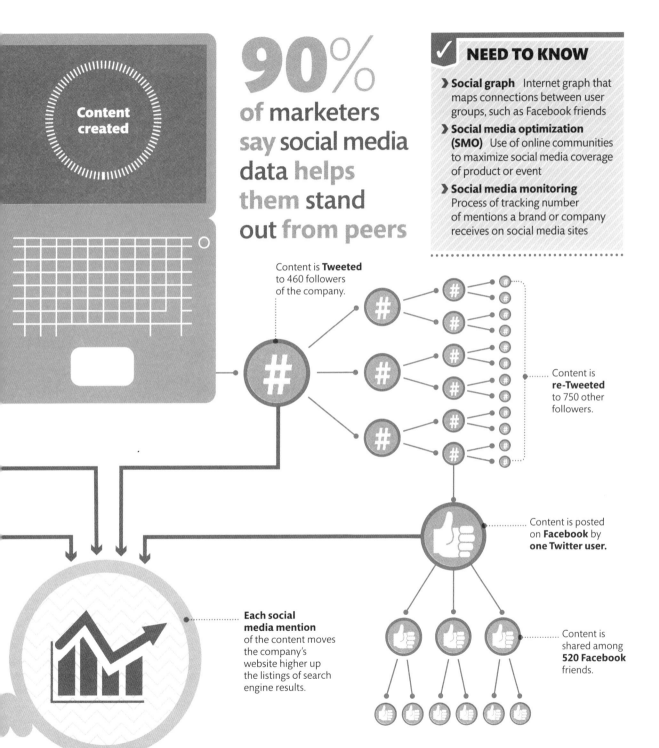

Content created

90%
of marketers say social media data helps them stand out from peers

✓ **NEED TO KNOW**

> **Social graph** Internet graph that maps connections between user groups, such as Facebook friends
> **Social media optimization (SMO)** Use of online communities to maximize social media coverage of product or event
> **Social media monitoring** Process of tracking number of mentions a brand or company receives on social media sites

Content is **Tweeted** to 460 followers of the company.

Content is **re-Tweeted** to 750 other followers.

Content is posted on **Facebook** by **one Twitter user.**

Each social media mention of the content moves the company's website higher up the listings of search engine results.

Content is shared among **520 Facebook** friends.

Search engine optimization (SEO)

SEO is a process marketers use to acquire traffic from search results on search engine sites. SEO software tools are available to help the user create web pages that will appear at the top of search engine listings.

How it works

Companies that have a web presence must ensure that their website has a high ranking on search engine listings. To achieve this, they frequently use SEO tools to monitor where their website appears when keywords are searched for, and take steps to keep it moving up the search results page. Some of the important measures marketers take include coming up with the right keywords, linking to other websites, and generating content that includes frequently searched keywords or phrases, so that their website remains relevant to a wide variety of search queries.

Search engines offer pay-per-click, a service that places a company's listing at the top of a search results page. Every click generates a fee payable to the search engine.

32%
of people click on the top Google search result

SEO process

These tools can be used regularly in a continuous attempt to move a website higher up the listings.

Keyword research
Use SEO tools to research the most popular keywords.

❯ **Brainstorm keywords**
❯ **Use tools to expand list**
❯ **Think how users will search**

Optimize pages
Create pages with the right elements to rank high.

❯ **Create similar content to top-ranked pages for keywords**
❯ **Write compelling title tags**
❯ **Use descriptive URLs, image tags, and file names**

Structure and technical SEO
Help search engines to find, crawl, and index your site.

❯ **Use logical site structure**
❯ **Ensure site is mobile-friendly and fast to load**
❯ **Make site secure with HTTPS**

Keyword selection
Use intuition and analysis with SEO tools to narrow your list.

❯ **Analyse traffic for keywords**
❯ **See how difficult it is to rank for each keyword**
❯ **Decide how best to compete**

NEED TO KNOW

❯ **Robot.txt** Text file that stops web-crawler software, such as Googlebot, from crawling certain web pages

❯ **Search algorithm** Step-by-step calculation that looks for clues to decide on search rankings

❯ **Metadata** Information that describes stored data – data about data

❯ **Black hat SEO** Frowned-upon SEO practices – such as stuffing in too many keywords – that go against search-engine guidelines

❯ **Bounce rate** The proportion of visitors who leave a website after viewing only one page

SEO TIPS

Avoid single words because multiple-word phrases rank higher.

Add blog to offer content that search engines will pick up.

Use reputable sites with relevant content to link back to your site.

Monitor search statistics, for example, using Google Keyword Planner or Semrush.

Prioritize good content and update it regularly with keywords.

Give headings keywords that relate to content on page.

Link-building
Add links from related websites to point back to own site.

❯ **Link to high-profile sites**
❯ **Contribute to social media**
❯ **Ask partners to link up**
❯ **Mimic rivals' web links**

Reporting and tracking
Use tools to track traffic and report on website ranking.

❯ **Focus on quality of visits**
❯ **Check server reports**
❯ **Tally sales from searches**

Keyword revision
Monitor search results from current keyword selection and make adjustments.

❯ **Check terms aren't broad**
❯ **Avoid specialist words**
❯ **Alter word order**

SEO spider
Software that crawls the internet, adding content to search engine databases

Business development

The overall aim of sales and marketing teams is to generate customer contact and convert it into revenue. This is the core of business development and it involves a continual process of drawing in potential customers, enticing them to purchase, and keeping them engaged. During this process, marketers and sales people use a range of strategies and channels to attract customers and to earn their long-term commitment to a brand and product.

Collaborative process

Marketing departments generate brand identity while sales teams do the selling. Working together, they aim to take potential customers on a journey from brand awareness to repeat sales, communicating the message through various channels.

Social media

Live events

Face-to-face communication

Build brand awareness

Target customer groups with content and/or ad campaigns to inform them about the brand and its values. This will lay the foundation for a long-term relationship to grow. *See pp.234-235.*

Generate leads

Use a combination of inbound and outbound marketing strategies to entice potential customers to seek out the brand or product. *See pp.236-237.*

Convert leads into sales

Once potential customers are interested, entice them to buy with targeted messages, offers, and well-designed e-commerce sites. *See pp.238-239.*

Advertising

Public relations

Email lists

Telemarketing

63%
of companies do not have a structured approach to optimizing their business

BUSINESS DEVELOPMENT STRATEGIES

Business development is reliant on growth. Sales and marketing teams can increase long-term profitability by building up a customer base and then trying to retain it. There are several ways to ensure the customer base remains buoyant.

❯ **Chart customer journey** from before to after sale.

❯ **Think of ways to reduce cost of sale** and increase customer satisfaction.

❯ **Integrate sales processes** with marketing to gain and retain customers; think about ideal customer.

❯ **Monitor and evaluate** these processes regularly.

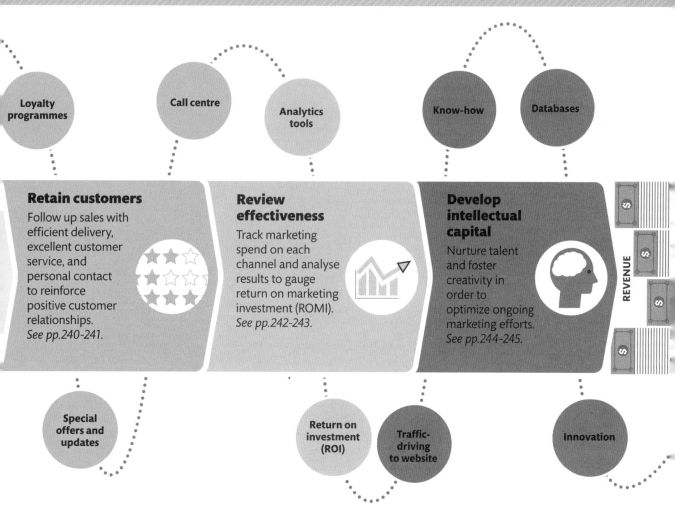

Loyalty programmes

Call centre

Analytics tools

Know-how

Databases

Retain customers
Follow up sales with efficient delivery, excellent customer service, and personal contact to reinforce positive customer relationships.
See pp.240-241.

Review effectiveness
Track marketing spend on each channel and analyse results to gauge return on marketing investment (ROMI).
See pp.242-243.

Develop intellectual capital
Nurture talent and foster creativity in order to optimize ongoing marketing efforts.
See pp.244-245.

REVENUE

Special offers and updates

Return on investment (ROI)

Traffic-driving to website

Innovation

Branding and rebranding

A brand is defined by the characteristics that mark a particular product. Branding is used to communicate a product's qualities to a consumer, and create a lasting bond between supplier and customer.

How it works

When a supplier develops a brand, it creates a defined set of values, expressed in product imagery, colours, logo, slogan, jingles, promotional imagery, and how employees relate to customers and suppliers.

The brand works for both supplier and customer, aiming to eliminate uncertainty and risk, and to convey key attributes. These days, social media helps to promote brands – for example, 90 per cent of Instagram users follow a brand.

The branding cycle

There are typical stages to branding a product. In order to rebrand (redevelop) a product, the supplier starts at the beginning again.

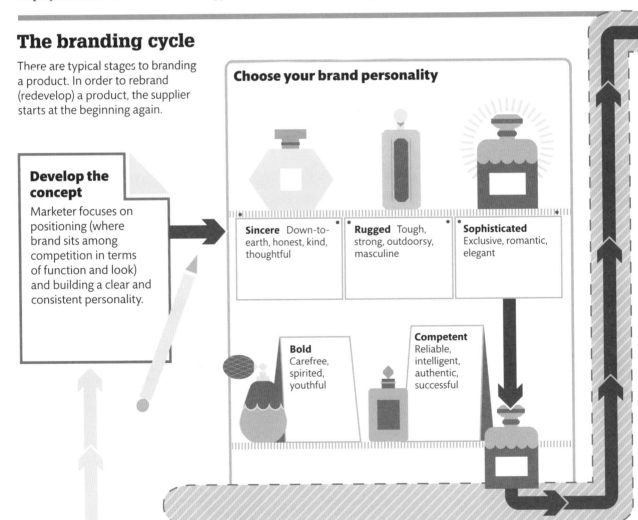

Develop the concept

Marketer focuses on positioning (where brand sits among competition in terms of function and look) and building a clear and consistent personality.

Choose your brand personality

Sincere Down-to-earth, honest, kind, thoughtful

Rugged Tough, strong, outdoorsy, masculine

Sophisticated Exclusive, romantic, elegant

Bold Carefree, spirited, youthful

Competent Reliable, intelligent, authentic, successful

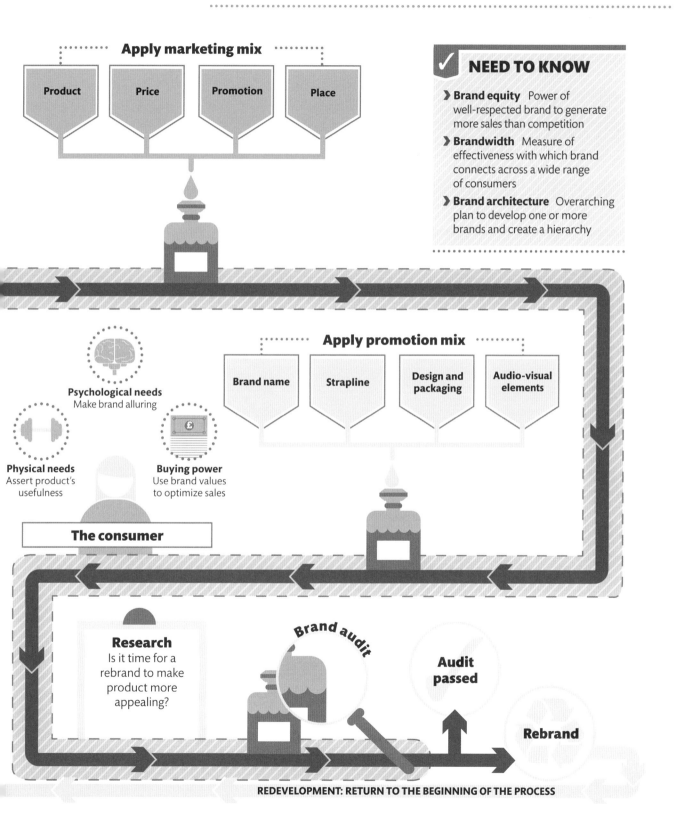

Apply marketing mix

- Product
- Price
- Promotion
- Place

Psychological needs
Make brand alluring

Physical needs
Assert product's usefulness

Buying power
Use brand values to optimize sales

Apply promotion mix

- Brand name
- Strapline
- Design and packaging
- Audio-visual elements

The consumer

Research
Is it time for a rebrand to make product more appealing?

Brand audit

Audit passed

Rebrand

REDEVELOPMENT: RETURN TO THE BEGINNING OF THE PROCESS

Lead generation

For a business to grow, one of its basic goals is to acquire new customers. Lead generation is the strategy it uses to locate, target, and nurture leads (potential customers).

How it works

The purpose of generating leads is to find consumers who may need or want to buy the product a business is selling. Sales teams do not want to waste resources on people who have no interest in the product in the first place, so the process of lead generation helps to define and capture the potential customers who seem most inclined to become actual customers – known as high-quality leads. To generate leads, marketing and sales typically collaborate on a campaign, offline or online, designed to identify and recruit promising customer prospects. Acquiring contact information is the first part of the process. Converting leads into sales is the next step (*see pp.238–239*).

Lead-generation process

Generating leads is a multi-step process that involves sales, marketing, and customer-service teams working together to plan, design, produce, test, and refine a campaign.

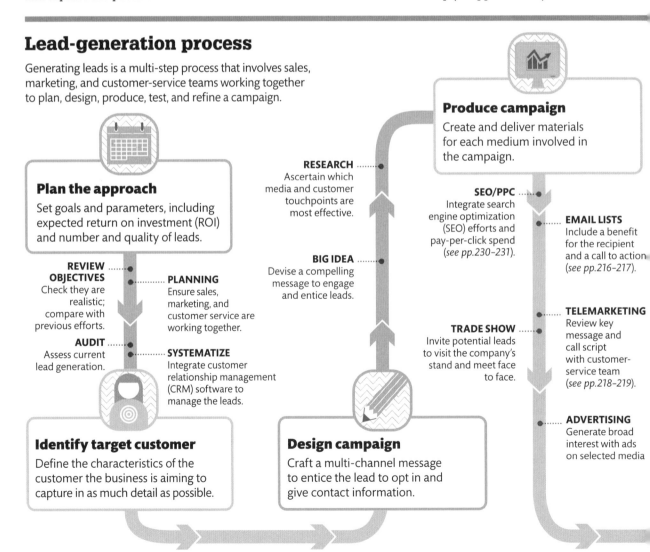

Plan the approach
Set goals and parameters, including expected return on investment (ROI) and number and quality of leads.

REVIEW OBJECTIVES
Check they are realistic; compare with previous efforts.

PLANNING
Ensure sales, marketing, and customer service are working together.

AUDIT
Assess current lead generation.

SYSTEMATIZE
Integrate customer relationship management (CRM) software to manage the leads.

Identify target customer
Define the characteristics of the customer the business is aiming to capture in as much detail as possible.

RESEARCH
Ascertain which media and customer touchpoints are most effective.

BIG IDEA
Devise a compelling message to engage and entice leads.

Design campaign
Craft a multi-channel message to entice the lead to opt in and give contact information.

Produce campaign
Create and deliver materials for each medium involved in the campaign.

SEO/PPC
Integrate search engine optimization (SEO) efforts and pay-per-click spend (*see pp.230–231*).

TRADE SHOW
Invite potential leads to visit the company's stand and meet face to face.

EMAIL LISTS
Include a benefit for the recipient and a call to action (*see pp.216–217*).

TELEMARKETING
Review key message and call script with customer-service team (*see pp.218–219*).

ADVERTISING
Generate broad interest with ads on selected media.

TOP FIVE STRATEGIES FOR LEAD GENERATION

❯ **Create content** such as a viral video or a newsworthy business report that takes leads to a sign-up page.

❯ **Use both online and offline channels**, as most customers will respond to just one channel.

❯ **Trace each customer touchpoint**, the point at which a customer comes into contact with the product, before, during, and after purchase. Touchpoints may range from online reviews to billing.

❯ **Tailor the call to action** to the channel, such as inviting trade-show visitors to enter a competition.

❯ **Design effective opt-in web forms** to capture data, such as asking customers to sign up for updates.

✓ NEED TO KNOW

❯ **Owned media** Channel owned by a business, such as a website, blog, or social media profile

❯ **Attention, interest, desire, action (AIDA)** Model for effective marketing messages

❯ **Cost per lead (CPL)** Amount it costs company to acquire one potential customer

QUALIFIED LEADS
Determine percentage of initial contacts with purchase capability.

ANALYSE PERFORMANCE
Identify adjustments needed to keep campaign on track.

Refine
Fine-tune the filtering process to ensure leads being generated are high quality and likely to buy.

RESPONSE RATES
Tally how many leads have been generated so far.

ONLINE CONVERSION RATES
Calculate percentage of web visitors converted to leads.

Measure
Track and measure the response from the various campaign activities to gauge effectiveness.

Test campaign
Monitor the initial hours and days of the campaign and make any corrections that are needed.

B2B LEAD GENERATION

Most businesses selling to other businesses (B2B) identify lead generation as one of their most important digital-marketing priorities. But which tactics do they find most effective?

- EMAIL 50%
- SEARCH (OPTIMIZATION & MARKETING) 43%
- CONTENT MARKETING 34%
- LIVE EVENTS 32%
- SOCIAL MEDIA 23%
- OTHER 19%
- PPC/ DISPLAY ADS 16%
- TELEMARKETING 13%
- RETARGETING 11%
- INFLUENCER MARKETING 10%
- PRINT 9%

% of B2B firms that place tactic in top three for generating leads with the highest return on investment in 2020

Lead conversion

The process of turning a customer's interest into a sale is called lead conversion. The task requires not only a sales pitch to promote the product or service, but also an approach tailored to the customer.

How it works

Sales and marketing departments are responsibile for generating sales income for a company. The first step is to locate or identify potential customers – lead generation. The second step is to make contact with those potential customers and entice or persuade them to buy – lead conversion.

A sales pitch is used to convert leads into customers. However, nowadays the stereotypical spiel delivered by an overzealous salesperson has been largely replaced by more sophisticated tactics, such as live chat on shopping websites, which inform customers and invite them to participate in a dialogue, rather than simply pestering them.

Raw lead
Potential customers, perhaps a website visitor or a person encountered at a live event

?

Pitch Find precise needs of suspect; show product's qualities and unique values to counter objections.

50/50

Prospect
One step away from becoming a customer, prospects need a final enticement to convince them to buy the product.

Pitch Reinforce product's value to prospect; offer payment options; highlight customer satisfaction policy.

Pitch Keep in touch with inactive prospect (with their consent) through updates, offers, product add-ons, or discounts.

✓ NEED TO KNOW

> **Lead scoring** System used to measure readiness of leads for conversion

> **Sales pipeline** Visual tracking of number of leads, suspects, and prospects at each stage in order to monitor sales process

> **Lead nurturing** Informal contact with a lead designed to gradually win them over as a customer

> **Cost per touch** Measurement of cost of sales labour each time lead is "touched" (contacted)

Customer
Raw lead has committed to buy; focus is now on retaining the customer and enticing them to make repeat purchase.

2.27%
the average lead conversion rate via e-commerce sites in 2021

Online lead conversion

A strategy is required for steering website visitors through every step of the lead-converting process. It is often presented as a funnel. Once visitors have arrived at a website, they are enticed to click on a "call to action" (CTA) button, which takes them further into the funnel.

Pitch Involve raw lead in website experience or conversation; identify need for product; show benefits.

Suspect

Raw leads show their interest by remaining on website or by not ending conversation with company representative.

Inactive

Prospect is not ready to buy immediately, but shows enough interest to suggest they might buy in the future.

Dead lead

Lead will not convert, but may be worth trying to revive in future.

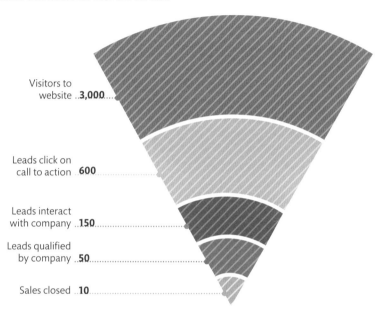

Visitors to website ..**3,000**....

Leads click on call to action ..**600**

Leads interact with company ..**150**..........

Leads qualified by company ..**50**...........

Sales closed ..**10**.........

THREE CLASSIC SALES PITCHES

High concept
Catchy introduction that captures the vision or key idea of a product or business; intended to grab attention and interest

Elevator
Short précis (under a minute long) that explains the why, what, and how of a business or product

20-minute deck
Presentation that explains the product or business in detail; how it can serve the need a prospective customer may have

Customer retention

Given that existing customers help businesses generate the majority of profit and growth through making additional sales and referrals, retaining these customers is a huge priority for marketers.

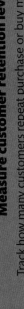

Measure customer retention level

Track how many customers repeat purchase or buy more products.

Identify satisfied customers

Customer referral

Measure the number of referrals an individual customer generates.

Loyalty

Pinpoint customers who are active in the brand's loyalty programme.

Identify the dissatisfied

Defection

Find out why certain customers have left and which competitor they have gone to.

Complaint analysis

Examine written customer complaints and call-centre records.

Introduce retention improvement strategy

Early warning systems

Anticipate any problems and alert customers in advance.

Recovery programmes

Apologize for any mistakes and make amends to woo dissatisfied customers back.

Customer feed-back surveys

Listen to customers and identfiy those at risk of defecting.

loyalty card

Loyalty programmes

Reward customers with improved incentives for staying loyal.

Boost customer service

Offer employees incentives to build customer relations.

Monitor and measure by analysing

Customer satisfaction

Assess rate of customer complaints and recommendations.

EXISTING CUSTOMERS   EXITING CUSTOMERS

Attrition rate

Calculate the number of customers retained (existing), lost (exiting), or gained in a given period.

Revenue targets

Measure revenue targets against cost of customer-retention efforts.

How it works

There are two stages to the process of customer retention: measuring the current rate of retention, and applying strategies to manage and improve it.

Practices include identifying the most valuable customers and nurturing relationships with them. The least valuable or most costly customers may be dropped if they show little development potential.

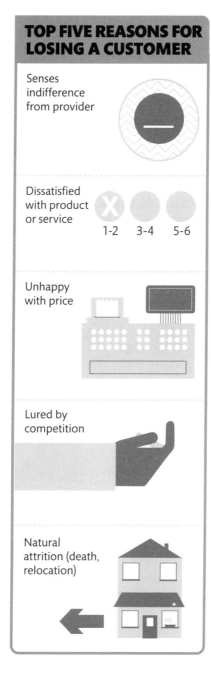

Upsell and cross-sell leads

Identify customers who may buy larger products, or related items.

1-2 3-4 5-6
7-8 9-10

Net promoter score

Gauge how likely a customer is to recommend the company to others.

Customer retention savings

Calculate savings made in marketing spend by retaining existing customers.

TOP FIVE REASONS FOR LOSING A CUSTOMER

Senses indifference from provider

Dissatisfied with product or service
1-2 3-4 5-6

Unhappy with price

Lured by competition

Natural attrition (death, relocation)

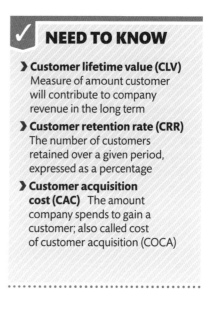

✓ NEED TO KNOW

› **Customer lifetime value (CLV)** Measure of amount customer will contribute to company revenue in the long term

› **Customer retention rate (CRR)** The number of customers retained over a given period, expressed as a percentage

› **Customer acquisition cost (CAC)** The amount company spends to gain a customer; also called cost of customer acquisition (COCA)

82%
of firms agree that customer retention is cheaper than acquisition – but most focus more on the latter

Return on marketing investment (ROMI)

Many organizations gauge the effectiveness of the amount they spend on marketing campaigns by measuring the return they make on marketing investment, which is commonly known as ROMI.

How it works

A subset of return on investment (ROI), return on marketing investment (ROMI) is one of the key calculations businesses use to work out the effectiveness of the money they spend on marketing.

ROMI is measured by comparing the revenue gained against the investment made in marketing, and is used to assess online campaigns, in particular. This calculation, however, only reflects the direct impact of marketing investment on a business's revenue and fails to take into account other gains, such as the word-of-mouth effect on social media, which are more difficult to quantify than the more clear-cut response received from advertising or direct mail.

As a result, nowadays, many digital marketers factor lag time or brand awareness into their ROMI calculations in order to quantify less tangible benefits and target future campaigns more effectively.

ROMI in practice

The diagram shows how a commercial air-conditioning company might use ROMI to measure the performance of a marketing campaign. The company spends US$2,100 on a direct-mail promotion, which it aims at offices in three major cities to generate sales leads and secure new contracts. The direct-mail flyer contains a contact form offering a 10 per cent discount to new clients who respond to the promotion within a specified period of time.

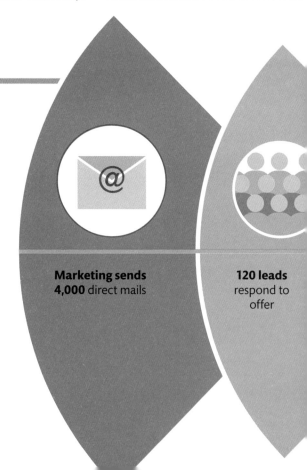

Marketing sends
4,000 direct mails

120 leads
respond to offer

$$\frac{\text{GROSS PROFIT} - \text{MARKETING INVESTMENT}}{\text{MARKETING INVESTMENT}} = \text{ROMI}$$

US$**36** is generated for every US$1 spent on email marketing

LONG-TERM BENEFITS OF MARKETING INVESTMENT

Some aspects of marketing investment are difficult to measure immediately. The benefits of providing excellent customer service, for example, or investing in research to help marketers retain customers, may not be evident right away but will reap long-term profits.

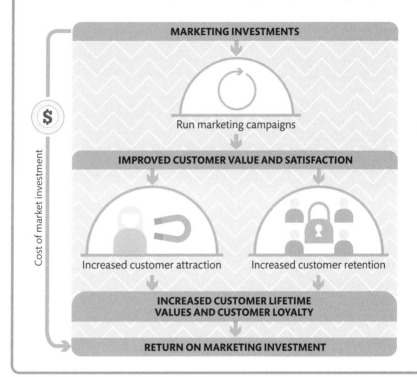

Cost of market investment

$

MARKETING INVESTMENTS

Run marketing campaigns

IMPROVED CUSTOMER VALUE AND SATISFACTION

Increased customer attraction

Increased customer retention

INCREASED CUSTOMER LIFETIME VALUES AND CUSTOMER LOYALTY

RETURN ON MARKETING INVESTMENT

14 qualified leads
(who are a good fit for the product) become sales opportunities

3 of these become customers

Results

Total new customers = 3
Average customer spend = US$6,500 (after 10% discount deducted from average US$7,222 total spend)
Revenue from marketing = US$19,500 (3 x US$6,500)
Campaign spend = US$2,100 + US$2,167 (3 x US$722) cost to company of promotional discount = US$4,267 total
ROMI = US$4.57 per customer / per US$1 spent on the campaign

$$\frac{US\$19,500}{US\$4,267} = US\$4.57$$

Intellectual capital

The knowledge within a company that is used to improve business performance is known as its intellectual capital.

How it works

Every business has capital, which refers to the physical, tangible assets that appear on the balance sheet of its financial statements.

A business also has intellectual capital – the knowledge and skills inside the company. This collective know-how is hard to quantify and measure, but it is essential to a company's ability to generate revenue. For instance, management must provide training and a handover period for new staff so that human capital does not go down when people leave the company, taking their expertise with them. Management academics have identified three main kinds of intellectual capital: human, structural, and customer.

✓ NEED TO KNOW

❯ **Strategic capital** Company's knowledge of its market and the business model needed for success

❯ **Intellectual property** Creations or inventions that are legally recognized as belonging to a particular entity or individual on a balance sheet

❯ **Intangible capital** All knowledge assets belonging to a business or organization; can be audited under various systems (*see far right*)

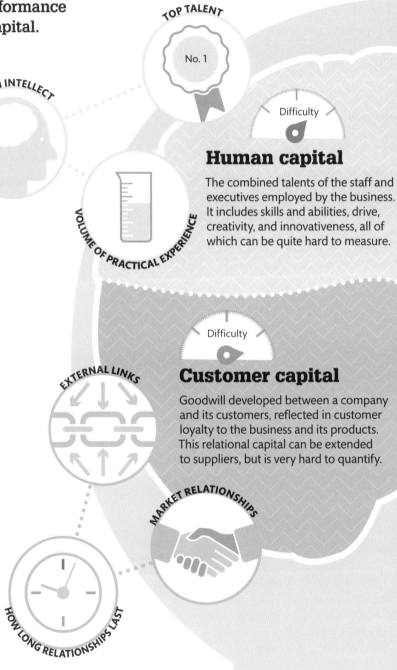

HUMAN INTELLECT

TOP TALENT

No. 1

Difficulty

Human capital

The combined talents of the staff and executives employed by the business. It includes skills and abilities, drive, creativity, and innovativeness, all of which can be quite hard to measure.

VOLUME OF PRACTICAL EXPERIENCE

EXTERNAL LINKS

Difficulty

Customer capital

Goodwill developed between a company and its customers, reflected in customer loyalty to the business and its products. This relational capital can be extended to suppliers, but is very hard to quantify.

MARKET RELATIONSHIPS

HOW LONG RELATIONSHIPS LAST

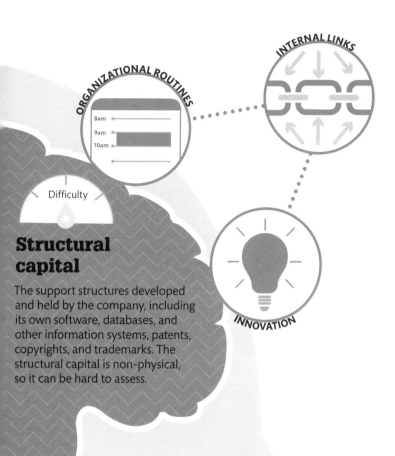

ORGANIZATIONAL ROUTINES

8am
9am
10am

INTERNAL LINKS

INNOVATION

Difficulty

Structural capital

The support structures developed and held by the company, including its own software, databases, and other information systems, patents, copyrights, and trademarks. The structural capital is non-physical, so it can be hard to assess.

"The only irreplaceable capital an organization possesses is the knowledge and ability of its people."

Andrew Carnegie, *industrialist*

MEASURING INTELLECTUAL CAPITAL

Measuring intellectual capital precisely is impossible because it is intangible, but its value to businesses means it is helpful to try to quantify it. There is no consistent way of doing this, but there are a few common approaches.

Market Value to Book Value Ratio

This looks at the difference between the financial value of the company, its book value - the difference between assets and liabilities – and the market value, which is the value of its shares. The difference includes intellectual capital and growth prospects.

The Skandia Navigator

This was developed by Leif Edvinsson, director of Swedish company Skandia, who created a model for quantifying intangible assets under five groupings – finance, customer, process, renewal and development, and human. This enables companies to understand how the difference between the market value and the book value of the business is created.

The Balanced Scorecard

Developed by US academics Robert Kaplan and David Norton, the Balanced Scorecard system (*see p.147*) uses four categories - learning and growth, business processes, customers, and finance - to measure intellectual capital alongside financial data. For example, analysing learning and growth provides insight into a company's human capital, while looking at business processes might reveal, say, if intellectual capital invested in manufacturing improvements is having an effect.

Information management

Monitoring the marketplace and making sense of the vast quantities of data available has become a priority for businesses; the data is crucial for digital marketing, which is taking on increasingly sophisticated forms. Nowadays, most businesses have a system in place for managing information – the most successful organizations use data not only to monitor day-to-day performance at every level, but to predict future outcomes and plan accordingly.

External

Outside the business, data flows in from production, supply chain, sales outlets, partners, and customers.

Internal

Within the business itself, data feeds into the marketing and IT teams from operations, finance, and HR.

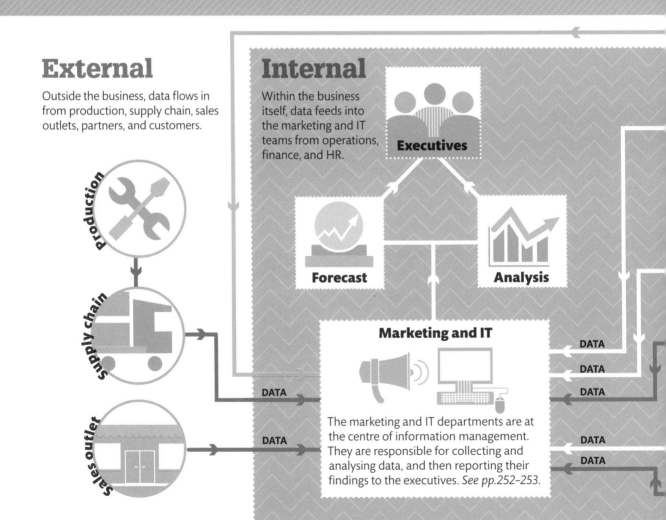

Production

supply chain

sales outlet

Executives

Forecast

Analysis

DATA

DATA

Marketing and IT

DATA

DATA

DATA

DATA

The marketing and IT departments are at the centre of information management. They are responsible for collecting and analysing data, and then reporting their findings to the executives. *See pp.252–253.*

DATA

DATA

50%
of organizations employed a chief digital officer in 2019 – up from 7% in 2014

LEGAL COMPLIANCE

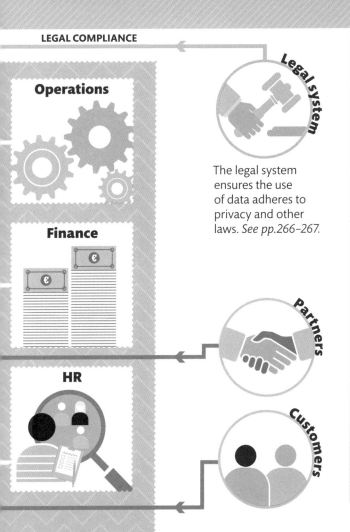

Operations

Finance

HR

Legal system

The legal system ensures the use of data adheres to privacy and other laws. *See pp.266–267.*

Partners

Customers

TRANSFORMING DATA INTO DECISIONS

With relevant data easily accessible (*see pp.262–263*) a business can identify its strengths and weaknesses in order to improve its processes and operations, as well as customer relationships (*see pp.264–265*).

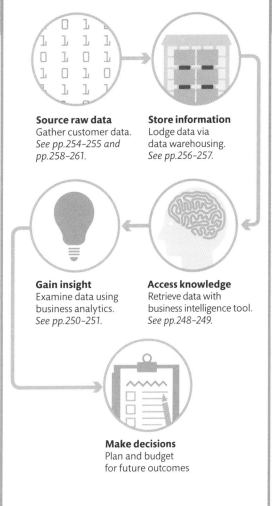

Source raw data
Gather customer data. *See pp.254–255 and pp.258–261.*

Store information
Lodge data via data warehousing. *See pp.256–257.*

Gain insight
Examine data using business analytics. *See pp.250–251.*

Access knowledge
Retrieve data with business intelligence tool. *See pp.248–249.*

Make decisions
Plan and budget for future outcomes

Business intelligence

Business intelligence (BI) is an umbrella term referring to the variety of software applications companies use to access and analyse the massive amounts of raw data they have at their fingertips.

How it works

BI relies on software programs and computerized systems for collecting and integrating data in order that a business can report on its activities, both past and present. The tools allow staff to pull relevant data from the company database. The marketer will then view the information on a computer screen using a data visualization tool known as a "dashboard", which can also be used for real-time monitoring of business operations.

Business intelligence process

BI tools allow retrieval of specific relevant data by specifying the terms of the intelligence they need (such as real-time sales compared to previous year's sales).

Collect source data

Company gathers raw data via several operation systems.

SUPPLY CHAIN MANAGEMENT (SCM)
Data from SCM sources

ENTERPRISE RESOURCE PLANNING (ERP)
Manages company data

WEB LOGS
Data relating to activity on corporate or e-commerce sites

TRANSACTIONAL DATABASE
Data of current commercial transactions

CUSTOMER RELATIONSHIP MANAGEMENT (CRM)
Data from CRM sources

EXTERNAL DATABASE
Information gathered from sources outside the company

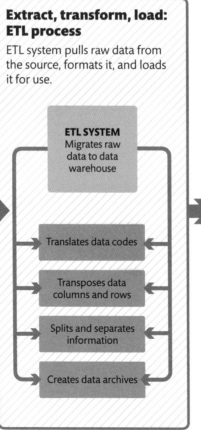

Extract, transform, load: ETL process

ETL system pulls raw data from the source, formats it, and loads it for use.

ETL SYSTEM
Migrates raw data to data warehouse

Translates data codes

Transposes data columns and rows

Splits and separates information

Creates data archives

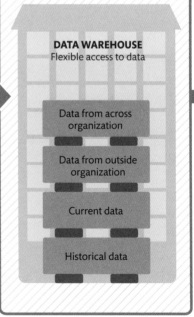

Store data

Business uses data warehousing to integrate and bank data in a readily accessible form.

DATA WAREHOUSE
Flexible access to data

Data from across organization

Data from outside organization

Current data

Historical data

21%

of employees worldwide are fully confident about their data literacy skills

Digital dashboard
Displays regularly updated business results using customized graphics.

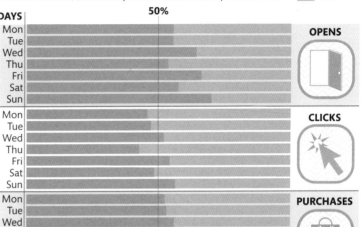

TRACKING EMAIL CAMPAIGN
This dashboard tracks the percentage of people who open an email, click on a website, and make a purchase on different days of the week.

YES
NO

DAYS   50%

Mon
Tue
Wed
Thu
Fri
Sat
Sun   **OPENS**

Mon
Tue
Wed
Thu
Fri
Sat
Sun   **CLICKS**

Mon
Tue
Wed
Thu
Fri
Sat
Sun   **PURCHASES**

Retrieve and analyse
Staff can fetch data to answer specific questions about what is happening in the company.

SPREADSHEETS
Form primary BI tool to display data (basic or advanced)

OLAP CUBES
Online analytical processing cubes enable 3-D analysis of three variables on spreadsheet

DATA MINING
Allows the sifting of data to find patterns and relationships

REPORTING TOOLS
Help users develop and produce reports

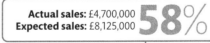

Actual sales: £4,700,000
Expected sales: £8,125,000
58%

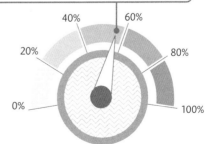

TRACKING SALES
This dashboard shows the sales a company actually makes as a percentage of expected sales.

40%   60%
20%   80%
0%   100%

Business analytics

More cutting edge than business intelligence (BI), business analytics (BA) allows advanced statistical analysis of data, which is used to help make future business decisions.

How it works

BA takes a scientific approach to interpreting information. Businesses use BA's advanced software tools to analyse information about past or current trends and behaviour to predict a future scenario. Unlike business intelligence or predictive analytics that analyse current and past data, BA allows businesses to forecast with a high degree of confidence. BA can be applied on a macro level to get a broad view of future business performance and on a micro level to assess, for example, the likelihood of individuals in niche markets making purchases.

Predictive modelling

Software program that predicts patterns of behaviour and the likelihood of specific sets of customers, or even individuals, making a purchase.

Business analytics process

A skilled analyst interprets the raw data using BA tools. The results influence the business actions that will be taken in the future.

BUSINESS INTELLIGENCE AND BUSINESS ANALYTICS

An example of a 5 per cent sales dip shows how BI and BA can be used to examine and understand the situation.

Business intelligence

> **Type of data investigation** Results reveal past and current events in the business

> **Questions answered** What has happened in the business in the past and what is happening currently?

> **Tools used** Reporting, dashboards, scorecards, online analytical processing (OLAP)

Business analytics

> **Type of data investigation** Examines past event in the business, and applies the patterns discovered to a future scenario

> **Questions answered** Why did it happen? Will it happen again? What can we do to stop it happening again?

> **Tools used** Statistical analysis, data mining, pattern matching, predictive modelling

81%
of managers globally have access to analytics, but only half of front-line employees do

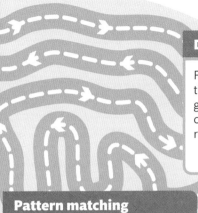

Data visualization

Formulation of graphs depicting the results of the data analysis; graphs may rank data, group common attributes, and compare relationships.

DATA USEFULNESS

Some data is more useful than other data – value is determined by the extent to which marketers can use it to make confident forecasts. Methods of interpreting data are increasingly sophisticated.

Pattern matching

Process of trawling through large quantities of data to find patterns between variables, which can be applied to other sets of data.

Predictive analytics

Program that conducts advanced analysis of data to forecast future outcome.

Data mining

Use of computerized processes and software programs to find relevant patterns in large sets of data.

Monitoring

Process that uses software to show what is currently happening in a business, providing real-time results to help key operations make decisions.

Statistical analysis

Software that organizes and investigates every piece of relevant data and interprets it to show trends and patterns.

In   **Out**

Raw data

This includes company records (past and current customer data and transaction histories) and external data (economic, trade, and industry reports).

Analysis

Software tools are used to process and study raw data. Analysts interpret results and make forecasts that help future business decisions.

Reporting

Method that draws on historical data to provide a general overview, revealing, for example, how the business performed in a given year.

Marketing and IT

The use of digital marketing strategies means that marketers are working more closely with IT specialists to develop the best ways of launching and managing online publicity campaigns.

Convergence of marketing and IT

Communicating with customers online is a vital part of many businesses. As a result, marketing relies so much on IT that in some companies marketing teams spend more money on technology than their IT departments do.

Marketer
Must grasp technology required to execute and track online campaigns.

Areas of overlap

◀ Digital marketing ▶

Developing a technology programme for publicity campaigns

Real-time transactions ▶

Installing a system for recording and tracking online sales as they happen

◀ Big data ▶

Locating key statistics from vast amounts of online information to improve marketing

◀ Data analytics

Using advanced tools to gather and analyse data for developing future marketing strategy

◀ Mobile technology ▶

Understanding and keeping up to date with advances in mobile applications and e-commerce potential

Data storage ▶

Building infrastructure and software for storing and retrieving sales, campaign, and customer history

◀ Social media ▶

Developing the best methods for increasing online traffic via social media channels

Tracking ▶

Following a customer through the online engagement and sales process

How it works

Marketers need to know how to use technology to increase revenue. At the same time, chief information officers (CIOs) have adapted to changes in external technology. The responsibilities of marketing and IT departments often overlap, with the hybrid professional role of marketing technologist (*see below*) sitting between the two fields.

8,000
marketing technology tools are available to businesses

IT person
Must find or develop software tools to implement and manage online campaigns.

✓ NEED TO KNOW

> **MarTech** Annual business conference that focuses on overlap of marketing strategy and technology

> **Actionable metrics** Measurement of campaign results that enable businesses to make informed decisions

> **Vanity metrics** Measurements of campaign results that appear positive but are not meaningful

> **Growth hacking** Low-cost online marketing techniques, such as using social media to improve sales

THE MARKETING TECHNOLOGIST

Online marketers rely on software to monitor and analyse campaigns, generate content, and extract data. The job of the marketing technologist, who has knowledge of both marketing and IT, requires a broad knowledge base.

- WEBSITE ARCHITECTURE
- SOFTWARE PROGRAMMING
- MARKETING SOFTWARE
- DATA AND ANALYTICS
- SOCIAL AND MOBILE PLATFORMS
- IT OPERATIONS
- CONTENT MARKETING AND SEO

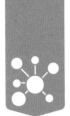

Collecting consumer data

Capturing key data is a priority for any business seeking to understand the marketplace. However, the task requires the use of innovative strategies to circumvent consumer sensitivity about privacy issues.

How it works

There are a number of methods that companies use in order to collect customer data. When there is contact between a customer and the company, marketers can use the opportunity to gather as much information as possible. This might happen at the point of sale in-store or online, where marketers are able to observe customer behaviour.

Marketers may also choose to solicit information directly by asking their customers to fill in registration forms and conducting telemarketing calls or customer surveys.

Collecting data to create consumer profile

Digital marketing and e-commerce have accelerated the rate at which customer information is gathered. Some methods require the customer's input, such as questionnaires that appear online. Others, such as website tracking, are possible without the need to contact the customer.

Surveys
Gather customer feedback via email, text/SMS, or postal, and face-to-face questionnaires.

Observations
Study customer's behaviour while they shop in-store or online.

Customer research
Conduct research on existing customers or on those who fit the customer profile.

Contact centre
Monitor customer calls and store data on preferences and purchase history.

⚠ WARNING

Data collection errors

> **Barraging** Using a customer's data to bombard them with information on products viewed or sites visited

> **Overlooking technical flaws**
Failing to integrate apps properly so that there is inconsistency (and errors) in collecting customer data

> **Using only automated systems**
Neglecting the opportunity to strengthen relationship with customer by communicating with them personally

Social media
View customer's profile information on social media.

Website trackers
Track website visitor's movement around site and see what attracts interest.

Competitions
Use competitions to collect information, from opinions to demographic data.

Transactions
Ask questions at checkout – in-store, online, or on the phone.

10%
of global internet users run ad-blocking software, which can stop online data tracking

TECHNOLOGY AT THE CHECKOUT

In this technological age, businesses have the means to learn about their customers without bombarding them with questions. Retailers, for example, typically use three methods in the shop to capture information about the customer.

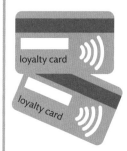

loyalty card

loyalty card

Loyalty programme
A company may collect information by inviting customers to register for a loyalty programme that offers an incentive. A loyalty programme also helps track customer preferences.

Point-of-sale software
Computer software programs that track a customer's purchases are available, allowing marketers to tailor offers to their spending habits.

Mobile technology
The use of smartphones enables marketers to compile data, for example the frequency of customer visits and the amount of time they spend in the store.

Data warehousing

The process of data warehousing involves information from a company's internal system, such as invoices and sales logs, as well as data from outside sources, being filed away in a secure digital vault.

How it works

The data warehouse is a repository that holds the company's sales and operational history, as well as relevant economic and trade information from other sources. The data goes through three stages as it enters the warehouse: first it is *extracted* from source, then it is *loaded*, and finally, it is *transformed* into usable formats. Together, this is known as the ELT process. Once stored, the data may be accessed by all areas of a company – from accounts to operations to sales. The data is often used to prove beliefs about the business. For example, the marketing manager of a power tools firm might presume that 25–35-year-old men are more likely to purchase its products than women in the same age bracket. The manager would be able to prove this belief by analysing the sales data and customer records accessed from the data warehouse.

US$51 billion
predicted size of the data warehouse market in 2028

Warehousing process

The data stored is regularly updated. When the business requires information from the warehouse, it is transformed into an accessible format and analysed using software tools. Data can be stored on in-house servers, or on external servers in the cloud provided by a third party.

Tapping data sources

The information a company collects includes online transaction processing (OLTP) data, historical data, and data from external sources.

Staging data

The ELT process converts raw data into a usable format.

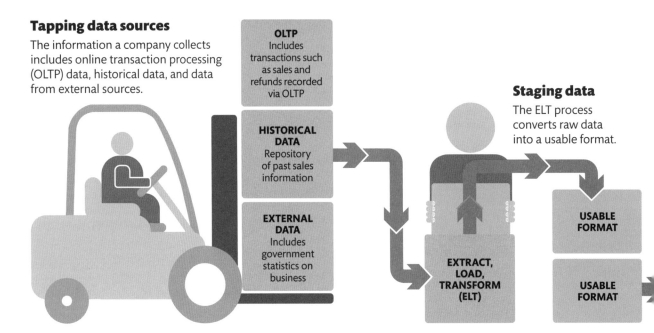

OLTP
Includes transactions such as sales and refunds recorded via OLTP

HISTORICAL DATA
Repository of past sales information

EXTERNAL DATA
Includes government statistics on business

EXTRACT, LOAD, TRANSFORM (ELT)

USABLE FORMAT

USABLE FORMAT

WHO USES THE DATA WAREHOUSE?

The key departments of a company can access the data warehouse to find out how they are faring. The method in which the data is formatted and stored makes it possible for them to seek answers to questions relevant to them. Typical questions various departments might ask include:

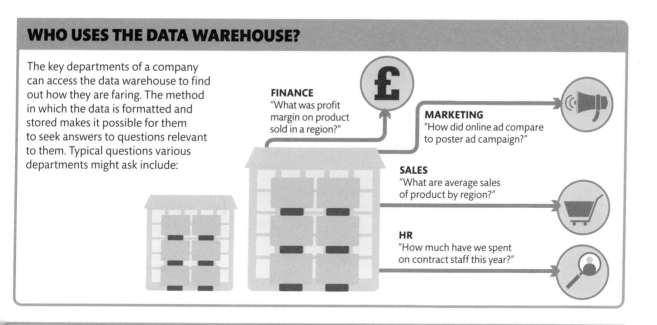

FINANCE
"What was profit margin on product sold in a region?"

MARKETING
"How did online ad compare to poster ad campaign?"

SALES
"What are average sales of product by region?"

HR
"How much have we spent on contract staff this year?"

Storing data

The data is stored in three categories: metadata, summary data, and raw data.

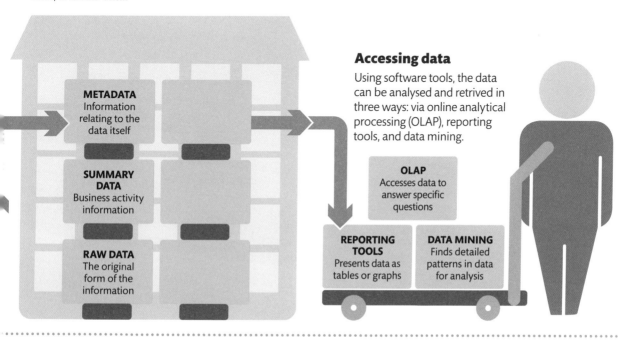

METADATA
Information relating to the data itself

SUMMARY DATA
Business activity information

RAW DATA
The original form of the information

Accessing data

Using software tools, the data can be analysed and retrieved in three ways: via online analytical processing (OLAP), reporting tools, and data mining.

OLAP
Accesses data to answer specific questions

REPORTING TOOLS
Presents data as tables or graphs

DATA MINING
Finds detailed patterns in data for analysis

Customer profiling

Marketers can create detailed portraits of customers using internal company data of their purchase habits, preferences, and lifestyle, and cite external data sources to learn about attitudes and social trends.

How it works

In order to best understand their audience, marketing departments define their ideal customer by developing a customer profile. They build this profile by gathering information about the kind of person who usually buys the type of product they wish to introduce to the marketplace. The information they look at includes basic data about a person, such as gender, age, occupation, and salary, as well as more detailed ideas concerning the person's typical spending habits, such as the places that they like to shop and the amount they tend to spend.

Psychographic view

> **Personality** Outspoken; likes to stand out from the crowd

> **Attitude** Positive outlook and enjoys the good things in life

> **Ethic** Works hard and believes in contributing to social causes

Segmentation model

By constructing a segmentation model, layered with a number of variables (different levels of information) about consumers, marketers can gradually build up a clear picture of their ideal target customer – in this case for a travel company.

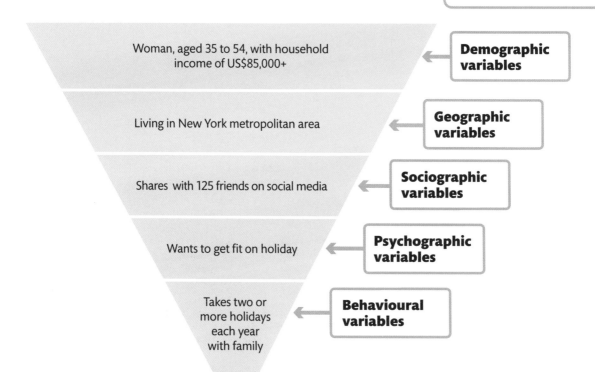

Woman, aged 35 to 54, with household income of US$85,000+ — **Demographic variables**

Living in New York metropolitan area — **Geographic variables**

Shares with 125 friends on social media — **Sociographic variables**

Wants to get fit on holiday — **Psychographic variables**

Takes two or more holidays each year with family — **Behavioural variables**

Behavioural view

> **Shopping location** Prefers to shop in smaller stores

> **Purchase habits** Buys in bulk to be thrifty, responds to discounts

> **Degree of loyalty** Faithful to a brand, but open to better offers

Sociographic view

> **Social media** Actively shares interests with connections

> **Community** Influential member who socializes and contributes to neighbourhood

> **Groups and clubs** Member of bird-watching and hiking group

83%
of consumers are happy to share their data to get a personalized experience

Geographic view

> **Continent** North America

> **City** Booming metropolis with work and social opportunities

> **Climate** Varies from below freezing in winter to hot and humid in summer

Customer profile dimensions

What does the ideal customer look like? Where do they live? What do they spend their money on?

Demographic view

> **Age group** 35–54 (helps gauge family priorities and income)

> **Status** Married (children affect spending choices)

> **Occupation and salary** Teacher, US$65,000

Creating a customer profile

By constructing a profile of an existing customer using data from within the company, marketers have a clearer view of the buying patterns and habits of an individual. They can then make projections about the long-term value of that person.

WEBSITE DATA
How often do they visit the site? Which web pages do they look at?

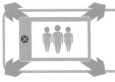

SOCIAL DATA
Which social media networks are they connected to? Do they share links?

TRANSACTION DATA
How much have they spent, how often, and on which products?

CRM DATA
What's their contact history with call centres? How have they responded to campaigns?

LOYALTY DATA
How loyal are they to the company? Do they use the company loyalty scheme?

MAIL DATA
What email contact has there been? What has the response rate to emailed content been?

POINT OF SALE
What observations have sales staff made from interacting with customer?

Customer profile

"Once you understand customer behaviour, everything else falls into place."

Thomas G. Stemberg, *founder of office supplies retailer Staples*

Assessing customer profile

Good customer

❯ Returns frequently to make repeat purchases

❯ Responds to marketing and in-store promotions

❯ Shares favourite products on social media networks

❯ Signs up for newsletters and special offers

Bad customer

❯ Bombards call centre with complaints

❯ Frequently returns products for full refund

❯ Never joins loyalty schemes or signs up for newsletters

❯ Spends less money than the cost of courting them

Three ways to use a customer profile

1 **Tailor content to suit customer** By sending out personalized messages and experiences, businesses engage customers and build a long-term relationship.

2 **Sell more to existing customer** Mining customer profile to see their spending habits, likes, and interests enables marketers to make personalized offers.

3 **Reward loyal customers** Identifying good customers and offering gifts and incentives tailored to their tastes increases customer lifetime value.

SOCIAL ECONOMIC SCALE

The UK has a system of grading people into social classes, which is used for general market research.

 A **Upper-middle class**
High managerial, professional/administrative

 B **Middle class**
Intermediate managerial, professional/administrative

 C1 **Lower-middle class**
Supervisory, clerical, junior managerial, prof/admin

 C2 **Skilled working class**
Skilled manual workers

 D **Working class**
Semi- and unskilled manual workers

 E **Non-working**
Pensioners, unemployed, casual/low-grade workers

✓ NEED TO KNOW

❯ **Omni-channel customer**
Consumer who shops using multiple channels, including store visits, via mobile apps and internet

❯ **Loyads** Customers who are loyal to a provider and champion them, bringing in other customers in the process

❯ **360-view** Profile that gives marketer a complete picture of customer, enabling them to predict their needs and behaviour

Big data

Business is trying to harness the huge amount of consumer data now available online. This information can be analysed and used to create detailed profiles to target customers more precisely.

How it works

Big data describes the mass of digital information transmitted via the internet every day. It is streamed at high speed and in many different formats, from database statistics to video, audio, and email documents. The challenge for most organizations is to sift through big data to find information that has the potential to add value to their business. Software tools are available that can analyse the masses of external data generated on the internet.

Internally and externally mined big data

Businesses are able to access data from sources such as mobile communications, social media networks, and commercial transactions, which show the activity of billions of people.

Big data store

External data source

An ever-expanding amount of data is being generated by outside organizations, which will prove increasingly valuable to businesses.

Big data

The volume of data is potentially so vast it cannot easily be moved and may overwhelm most organizations.

Social media

Data reveals what people are saying about the organization and its products.

Audio

Data includes news broadcasts, interviews, call-centre recordings, and podcasts.

Photos and video

Data comprises blogs, images, video recordings from entertainment media, and surveillance.

Public data

Information is produced by large organizations, but there are many legal constraints on its use.

Big data vendor

Provides services, systems, and tools enabling companies to store, access, and analyse data. Vendor offers applications to suit individual business needs.

50–80%
of data scientists' time is spent preparing data before it can be used

Internal data source

Internal data sent to the big data vault where it is traced and recorded is drawn from all parts of the organization and forms a unified database.

Transactions
> Spend per customer
> Foot traffic in shops
> Time spent per visit

Log data
> Customer reviews
> Customer service
> Audio files of customer service calls, for example

Emails
> Internal communications
> Customer contacts
> Email campaigns

✓ NEED TO KNOW

> **Apache Hadoop** Open-source software library for storing and processing big data
> **Terabyte** One trillion bytes
> **Petabyte** Unit of digital data equivalent to 1,024 terabytes (one petabyte equates to 341 million three-minute songs on MP3)
> **Exabyte** Unit of digital data equivalent to 1,024 petabytes (five exabytes equates to all words ever spoken by human beings)

INFORMATION OVERLOAD

The volume of data typically generated online every second:
> **Emails** 3,048,134 sent
> **Tweets** 9,570 sent
> **Instagram** 1,088 images uploaded
> **Skype** 5,853 calls
> **Internet** 123,432 GB of traffic
> **Google** 93,823 searches
> **YouTube** 90,694 videos watched

DATA MANAGEMENT

Organizations can choose either offline or online options to store big data and various software programs for access and analysis.
> **Big storage hardware** Servers; storage and network equipment capable of supporting many terabytes of data
> **Software** Includes programs for research and analysis, storage and access, and graphic visualization of data
> **Cloud services** Third-party providers that offer storage networks for big data management and access

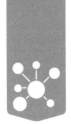

Customer relationship management (CRM)

CRM is a computerized system that a company uses for managing and coordinating marketing, sales, and customer-support data. The data is used to maintain good customer relations, which improves profitability.

How it works

CRM is a software tool in the company's IT system that records all interactions the business has with customers. The information can be used in a number of ways: the sales team may use it to find new business leads and improve relationships with current customers, the marketing team may use it to reward loyalty, and customer service may use it to deal with any issues.

 NEED TO KNOW

> **Technology-enabled relationship management (TERM)** Use of automated processes to manage customer relationships

> **Enterprise resource planning (ERP)** Precursor to CRM

> **Cloud-based CRM** Computerized CRM system that exists on a technology cloud

CRM system

The system uses reliable processes, which allow companies to connect more efficiently with customers and ultimately offer a better service, resulting in long-term gains for the company.

Customer

Customers' data flows into the CRM system through their transactions.

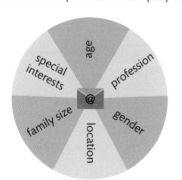

AUTOMATION

CRM can use automation as a tool to respond to customers who visit and use their website.

Customer segmentation

The market can be segmented into groups relevant to the product the company sells.

age · profession · gender · location · family size · special interests · @

Email campaign management

Different emails are sent automatically to the relevant groups.

Age

Gender

Profession

Location

Family size

Special interests

871%
the average return on investment delivered by CRM

Marketing
Target groups for special campaigns; monitor and reward loyalty; generate leads

Sales
Convert new leads; find new prospects; cross-sell and up-sell opportunities; customize pitches

Customer contact form
CRM uses the information to group customers according to their buying behaviour.

Quote request
The company sends a quotation in response to the customer's interest in their product.

Customer feedback
The company asks questions and monitors social media to glean information about customers' views.

E-commerce transaction
The customer pays for the product via the internet.

Support ticket
An automated ticket allows the customer to track delivery of the product.

Operations
Improve efficiency of manufacturing, product delivery, ordering, and tracking

Customer service
Respond to service issues immediately; manage customer cases; gather feedback

Finance
Generate invoices in a timely manner; manage payment process

Compliance

In most countries, companies have to adhere to laws and industry regulations that govern how they can sell and market their products. The rules are there to make sure that businesses operate fairly.

How it works

Governments impose rules on marketers to prevent any unscrupulous, misleading, or unwelcome practices, such as false advertising, the failure to disclose all terms and conditions, and spam marketing (sending unsolicited emails). The regulatory body is able to investigate any company accused of breaking the rules and impose penalties if it finds the company guilty.

Marketing regulations

To protect the consumer, regulatory bodies produce guidelines instructing companies on how they should market their products.

Business areas subject to regulation	Example of marketing practice
Comparative claims	"Our model is much better than our competitor's!"
Endorsements	"I owe my success to their product!"
Special offers	"Buy one, get one free!"
Sweepstakes and contests	"Enter the prize draw for the chance to win a holiday of a lifetime!"
Telemarketing	"Good morning. Would you like to make huge savings on your energy bills?"
Marketing to children	"Roll up, roll up, enter the house of toys..."
Customer data	"Please fill in the registration form."
Email marketing	"Ends today, 24-hour online sale!"
Use of spam	"Congratulations! You have been selected..."
Negative-option billing	"Please untick box if you do not wish to..."

50%
of all email traffic
in 2020 was spam

Typical regulations to protect consumer

☑ A marketer making a claim that its product is superior to a rival's must be able to substantiate it with proof.

☑ A marketer must be able to prove that an endorsement by a person that they have used to promote a product is genuine.

☑ A marketer promoting a product with a special offer must set out the terms and conditions in writing. In the UK, use of the word "free" is subject to regulation.

☑ All competitions and prize draws must adhere to legal guidelines to ensure they are fair and impartial.

☑ Telemarketers in the UK must provide key facts before an order is placed, including business name and contact, cost and quantity, restrictions and conditions, and refund policy.

☑ Marketers must stick to specific guidelines governing how they advertise and promote products to children.

☑ Customer information must be stored, managed, and used in accordance with privacy laws.

☑ Marketers in the UK must not send emails to individuals unless they have given specific consent, or they are existing customers. Every message must include an opt-out option.

☑ Marketers must never send bulk unsolicited emails, the most common form of spam, or other types of unrequested message.

☑ Any item offered alongside the main product purchased must be presented as an option to buy, not an item the consumer must take action to refuse.

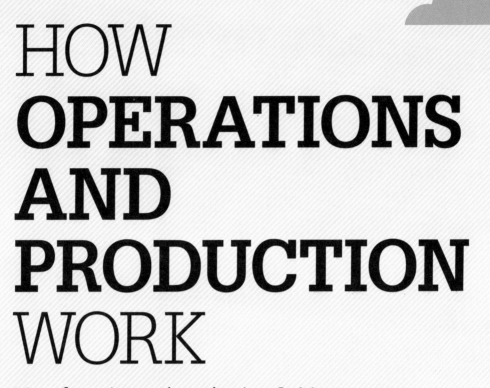

HOW
OPERATIONS
AND
PRODUCTION
WORK

Manufacturing and production ❯ Management
Product ❯ Control ❯ Supply chain

Manufacturing and production

Once a firm has decided what goods or services to supply, its directors have to choose a method of production that best suits consumer demand, the product, and the market, as well as the one that will be the most profitable. Companies work in three general areas of industry, which together form a production chain to provide consumers with finished goods or services.

Production methods

Before the Industrial Revolution, products were made by craftsmen. Then factories brought people together to work on machines. Typically, this was job production, with one person making one item. Economist Adam Smith first introduced the concept of division of labour, which led to mass production, with car maker Henry Ford popularizing the moving assembly line at the start of the 20th century. Today, manufacturers can combine the best of all methods, with large-scale production of personalized products. Production typically involves three stages – here, from haricot bean to baked beans sold in supermarkets.

Primary production

The acquisition and processing of raw materials – in this case, haricot beans, as well as tomatoes for the sauce

> **PRODUCTION IN PRACTICE**
> Native to South America, haricot beans are grown either for the immature green pods, eaten fresh as green beans, or for the beans themselves. These are dried and used most commonly in baked beans, a dish that originally came from Boston in the US.

CHOOSING THE BEST METHOD

> **Job production** Items are made individually. *See pp.272–273.*

> **Batch production** A number of items are all made together at the same time. *See pp.274–275.*

> **Flow production** Suitable for mass-producing identical items on an assembly line. *See pp.276–277.*

> **Mass customization** Mass product is customized by buyer. *See pp.278–279.*

> **Continuous production** 24/7 line of production, for products with consistent demand. *See pp.280–281.*

> **Hybrid processes** Mixing batch and flow production or combining other processes. *See pp.282–283.*

US$3.85 trillion

the value of China's annual manufacturing output in 2020, the highest in the world

KEY PRODUCTION FACTORS

To create products, businesses need resources, including:

❯ **Capital** Finance invested in business, including money spent on production tools, such as equipment, machinery, and buildings

❯ **Land** Natural resources used to create goods and services – for example, physical land or extractable resources such as minerals, timber, oil, or gas

❯ **Labour** People employed in a business with the necessary skills to produce the goods and services

❯ **Enterprise** Entrepreneurs and/or leaders who bring the factors of production together to make the whole process happen

Secondary production

The manufacture and assembly of raw materials to turn them into a product or service; in this instance, baked beans

Tertiary production

Services that support the production and distribution of the baked beans, such as transport, advertising, warehousing, and insurance

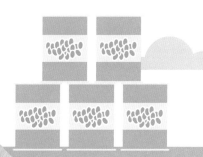

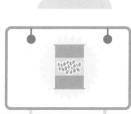

The raw beans are mixed with tomato sauce, sugar, salt, and secret spices. The ingredients are cooked in vast pressure cookers, ensuring consistent texture and a long shelf life, and then sealed in tins.

The labelled tins are transported to warehouses and from there to supermarkets and other outlets ready to be sold. Several brands vie for market supremacy of this popular convenience food, using advertising, price, and taste differentiation.

Job production

In job production, items are made individually. Each item is one job, which is usually finished before another is started. This method is typically used for small-scale production or for large one-off projects.

How it works

Job production is best suited to a business that has to meet specific customer requirements. Typically, these are unique requests, which an individual or a team handles from start to finish. Made-to-measure suits or custom-made furniture are examples. The scale may be small, and firms often start with job production because it is simple and little investment is required. Job production can also be used for complex projects and those involving leading-edge technology, including film production, major constructions such as ships for the navy, architect-designed buildings, and civil engineering projects including bridges and tunnels.

SERVICES

Job production can also apply to services, such as hairdressing or processing an order for customer collection. Flights come under the same umbrella – air stewards tailor their services to passengers' dietary requirements and special needs for items such as wheelchairs.

Wedding dress production

A bride-to-be can choose to buy a dress off-the-peg (typically made by batch production) or have one specially designed and made for her, which costs significantly more.

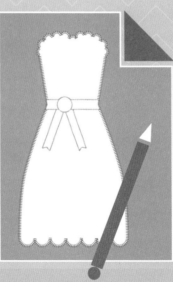

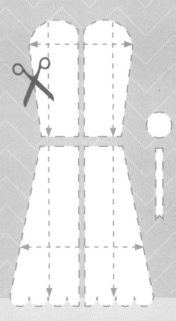

Bride-to-be at the shops

The bride-to-be cannot find the dress of her dreams off-the-peg, so opts to pay to have a one-off garment made.

Dressmaker commissioned

A specialist dressmaker is engaged to design a wedding dress to the bride-to-be's specifications.

Cutting out the dress

The dressmaker makes a pattern and cuts one dress from the bride-to-be's chosen fabric.

JOB PRODUCTION PROS AND CONS

Pros	*Cons*
❯ Products generally of high quality	❯ Does not allow for economies of scale, so high one-off costs
❯ Great job satisfaction and pride in work as follow through from start to finish	❯ Labour-intensive
❯ Producer can satisfy individual customer needs	❯ Special materials and investment in skills may be required
❯ Can make a profit with only a few customers	❯ High price may put off customers, especially in times of recession
❯ For small jobs, word-of-mouth recommendations reduce marketing costs	❯ Heavy reliance on just a handful of customers

US$1,600
the average cost of a wedding dress in the US in 2019

Sewing the dress
The dressmaker focuses on stitching and finishing the one garment.

Dress fitting
After any alterations, the dressmaker is satisfied that the dress fits the bride-to-be and meets her requirements.

Completing the dress
The price is high, but the dress is exactly what the bride-to-be wants. Now the dressmaker can start on another dress.

Batch production

When a number of the same items are made together, it is called batch production. One batch finishes each stage of the production process before the next batch starts, using the same equipment and steps.

How it works

Batch production allows a firm to make a quantity of items in one production run. Factory equipment is geared up in terms of scale and special tools that can be changed for each batch. For example, equipment is set up to make 200 size 10 dresses in red fabric and then adjusted to produce 400 size 12 dresses in blue fabric. Quantities can vary from as few as four identical items for a local supplier to thousands for a department store, and batches can be made as often as required. Batch production is common in the food, clothing, footwear, paints, adhesive, and pharmaceutical ingredients industries. Each batch must be traceable, with clear date stamping, in order to comply with laws and standards.

As easy as sliced bread

Bread is commonly made in batches. A baker might make 100 white rolls then 50 large brown loaves.

Mix bulk ingredients

Ingredients for the batch of white rolls are mixed to form a dough.

Batch 1

Divide dough

After machine-mixing, the bulk dough is divided into small tins.

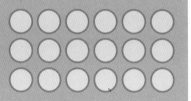

Prove dough

The dough is left to rise (prove) in tins.

Adjust for second batch

The equipment is recalibrated to make 50 large brown loaves. Bulk ingredients for the batch of brown bread are mixed to form a dough.

Batch 2

Divide dough

After machine-mixing, the bulk dough is divided into large tins.

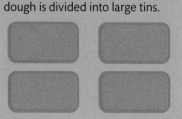

Prove dough

The dough is left to rise (prove) in the tins.

11 million

loaves of bread are sold every day in the UK

BATCH PRODUCTION PROS AND CONS

Pros	*Cons*
❯ Economies of scale: low unit costs, as large number is made	❯ Repetitive work (even if automated), so workers may be less motivated
❯ Customer offered choice of, for example, size, weight, and flavours	❯ Costly because may require storage of raw materials, work in progress, and finished items (*see p.139*)
❯ Output and productivity increases with use of specialist/ dedicated machinery	❯ Requires detailed planning and scheduling

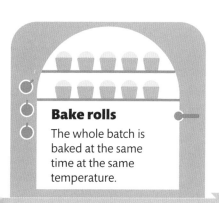

Bake rolls

The whole batch is baked at the same time at the same temperature.

De-pan and cool rolls

The rolls are removed from their tins.

Bag up to complete

All the rolls finish the production process together.

Bake loaves

Baking time is longer than for Batch 1, as the units are larger.

De-pan and cool bread

The large brown loaves are removed from their tins.

Slice and bag loaves

The loaves are sliced and packed for sale.

Flow production

The purpose of flow (mass) production is to produce a large number of identical, standardized items. This usually happens on a moving line, which can be interrupted when the product is changed.

How it works

Flow production typically involves large factories equipped with conveyor belts and expensive machinery, the assembly of individual components, which may be bought in from other companies, and the automation of tasks. An example of this is car manufacturing, where elements of the product are put together along a line; robot arms may fit wheels and workers may perform specialized jobs. Significant output is possible with even a small number of workers. Newspaper printers, oil refineries, and chemical plants also use flow production.

The production line

In flow production the item being made, such as a car, moves on a conveyor belt through different stages until completion. Components to build the car may have been outsourced or produced in another of the firm's factories. They are all ready to be used along the line.

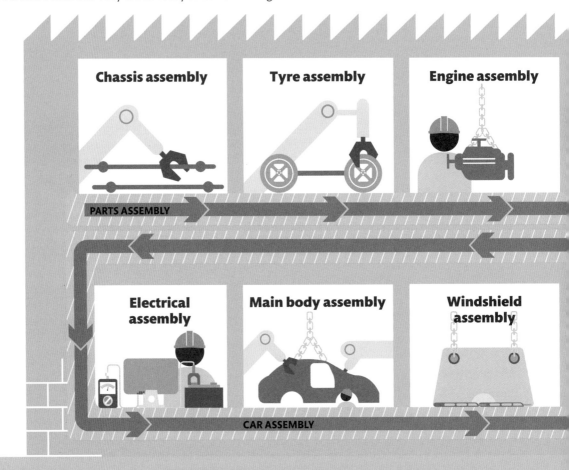

Chassis assembly

Tyre assembly

Engine assembly

PARTS ASSEMBLY

Electrical assembly

Main body assembly

Windshield assembly

CAR ASSEMBLY

FLOW PRODUCTION PROS AND CONS

Pros

> Economies of scale: can produce large number of goods cheaply

> Unskilled labour and automation keep costs low

> Materials bought in large quantities, so low cost

Cons

> Expensive machinery requires significant investment

> Repetitive work means workers may be less motivated

> Reliant on equipment: if line breaks, production is halted

78 million
vehicles **were** produced globally **in 2020**

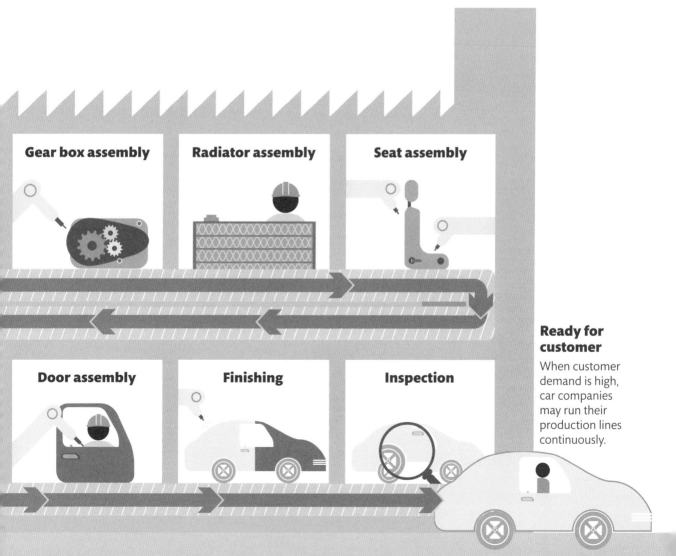

Gear box assembly

Radiator assembly

Seat assembly

Door assembly

Finishing

Inspection

Ready for customer

When customer demand is high, car companies may run their production lines continuously.

Mass customization

Sophisticated technology and manufacturing developments enable mass products to be personalized. The low unit costs of mass production combine with the marketing opportunities of custom-made.

How it works

Mass customization offers new opportunities for the manufacturing and service industries. Social media, online technology, 3-D modelling tools, e-commerce software, and flexible production systems and processes are allowing customers to configure products to match their own taste and needs. Industries such as footwear (particularly trainers), clothing, cars, jewellery, and computers already allow consumers to customize their purchases. The price is generally higher than for standardized goods.

Revolutionary new technologies are expected to further extend customization, allowing individuals to, for example, scan their body contours and use augmented reality to design and order unique clothing.

FOOD MIXES

The generation raised on social media expect to personalize every aspect of their lives, and food and drink is set to be a growth area for mass customization. Websites allow consumers to make their own cereal mixes, which is especially useful for those with allergies, and to create their own blends of tea and coffee.

Customers design own products

Mass customization has enormous potential to change consumerism. For example, consumers can buy trainers designed to their own specification via the internet. This is a high-status commodity among certain groups.

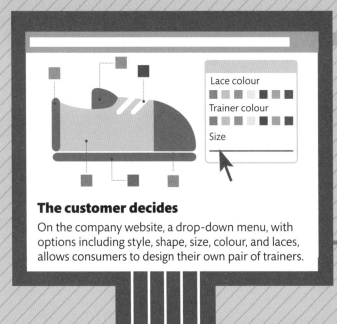

The customer decides

On the company website, a drop-down menu, with options including style, shape, size, colour, and laces, allows consumers to design their own pair of trainers.

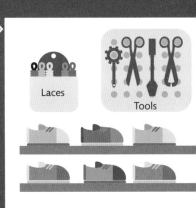

Sends order to factory

The firm holds no finished stock but manufactures to order from a range of parts, getting paid by the customer before production.

25.3%

the average amount more that consumers are willing to pay for personalization

FOUR TYPES OF MASS CUSTOMIZATION

In his book *Mass Customization: The New Frontier in Business Competition*, B. Joseph Pine II outlines four distinct types:

❯ **Collaborative customization**
Work with individual customer to develop specific product to suit their needs. Technology firms, for example, assemble computers to customer's specification.

❯ **Adaptive customization**
Produce standardized products that are customizable by end-user. For instance, US company Lutron produces a lighting system that lets customers choose own setting from preprogrammed options.

❯ **Transparent customization**
Provide unique products to individuals without overtly stating items are customized. Many hotel groups, for instance, keep a database of guests' preferences to help personalize their stay.

❯ **Cosmetic customization**
Make a standardized product, but market it differently. Branded bags, T-shirts, and pens used to promote a business are examples.

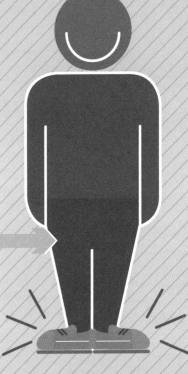

Trainers shipped to customer
The customer receives a differentiated product and has the psychological benefit of personalized design – at a price.

Patterned laces
Cushioned sole
Size 7.5, narrow fit

Continuous production

During continuous production, a product is made 24 hours a day, seven days a week. The production line runs continuously to cope with demand and staff work round the clock in shifts.

How it works

With flow or mass production, the line is stopped to change products or models. Continuous production uses the same concept, but it runs throughout the year so output is non-stop. This method is used for identical commodities with high, consistent demand, including paper, cardboard, packaging, washing powder, electronic components, and oil products. As with mass production, processes are automated, staffing levels are kept to a minimum, and quality control is essential.

There is high competition in industries using continuous production. Margins may be low, but demand is often relatively stable, encouraging investment in capital equipment.

The paper trail

Paper is used throughout the world, and factories operate 365 days a year to satisfy constant demand. Timber is the raw material for papermaking. Once the timber has been debarked, chipped, and pulped, the fibres are washed and dyed. At the end of its life cycle, some paper is recycled.

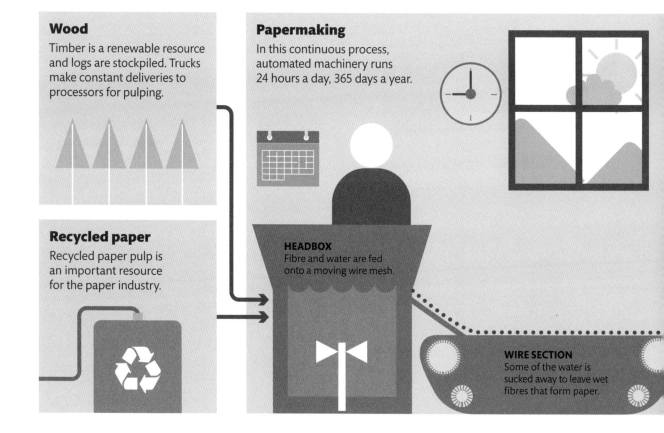

Wood
Timber is a renewable resource and logs are stockpiled. Trucks make constant deliveries to processors for pulping.

Papermaking
In this continuous process, automated machinery runs 24 hours a day, 365 days a year.

Recycled paper
Recycled paper pulp is an important resource for the paper industry.

HEADBOX
Fibre and water are fed onto a moving wire mesh.

WIRE SECTION
Some of the water is sucked away to leave wet fibres that form paper.

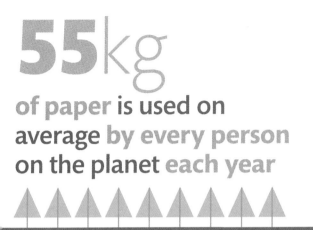

55kg
of paper **is used on average** by every person on the planet **each year**

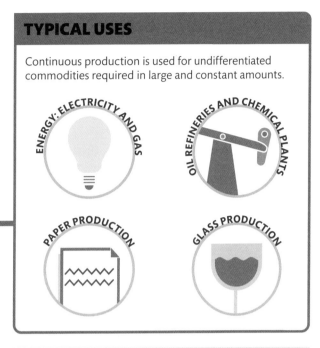

TYPICAL USES

Continuous production is used for undifferentiated commodities required in large and constant amounts.

ENERGY: ELECTRICITY AND GAS

OIL REFINERIES AND CHEMICAL PLANTS

PAPER PRODUCTION

GLASS PRODUCTION

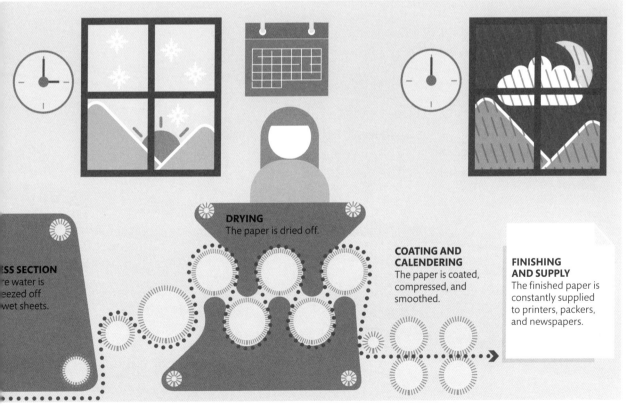

DRYING
The paper is dried off.

SS SECTION
re water is
eezed off
wet sheets.

COATING AND CALENDERING
The paper is coated, compressed, and smoothed.

FINISHING AND SUPPLY
The finished paper is constantly supplied to printers, packers, and newspapers.

Hybrid processes

Manufacturing firms may adapt existing processes or combine two production methods for optimal performance, particularly if they make a wide range of products.

How it works

There are many examples of hybrid processes. One is linked batch flow production, where only two or three pieces of equipment are required and a batch flows from one process to another. This is common in the chemicals and pharmaceuticals industries. For instance, a company may make headache medication and a hay fever remedy in tablet, capsule, and liquid form, and in varying doses; each batch flows through a series of steps, depending on composition and form, from bulk processing to packaging. Another example is cell manufacturing, which combines job production with flow (mass) production.

Combining methods

On the classic assembly line, each worker is skilled in producing one type or part of an item. At the other end of the scale, one person completes all stages, creating the finished product from beginning to end. Cell manufacturing combines flow production with job production to create autonomous units. A number of workers are dedicated to production, or part production, of a set of goods.

Flow production

One process is handled by one or more workers, and that job is completed before the product or part moves on to the next workstation. Worker 1 uses only one set of tools for the process, before the product moves on to Worker 2, and so on down the line. *See pp.276–277.*

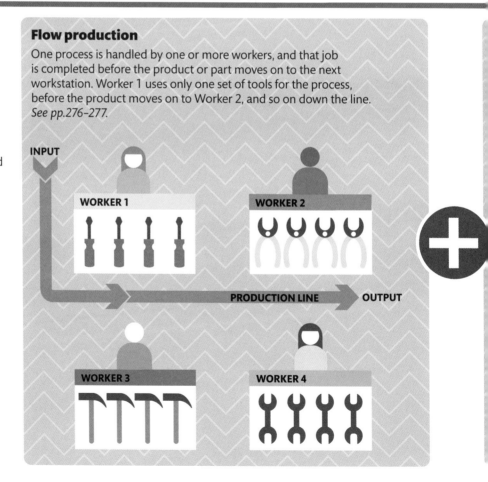

HYBRID PROCESSES FOR INNOVATION

By combining manufacturing processes, companies can create products with new and original qualities. For instance, a food company that makes sliced bread and oven chips may speed up chip production by baking them in the bread oven first. This has the unintended but beneficial consequence of making the fries healthier. A new product is created, which may now be marketed as a new proposition to a different set of consumers.

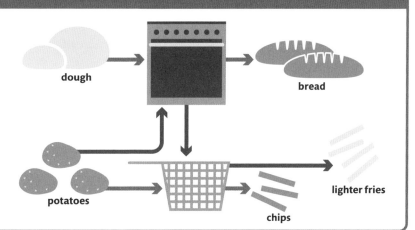

dough

bread

potatoes

chips

lighter fries

Job production

One worker creates a one-off product, such as a fitted kitchen, from start to finish. This way of working can be more rewarding for the worker, who uses a range of skills, but it tends to be costly for the customer. *See pp.272–273.*

RKER

Cell manufacturing

Combining the best of flow and job production, here a group of products or parts is produced in separate small units (cells) made up of a number of workers in the factory. Workers are skilled to produce all the items in the set. Dissimilar items can be produced without slowing the production line. The idea is to improve performance by giving each cell a degree of autonomy.

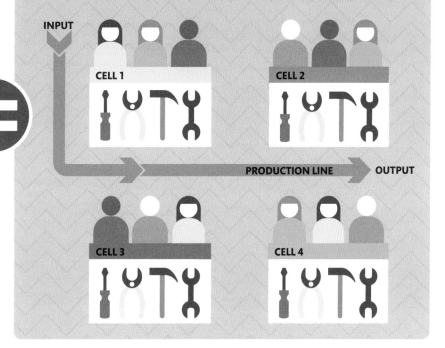

INPUT

CELL 1

CELL 2

CELL 3

CELL 4

PRODUCTION LINE

OUTPUT

Management

Every manager in a business, particularly in manufacturing, has to ensure that all resources – from materials to equipment and staff – are used efficiently, while keeping the customer continually in mind. Managers make key decisions to lay down procedures and set standards and then work continuously to improve processes to ensure that the company remains profitable.

Which approach?

How people and processes are organized in making and delivering the product to the customer is critical if a company is to survive fierce competition and rapidly shifting consumer demands in a global market. In making decisions about how a business can meet its goals, managers may combine a number of approaches as many are interlinked and achieve similar outcomes.

MANAGER OR LEADER?

Management and leadership are not the same, but are closely linked:

> Managers **plan**, **organize**, **coordinate**, **ask questions**, and **motivate**; leaders also **create a vision** and **inspire**.

> Managers organize workers to **maximize efficiency** and **nurture skills**; leaders also **develop future talent**.

> Managers focus on the **bottom line**; leaders also **look to the horizon**.

> Managers explain to workers what **needs to be done** and **provide the support to do it**; leaders also persuade workers to **want to do more** than needs to be done.

> Good managers **require leadership skills**, while great leaders **know what it takes** to be good managers.

The following classic distinction has been attributed to two different business leaders and writers, Peter Drucker and Warren Bennis: management is doing things right; leadership is doing the right things.

Agile production

How can we be more responsive to shifts in customer demand? *See pp.296–297.*

Time-based management

How can we use time effectively? *See pp.294–295.*

No. 1

European country for innovation in 2020: Switzerland

Kaizen

How can we drive continuous improvements? *See pp.298–299.*

Economies and diseconomies of scale

What scale of operation is best for us? *See pp.286–287.*

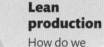

Lean production

How do we minimize resources to reduce costs? *See pp.288–289.*

INNOVATE

INVOLVE
EMPLOYEES

FOCUS
ON VALUE

STRATEGIC
ALLIANCES WITH
SUPPLIERS

MINIMIZE
WASTE

UNINTERRUPTED
WORKFLOW

CUSTOMERS
AT THE HEART
OF WHAT
WE DO

Just-in-time

How can we meet customer demand and minimize stock? *See pp.290–291.*

Total quality management

How do we improve customer satisfaction? *See pp.292–293.*

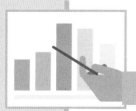

Economies and diseconomies of scale

Economies of scale are one of the advantages of large-scale production and result in a lower unit cost of each item produced. However, costs can also go up as the operation grows, resulting in diseconomies of scale.

How it works

Economies of scale is a simple concept: the more items produced or handled, the cheaper the average (unit) cost, as efficiencies and fixed costs are shared across all items. This gives a business a competitive advantage.

Supermarkets, for example, buy food in bulk at low unit costs, which they pass on to consumers. However, diseconomies of scale may occur when the operation experiences high administration costs, wastage from lack of control, or lack of employee productivity.

Economies of scale

While it may be inefficent for a small dairy to supply milk to a supermarket, it is cost-effective for a concern running to thousands of bottles. Make the delivery too large, though, and wastage creeps in due to associated costs.

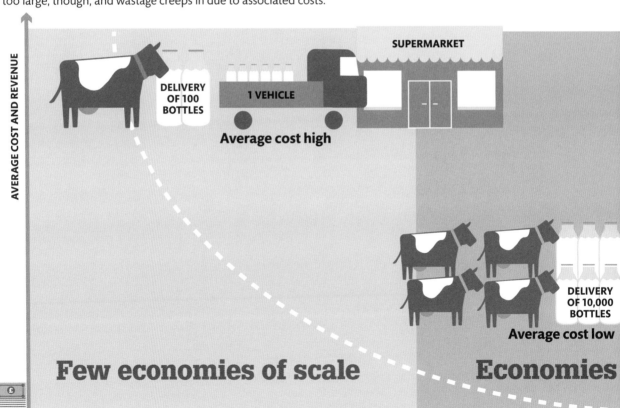

AVERAGE COST AND REVENUE

SUPERMARKET

DELIVERY OF 100 BOTTLES

1 VEHICLE

Average cost high

DELIVERY OF 10,000 BOTTLES

Average cost low

Few economies of scale

Economies

NETWORK ECONOMY

Online networks, such as eBay and Facebook, rarely stray into diseconomies of scale. They can deliver economies of scale even at an international level: the cost of adding one more user to a network is almost nil. However, the resulting benefits may be huge, because each new user in the network can interact or trade with other members of the network.

9%

higher net profit at Netflix in 2020 compared with 2016 after adding 115 million more subscribers

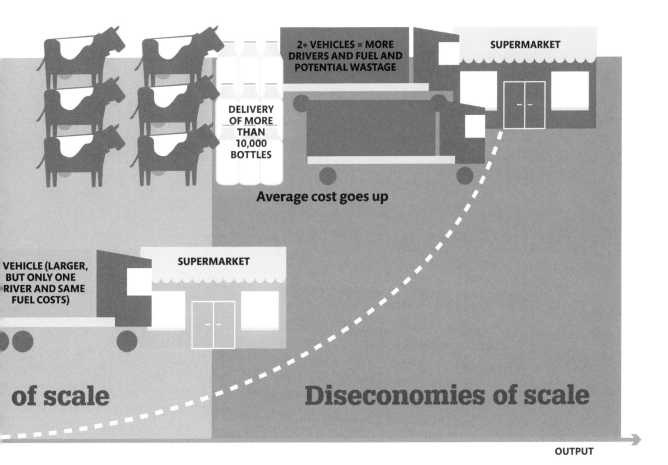

2+ VEHICLES = MORE DRIVERS AND FUEL AND POTENTIAL WASTAGE

SUPERMARKET

DELIVERY OF MORE THAN 10,000 BOTTLES

Average cost goes up

VEHICLE (LARGER, BUT ONLY ONE DRIVER AND SAME FUEL COSTS)

SUPERMARKET

of scale

Diseconomies of scale

OUTPUT

Lean production

The aim of lean production is to reduce the resources used to supply goods and services to consumers. By cutting down human effort, materials, space, capital, and time, lean production cuts costs.

How it works

The focus in lean production is on efficiency to maximize value for the customer, but without affecting quality. Lean seeks to eliminate all activities that do not add value to the production process, including holding inventory (stock), repairing faults, and unnecessary movement of people and products around a manufacturing plant.

Optimizing the flow of products and services through value streams, which are sequences of activity that flow horizontally across technologies, assets, and functions to customers, allows the business to respond to consumer demand faster. Efficiency also makes it simpler and more accurate to manage information.

Case study: how Toyota eliminates waste

Lean production is about getting rid of waste, sometimes called non-value-added activities. Car manufacturer Toyota has identified eight areas of waste and a lean approach to counter these.

Overproduction

Waste
Items produced surplus to customer demand

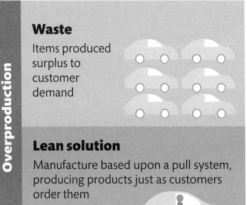

Lean solution
Manufacture based upon a pull system, producing products just as customers order them

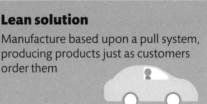

Waiting

Waste
Unproductive time spent waiting for material, information, equipment, tools

Lean solution
All resources provided on a just-in-time (JIT) basis – not too early, not too late

Excess inventory

Waste
Extra, unwanted stock held in inventory

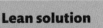

Lean solution
Kanban cards used to indicate material order points: how much, from where, and to where

Defects

Waste
Consumes materials and uses up labour; results in customer complaints

Lean solution
Total quality management used to improve all areas

CREATING A LEAN COMPANY

In their 1996 book, *Lean Thinking: Banish Waste and Create Wealth in Your Corporation*, James Womack and Daniel Jones identify the five principles of lean manufacturing:

❯ **Value** Use surveys, interviews, analytics, and other sources to define customer value – what customers really want from your products and what they are willing to pay.

❯ **Value stream** Map the value stream by determining all company activities that contribute to creating customer value. Those that do not may still be necessary to the business, but anything else should be eliminated.

❯ **Flow** Make sure all the remaining steps run smoothly together, without disruption.

❯ **Pull** Implement a "pull system", so work only occurs when there is actual demand. Make sure the necessary materials and information are available to create the right quantity of products at the right time, cutting labour, resources, and storage waste.

❯ **Perfection** Make the process of continuous improvement part of the organization's culture, and keep trying to get better every day.

9.5 million

the number of cars Toyota sold in 2020

Transportation in stages

Waste
Superfluous stages in the transportation process

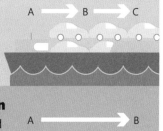

Lean solution
Material shipped directly from the supplier to the assembly line

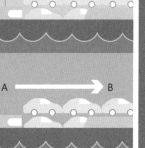

Non-value-added processing

Waste
Unprofitable stages in the production or reworking of a product

Lean solution
Map the value stream to identify non-value-added steps in the process; get it right the first time

Excess motion

Waste
Poor workflow, poor layout, and inconsistent working methods

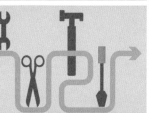

Lean solution
Workplace organization, a systematic method for standardizing the workplace

Underused people

Waste
Underutilization of employees' mental, creative, and physical skills and abilities

Lean solution
Work cells replace assembly line; better use of labour, employee involvement, and communication

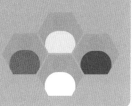

Just-in-time

The system of production in which an actual order is the trigger for an item to be manufactured is called just-in-time. It enables a firm to produce only the items required, in the right amount, at the right time.

How it works

Also called demand-pull production, just-in-time means that stock levels of raw materials, components, work in progress, and finished goods are kept as low as possible, reducing costs. The system requires detailed planning, scheduling, and flow of resources throughout the production process, now enabled by sophisticated production-scheduling software. Supplies have to be delivered directly to the production line when they are needed, requiring strong relationships and interconnected systems with suppliers. The benefits of reduced inventory are balanced against the cost of frequent deliveries and loss of purchasing economies of scale (discounts for bulk-buying). The system goes back to 1953, the year Toyota brought in just-in-time manufacturing. The phrase is sometimes used in a more general sense today to mean eliminating waste of resources.

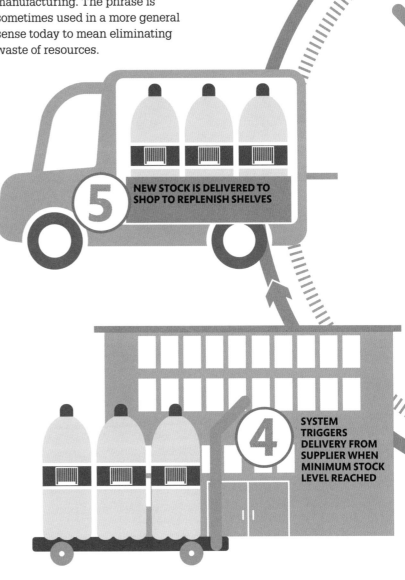

5 NEW STOCK IS DELIVERED TO SHOP TO REPLENISH SHELVES

4 SYSTEM TRIGGERS DELIVERY FROM SUPPLIER WHEN MINIMUM STOCK LEVEL REACHED

JUST-IN-TIME PROS AND CONS

Pros

> **Lower stock** so less storage space and less working capital needed
> **Demand-pull** avoids obsolete, out-of-date stock
> **Staff** spend less time checking and moving items

Cons

> **No room for error** – for instance, if there are any faults in the stock delivered, the whole day's production is halted
> **Operation** is reliant on suppliers
> **No cushion** for sudden upsurge in demand

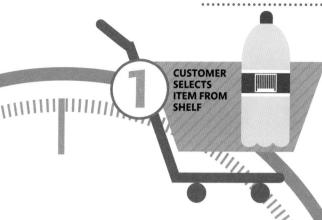

1 CUSTOMER SELECTS ITEM FROM SHELF

9.7%

the average annual growth expected in the global print-on-demand T-shirt market from 2021 to 2028

Just-in-time in retail

To reduce stockholding, many supermarkets now use just-in-time deliveries, relying on computer data systems. In manufacturing, systems are often based on Kanban cards, dockets for withdrawing and ordering items at each workstation of the production process.

2 ASSISTANT SCANS BARCODE

3 COMPUTER SYSTEM SIGNALS WAREHOUSE

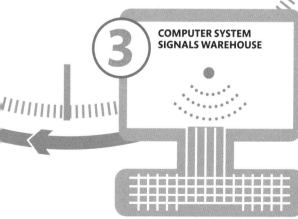

🔍 CASE STUDY

Print-on-demand publishing at Peecho

Amsterdam-based Peecho offers just-in-time print-on-demand services, only printing the products they host, such as books and images, when ordered by a customer:

❯ Content owner uploads their product, such as a book or image, to Peecho.com.

❯ Customer places order, and Peecho prints only the number of copies needed to fulfil order.

❯ Content owner avoids upfront costs of producing and storing large print run, and can easily distribute their printed products anywhere.

Total quality management

Success through customer satisfaction is the ethos of total quality management (TQM). Everything a company does is relevant, and the focus is on managing and improving processes rather than outcomes.

How it works

Companies use TQM to create a customer-focused organization that involves all employees in continuous improvement. It is a strategic and systematic approach that puts quality at the heart of the firm's activities and culture. Customers determine the level of quality, measured through their satisfaction. The organization is viewed as a series of horizontal processes that take inputs from suppliers through to the delivered outputs. Measuring performance data is critical, as is good communication to maintain momentum. Although similar to the now more widespread Six Sigma (*see pp.320–321*), TQM differs in its focus on internal quality standards, rather than on reducing defects and producing quantifiable results.

WHAT TQM MEANS

> **Total** Involves everyone and all activities in the company
> **Quality** Conformity to meeting customer requirements
> **Management** Quality can and must be managed

Case study: The Walt Disney Company

Manufacturing companies, in which the focus is on meeting or exceeding customer expectations by making products within certain specifications, are often used as TQM examples. TQM can also be applied in service industries, of which Disney is a good example.

The Walt Disney Company

Disney's aim is to maximize long-term shareholder value, and part of this involves delivering a magical customer experience at its theme parks.

Focus on the customer

Disney incorporated the TQM concept of quality into its approach to customer service. Its visitors are seen as guests and treated as VIPs and individuals.

Involve everyone in quality

Founder Walt Disney firmly believed in quality and saw it as everyone's job, something that could not be delegated.

Perfect processes

Walt Disney viewed the theme parks as factories producing delight. He built quality by designing processes and repeating them at scale.

> "Quality control is applicable to any kind of enterprise. In fact, quality control must be applied in every enterprise"
>
> Dr Kaoru Ishikawa, *engineering professor*

70,000

Disney World cast members are employed to make guests happy

Employees
Disney calls its employees "cast members". They are trained in every aspect of delivery, including posture, gestures, facial expressions, and tone of voice.

Exceptional service
Cast members (employees) are focused on delighting the customer – their sole job is to make visitors happy.

Suppliers
Disney collaborates with suppliers – for example, its partnerships with McDonald's and Coca-Cola – to ensure consistent quality.

Continuous improvement
Walt Disney saw the theme parks as an incomplete product; today, improvements come from the bottom up.

"When does the Three O'Clock Parade start?"
Cast members are trained to answer this common question by responding with the time the parade will be passing a particular point in the park.

Shared purpose
Walt Disney started by defining a company culture based entirely on creating a genuine shared purpose that people would be proud to support.

Integrated systems
Technology supports the experience: for example, the volume of ambient music is the same in all theme parks, delivered through thousands of perfectly placed speakers.

Time-based management

The general approach that recognizes the importance and value of time and seeks to reduce the level of unproductive time in an organization is called time-based management.

How it works

The fast pace of competition means a business that can manage time efficiently will enjoy a significant competitive advantage. This applies to new product development, faster response times to meet changing market and customer needs, and reduced waste. For a business to operate a time-based management system, its people have to be multi-skilled and able to move swiftly between different tasks, its machinery has to be flexible so that production runs can be changed at short notice, and there has to be a culture of mutual trust between workers and managers. Time-based management is a key aspect of lean production.

Case study: managing time at Amazon

With approximately 37 million square metres of storage space in its warehouses and hundreds of millions of customers worldwide, Amazon is an undisputed leader in online retail. One of its key strengths is being able to deliver products quickly, with many customers paying a premium to get their items even faster through its Prime subscription service. To be able to do this at a reasonable cost, the company ensures every process adds value and takes a minimum amount of time–from making sure there is enough stock and space to store it, to picking the right product and delivering it. Much of this is achieved through the use of information technology.

Storage

Amazon uses every available inch of warehouse space to store inventory by utilizing the idea of "chaotic storage". Items are placed in the location that optimizes the use of space, rather than in an ordered categorized section. The inventory management system keeps note of where that item is stored and can locate it instantly, saving time and space.

Analysis

The time and cost of each of these processes is analysed to ensure they are completed in the best possible way.

34%
of **organizations**
mostly or
always complete
projects **on time**

PART OF PROJECT MANAGEMENT

Time-based management is a critical part of project management. Timing aids include:

> **Tools** such as Gantt charts show the project schedule as a bar chart, making it easy to plot and monitor daily progress and targets.

> **Project management systems** methods such as PRINCE2 (PRojects IN Controlled Environments) help to structure projects step by step in logical, organized ways.

> **Methodologies** such as agile help project managers working in software development respond to the unpredictable; they are often implemented via the Scrum framework, in which one person takes charge of constant reprioritizing. Based on the premise that software cannot be built up like a product on an assembly line, as it would be out of date before it was released, every area of development is constantly reappraised.

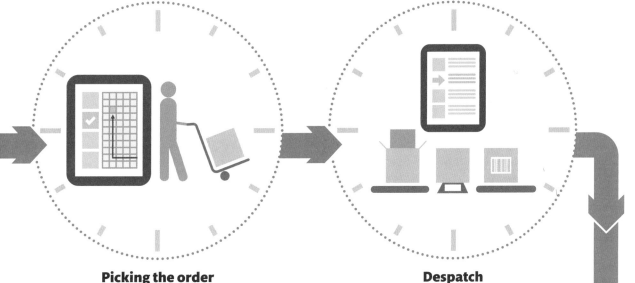

Picking the order

Computer systems direct the pickers to the nearest location for that product, which not only saves time, but also avoids costly and time-wasting picking errors where the wrong product is inadvertently selected.

Despatch

After picking, the product moves along a conveyor for packing, weighing, and labelling. This is then tracked and scanned by the computer system, before being sent to the sorting centre, where packages are distributed by location and delivery speed.

Agile production

Speed and agility are the key competitive advantages of agile production: the focus is on rapid response to the customer, enabling the business to take advantage of short windows of opportunity.

How it works

The goal of agile production is to stay ahead of the competition. Often incorporating concepts of lean production (*see pp.288–289*), agile has an extra dimension: meeting customer demand rapidly and effectively. It relies on flexible and collaborative workers who can deliver swiftly and effectively. The company has to be able to change or increase production quickly. Design of products might incorporate modular concepts, allowing for customization, and strong relationships with suppliers are essential.

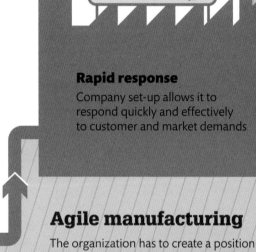

Rapid response
Company set-up allows it to respond quickly and effectively to customer and market demands

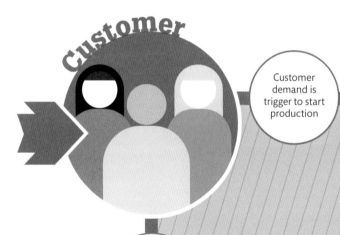

Customer

Customer demand is trigger to start production

Agile manufacturing

The organization has to create a position from which it can alter course as nimbly and swiftly as a cheetah. It needs to be able to retool facilities quickly, modify agreements with suppliers, and continually introduce new ideas and improvements.

Integrated technology
Effective information systems, often linked to suppliers

Product reaches consumer

Continuous innovation
Constant search for new and better ways to deliver for customer

Modular products

Independently created parts used in different/ customized products

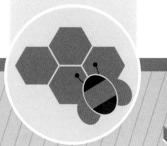

Knowledge culture

Capturing experience, learning from mistakes

71%

of organizations use agile approaches for projects at least sometimes

Strategic partnerships

Supplier collaboration rather than contract negotiation

Transport system

Systems, facilities, infrastructure to speed product to customer

Flexible workforce

Self-organizing, adaptable teams

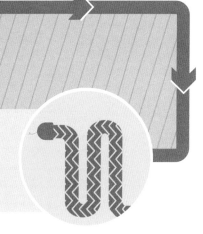

Kaizen

Started in Japan, kaizen is a system of continuous improvement that involves all employees. From senior managers to workers on the shop floor, everyone is encouraged to suggest improvements day to day.

How it works

The kaizen philosophy is "to do it better, make it better, improve it even if it isn't broken, because if we don't, we can't compete with those who do". Kaizen is rarely about ideas for major change but is more to do with ongoing, systematic, incremental improvement. A relentless attempt to eliminate unnecessary activities, delay, or waste (*muda*), kaizen starts by setting high standards and then looks for ways to continually improve those standards. It is supported by a framework of training, communication, and supervision, and results in improved efficiency, productivity, quality, lead time, and customer loyalty.

Creating good change

Kaizen events are implemented through a cycle of activity, known as plan, do, check, act. Central to kaizen are quality, ongoing effort, involvement of every employee as part of their daily work, willingness to change, and communication.

BETTER AND BETTER

Kaizen was created in Japan after World War II. It comes from the Japanese words *kai*, which means "change" or "to correct", and *zen*, which means "good". Companies such as Toyota and Canon have seen significant improvements by involving their employees in recommendations for change.

KAI	ZEN
改	善
CHANGE	GOOD

29
seconds saved building each car at Toyota UK **from one** new idea **to** automate adding stickers

Innovate – find and implement better ways to meet requirements and increase productivity.

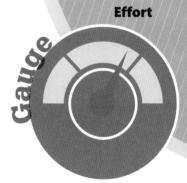

Quality

Effort

Gauge measurements against required standards.

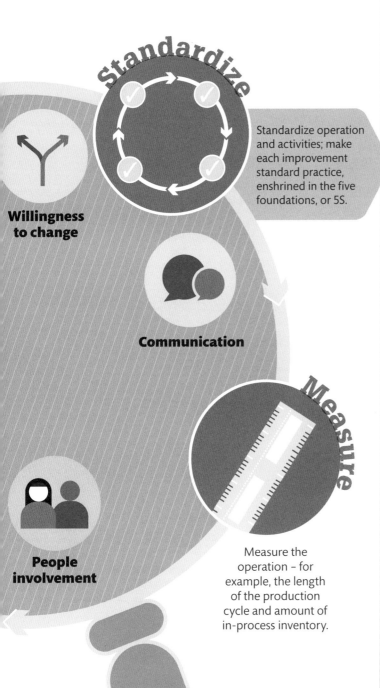

Standardize

Standardize operation and activities; make each improvement standard practice, enshrined in the five foundations, or 5S.

Willingness to change

Communication

Measure

Measure the operation – for example, the length of the production cycle and amount of in-process inventory.

People involvement

FIVE FOUNDATIONS

The five steps of workplace organization, known as 5S, are the foundations for continuous improvement in kaizen.

Seiri (Sort)

Keep only essential items in the work area. Remove and store all unnecessary items.

Seiton (Streamline)

Retrieve ordered items swiftly and easily to create efficient workflow.

Seiso (Shine)

Keep the workspace clean, as cleanliness leads to efficiency.

Seiketsu (Standardize)

Keep consistent work practices, tools, and workstations, and make roles clear.

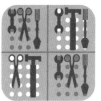

Shitsuke (Sustain)

The four cornerstones above become the standard way to operate all the time.

Product

The items that firms sell to satisfy a consumer need and to make a profit for the business are broadly termed product, whether they are something tangible like toothpaste or an intangible service such as an insurance policy. In a typical life cycle, a product is developed and launched, and a few customers take it up. The domino effect causes wider distribution. Growth eases as the market becomes saturated, and sales flatten and decline until the product is no longer viable.

Product evolution

From start to finish, every product, such as a tube of toothpaste, goes through a process of testing, innovation, and quality control to ensure that it will make the biggest impact on release and throughout its lifespan. Successful companies understand the limited lifespan of products and so invest in the early stages to maximize growth later on.

> "A lot of times, people don't know what they want until you show it to them."
>
> Steve Jobs, *Apple Inc. cofounder*

New product idea

A company decides to release a tube of toothpaste with a new flavour. Its viability is evaluated and potential competition researched. The new toothpaste also requires other qualities, such as whitening and enamel protection, to capture its segment of the market. *See pp.304–305.*

Testing and development

A focus group is assembled to taste the new flavour, along with some variations. Their preferences and comments are noted, and the toothpaste is developed into a usable product. *See pp.302–303.*

€2.8 trillion

the value of goods traded between EU member states in 2020

PRODUCT LIFESPAN

Home entertainment offers different products to consumers. These are four examples of products at different stages in their life cycle (*see pp.184–185*):

❯ **Introduction** 8K ultra-high definition televisions only recently available for the home

❯ **Growth** Streaming services – increase in take-up due to convenience, value, and content choice

❯ **Maturity** Regular high-definition televisions, challenged by more sophisticated technology

❯ **Decline** DVD players – DVD discs superseded by cheaper, higher-resolution streaming services

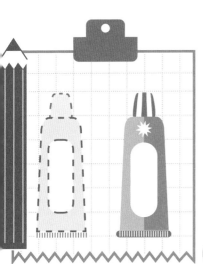

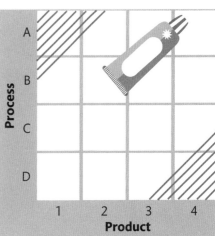

Packaging and design

The toothpaste tube is given a bright, clean, and attractive look. Design considerations include functionality, expense of materials, and an appeal to current trends. *See pp.306–307.*

Quality management

A period of quality control begins in which standards of safety and performance are thoroughly checked. It is far cheaper to correct defects in the design phase than later in production. *See pp.308–309.*

Product-process matrix

Using a product-process matrix, the company identifies the correct production method for the toothpaste. Because the company makes only a few products, each at a high volume, it decides to use assembly-line production. *See pp.310–311.*

New product development

Companies cannot stand still. In today's fiercely competitive marketplace, they have to budget for research into new ideas and identify new products to bring to market simply to stay in business.

How it works

New product development is a process with a number of critical stages to ensure that a business focuses its investment on products that will sell and, above all, make a profit. It starts with an idea, possibly to improve and relaunch an existing product. Some companies run sessions to encourage creativity and generate a pool of ideas, a few of which can be explored. They might work with potential customers and also with suppliers, if part of the manufacturing process is to be outsourced, to refine and develop ideas before finally bringing the product to market.

TRENDING CLAIMS

New products are influenced by trends, reflected in the claims on packaging and in advertising. The top claims on new food products in the US in 2020, for example, were "kosher", "low allergen", "gluten-free", and "no additives".

The development process

The nature of the idea and the size of the company affect each stage and influence how long the product takes to reach the market but the process is generally the same.

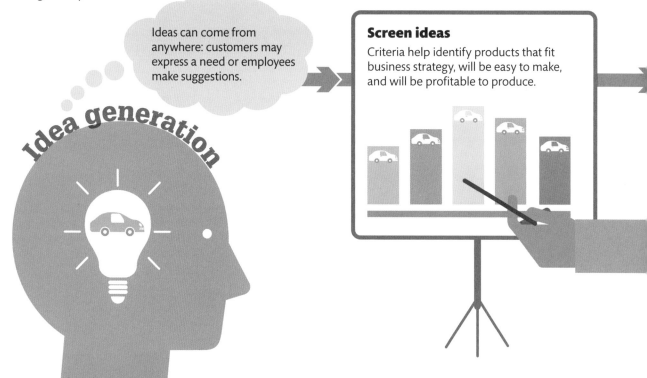

Ideas can come from anywhere: customers may express a need or employees make suggestions.

Idea generation

Screen ideas

Criteria help identify products that fit business strategy, will be easy to make, and will be profitable to produce.

Test concept

Feedback from consumers, via focus groups, interviews, or online evaluation, determine whether an idea is worth pursuing.

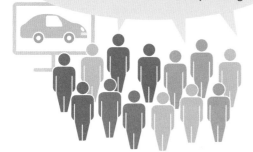

Analyse market

Analysis of opportunity, influenced by predicted growth and trends, helps build a picture of potential sales.

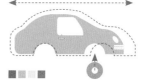

Test market

Product is tested on section of market, perhaps a selected geographic area with good representation of target audience.

Develop products

Features are confirmed, actual product designed, taking test-concept stage results into account, and a prototype developed.

Launch

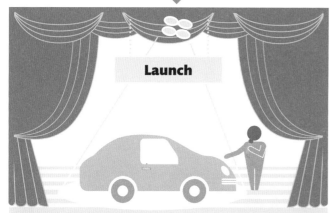

Companies ensure distribution and tell customers about new product, through social media or advertising, to kickstart sales.

US$**5.3** billion

reported loss by **Samsung** after its disappointing **Galaxy Note 7** phone launch

Innovation and invention

Innovating is more than just having a bright idea – it is the way inventions and ideas reach commercial success. It is the lifeblood of any company, as keeping ahead of the game is essential for survival.

How it works

Innovation needs a culture that encourages people to be inventive and explore ideas. It also requires processes that can take initial ideas and develop them. Successful businesses such as the Apple, Sony, and Huawei technology companies know how to do this. Innovation is not small, incremental changes, but transformational ones, such as solving an existing problem in a radically different way, or identifying an unknown problem and inventing the solution.

From idea to product

Innovation is stimulated by many triggers. The idea then requires people to be working in a conducive environment to ensure it is implemented and makes a difference.

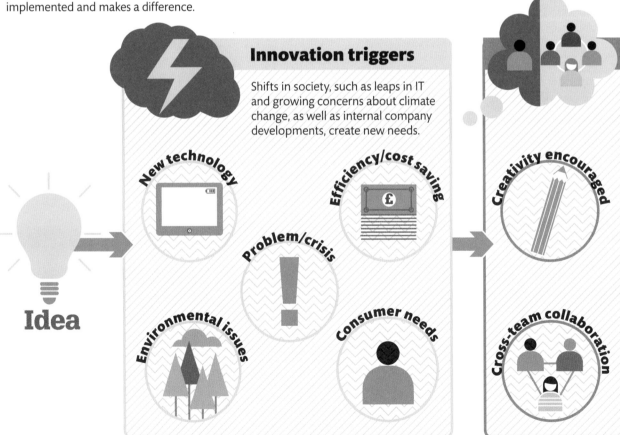

Idea

Innovation triggers

Shifts in society, such as leaps in IT and growing concerns about climate change, as well as internal company developments, create new needs.

New technology

Efficiency/cost saving

Problem/crisis

Environmental issues

Consumer needs

Creativity encouraged

Cross-team collaboration

DIFFERENT TYPES OF INNOVATION

Sustaining innovation Significantly improving existing products, typically through technology – for example, more pixels in cameras, smaller and more powerful laptops

Sustainable or eco-innovation New product that has minimal impact on the environment

Frugal innovation Low-cost product for emerging mass market

Breakthrough innovation Product or service that simultaneously shifts a market and has significant outcomes for the world at large, such as cloud computing or self-driving vehicles

Disruptive innovation Displaces established competitors or changes the norm – for instance, online gambling replacing high-street betting shops

"Genius is one per cent inspiration, and ninety-nine per cent perspiration."

Thomas Edison, *US inventor*

Intellectual property (IP) is the expression of an idea. IP might be a design, an invention, or other type of intellectual creation, and it can be protected by law, for example, with a patent.

Brainstorm

Individuals and teams need the time and mental space to think originally.

Action

The culture and processes of the company have to be favourable for testing the viability of ideas.

Listening at all levels

Failure allowed

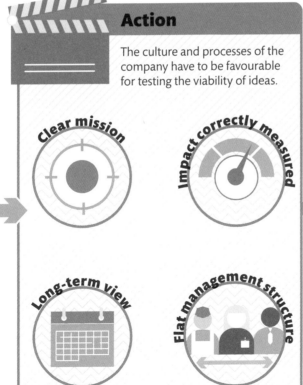

Clear mission

Impact correctly measured

Long-term view

Flat management structure

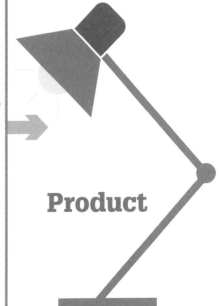

Product

Design

Any product has to be well designed to succeed. Excellent designs for everyday items – from the Anglepoise lamp to reflective road signs – have shaped our modern world.

How it works

The starting point for design is an idea for a product that fulfils a need, whether it is a specialist item or something in day-to-day use. The designer has to think of ways in which a product can serve its purpose and meet other criteria, including aesthetics, cost, durability, and environmental considerations. The design may be integral to the product, such as Apple's rectangular devices with rounded corners, for which it obtained a design patent. Some designs are iconic, such as the Coca-Cola bottle. Yet design is more than just shape. Along with functionality, it includes materials and colour, and extends from the products to their packaging.

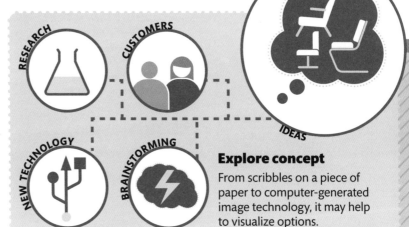

RESEARCH

CUSTOMERS

IDEAS

NEW TECHNOLOGY

BRAINSTORMING

Explore concept
From scribbles on a piece of paper to computer-generated image technology, it may help to visualize options.

Product-design process

Designs for mass-produced items, such as furniture, lighting, domestic appliances, and communications technology, take a lot of hard work. The process of creating a functional design that looks good has several steps.

CONSIDERATIONS FOR DESIGN SUCCESS

> **Functional** Serves a purpose
> **Aesthetic** Pleasurable to use
> **Innovative** Different and new, possibly using innovative technology
> **Easy to use** Understandable, and with useful features
> **Simple** Unobtrusive, subtle
> **Long-lasting** Sustainable, not too fashion-sensitive
> **Environmentally friendly** Minimizes resources and pollution

Redesign
Next year, the product may need revamping.

End product
The final version of the design that goes on sale may look very different from the initial concept.

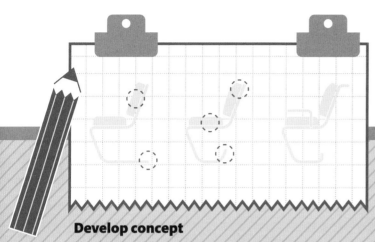

Develop concept

The design can be broken into components, such as functional requirements and production options, and each evaluated independently.

Make prototype

This might be a one-off, or a series of prototypes, to test and refine the product's functionality.

32%

higher revenue generated by the most design-focused companies over five years

Feedback

Now is the time to find out what people think of the product and how it could be improved.

CUSTOMERS (EXTERNAL)

MANUFACTURING

MARKETING (INTERNAL)

Design decisions

Before full-scale production begins, all decisions have to be made and paperwork, such as intellectual property rights, finalized.

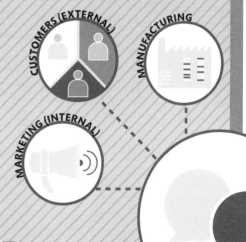

Quality management

For businesses, quality is not a vague term but a philosophy of going beyond consumer expectations. Excellent quality management can give a company a key competitive edge.

How it works

Many consumers might find it hard to define quality, because it can be subjective, but they know it when they see it. However, companies need to define and measure it. They know that to build a good reputation and thrive they have to exceed customers' expectations in terms of quality for both products and services. To do this, they apply a number of quality standards, or key performance indicators (KPIs), for the manufacturing process, and continually measure themselves against these. Quality does not apply just to the product or service itself; it ripples out to the associated people and processes, and across the organizational environment.

Cost of quality

Quality management is essential to ensure that any defects are nipped in the bud – the earlier the better – and definitely before they become apparent to the consumer.

CUSTOMER FIRST

Before the 1970s, quality was seen as something to be inspected and corrected. Then US businesses began to lose out to Japanese companies – for example, Toyota and Honda were able to produce cars at lower cost and with a much higher quality. The difference was that quality had a strategic meaning for Japanese firms – they made the customer their priority and were the first companies to define quality as meeting or exceeding customer expectations.

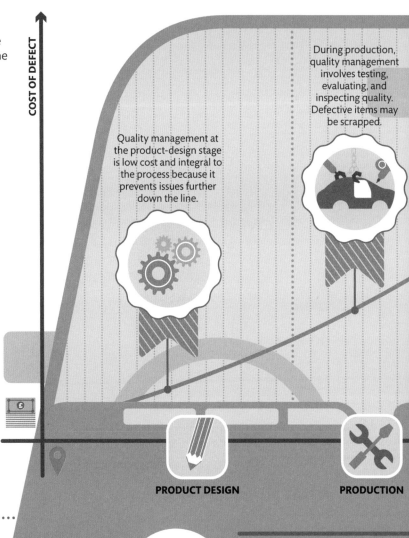

COST OF DEFECT

Quality management at the product-design stage is low cost and integral to the process because it prevents issues further down the line.

During production, quality management involves testing, evaluating, and inspecting quality. Defective items may be scrapped.

PRODUCT DESIGN

PRODUCTION

60%

of organizations **agree that** customers **are the** key drivers **of their** quality programmes

Once the product is with the customer, the cost of correcting defects is significant. Financial cost includes returns, repairs, and recalls, but the impact on the company's reputation may be even more damaging.

LOCATION OF DEFECT

PRODUCT WITH CUSTOMER

WHAT MAKES QUALITY?

Manufacturing industry

> Conformity to specifications/standards
> Performance
> Reliability
> Functionality/features
> Durability
> Serviceability

Service industry

> Getting the desired result
> Consistency
> Responsiveness to customer needs
> Courtesy/friendliness
> Promptness
> Psychological factors, such as good atmosphere

★ ★ ★ ★ ★

Product-process matrix

A product-process matrix is a tool that can help a business identify the best way to make a product, based on volume and the level of customization.

How it works

The production process has different stages. Businesses typically start with low volumes and are highly flexible, but not very cost-efficient. A small printing firm or dressmaker, for example, would be positioned in the bottom left-hand corner of the product-process matrix, where each job is unique and job production is the most effective method. Production stages then progress through increasing standardization and mechanization to full automation. Companies in the top right-hand corner of the matrix have high-volume products and a small range, so continuous flow production is the best option for them.

Choosing the best method

A business, or a business unit in a large company, occupies a particular region in the matrix. Different processes suit different products, depending on the stage of their life cycle and the scale of the business.

EVOLVING PROCESS

The product-process matrix was first introduced by Harvard academics Robert H. Hayes and Steven C. Wheelwright in the *Harvard Business Review* in 1979. Since then, some companies have worked out the apparent contradiction of how to customize high-volume products (mass customization). Nevertheless, the product-process matrix remains relevant in many industries.

over **1/4**

29%
of all goods are manufactured in China

NOT VIABLE

Product

Low volume
Low standardization; unique, one-off products

Dressmaker

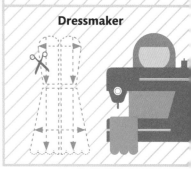

Process

Mass production
Continuous flow; non-stop process
(*see pp.280–281*)

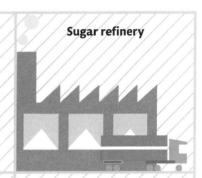
Sugar refinery

Car assembly

RARELY VIABLE
An assembly line is not normally a suitable process for making multiple products at low or medium volume.

Assembly line
Connected line flow; process repeated for each product
(*see pp.276–277*)

Low–medium volume
Some standardization; multiple products

High volume
Standardization; products manufactured in large quantities

Very high volume
High standardization; single commodity product

Bakery

Batch production
Disconnected line flow; similar process adjusted for each batch
(*see pp.274–275*)

RARELY VIABLE
Batch production is not normally a suitable process for making standardized products at high volume.

Job production
Jumbled flow; complex, unique process design for each order
(*see pp.272–273*)

NOT VIABLE

Control

Essential in any type of organization, control is fundamental when the primary goal is to generate profits. Control needs to cover costs, resources, and quality of the product or service to ensure that the operation runs smoothly. As well as crossing departments, control has to run from top to bottom, with directors formulating strategy while managers allocate resources, people, materials, and equipment, and oversee the work of individuals and teams.

The chain of control

It is simplest to think of a business as an end-to-end chain. Leaders have to make decisions on business goals, strategy, and policies at the start of the chain. This is critical for control along the chain. If there is no clear direction from the start, problems become exacerbated as they travel further along the line. Controls are put in place all the way along the chain to ensure that the organization is working to its goals, that it meets the desired standards, and that individuals and teams are clear about what is involved in specific tasks.

Control in practice: strategic control

ABC Cakes Company's goal is to be the top-selling cupcakes business. Its directors decide the quantity and quality of cupcakes the company needs to sell and so invest in a new factory. They also decide the scale of investment and estimate when it will begin to yield returns, and how long it will take for the project to repay its full cost (payback period).

Management control

The management team ensures that everyone meets their targets, liaises with other links in the chain, and works seamlessly to be a top-selling cupcakes business.

FUNCTIONS ALONG THE CHAIN
While directors work on strategic investment, policy, and process control, management may use tools such as Six Sigma to perfect operational control. *See pp.320–321.*

Investment relies on cash flowing back into the business from the cupcake sales, balanced by the cost of production.

Policies on, say, maintaining the optimum level of inventory, are supported along the chain by finance, HR, and IT.

Processes are in place to control costs, with continual reviews of the most efficient use of resources.

Procurement purchases raw materials from companies that meet its stringent standards.

84:1
the median ratio of CEO to employee pay of FTSE 100 companies in 2019

LEGALLY IMPOSED CONTROL

Many industries are subject to external controls as well as their own:

❯ **Financial institutions** National and international regulatory controls

❯ **Advertising industry** National regulation to protect public interest

❯ **Health and social care** National laws to protect vulnerable members of the public

❯ **Manufacturing** National regulations on health and safety

"Drive thy business, or it will drive thee."

Benjamin Franklin, *US statesman and scientist*

ABC CAKES

Task control

Metrics and key performance indicators are set for each task. They control, for example, how long it takes to ice and decorate a batch of cupcakes.

ABC CAKES COMPANY

Goods received
checks on-time delivery and that all inputs are consistently of the right quality.
See pp.318–319.

Stock control
uses sophisticated systems to ensure the optimum level of inventory.
See pp.316–317.

Production
has metrics for the quantity and quality of the cupcakes.
See pp.314–315.

Marketing
benchmarks the price and reviews the promotion of the product against competitors
See pp.332–333.

Sales
works to detailed targets.
See pp.314–315.

Managing capacity

In terms of production, capacity means how much work can be achieved in a given time. Ideally, a business matches its capacity to customer demand, so it uses its resources with maximum efficiency.

How it works

Every business has to consider how much capacity it needs for its operation, and how to manage this capacity both day-to-day and in the future. Management has to decide its priority: whether to deliver excellent customer service by having extra capacity, and so price its products or services high; or to manage its resources efficiently for a better return on investment, at the risk of disappointing customers if and when demand goes beyond its capacity. Businesses may offer consumers incentives to help manage capacity – for instance, cheaper off-peak rail fares encourage passengers to travel outside the rush hour, so easing overcrowding on trains that are full to capacity in the early morning. Likewise, many hotel chains do not charge a fixed price for rooms, pricing them according to demand to maintain capacity.

Capacity decisions

The fundamental decision is whether to compromise on demand or capacity – whether to put customers or the streamlining of operational costs first.

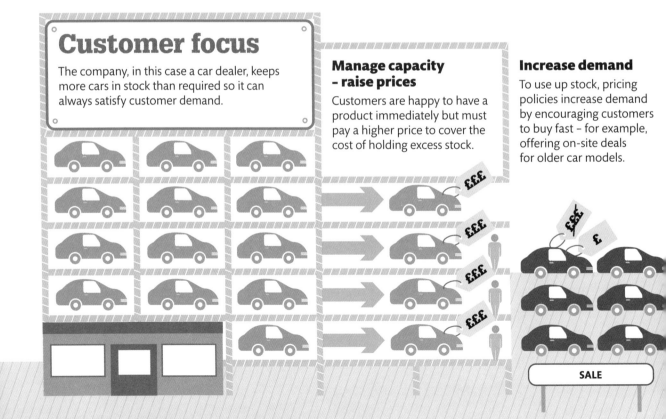

Customer focus

The company, in this case a car dealer, keeps more cars in stock than required so it can always satisfy customer demand.

Manage capacity – raise prices

Customers are happy to have a product immediately but must pay a higher price to cover the cost of holding excess stock.

Increase demand

To use up stock, pricing policies increase demand by encouraging customers to buy fast – for example, offering on-site deals for older car models.

SALE

HOW CAPACITY AFFECTS A COMPANY

Capacity management is critical to ensure, for example, that a manufacturing operation has the right level of resources to work to a production schedule. It affects many areas of the business, as all are interlinked and cost the company money:

❯ Factory or office size
❯ What and how much equipment is needed
❯ Staffing levels
❯ Use of labour, for example, shift work
❯ Which materials to use, how much/how often to order
❯ Inventory (stock) levels
❯ Production scheduling
❯ Speed and ease of processes
❯ Type of information technology used

✓ NEED TO KNOW

❯ **Potential capacity** The capacity that can be made available long term, a factor that affects investment decisions and business growth
❯ **Immediate capacity** The maximum potential capacity available in the short term
❯ **Effective capacity** The total capacity that is realistically achievable when all resources are being used optimally

Resource focus

The company uses resources as efficiently as possible. Wastage is kept to a minimum, but satisfying demand is hard because work is at full capacity and output cannot rise.

50%

expected average annual **growth in** vehicle deliveries at **Tesla to meet demand**

Manage capacity – keep stock low

It produces stock according to demand and holds low inventory to minimize unnecessary spending and storage costs.

Demand not satisfied

Company is unable to meet surges in demand, customers may have to wait while production catches up, and business may be lost to competitors.

Inventory

Firms have to manage inventory (stock) to meet customer demand, even if they trade online and have no physical shop front. Successful inventory management is a complex process.

How it works

Stock may include finished goods, work in progress, and raw materials. Getting the right level is a balance between having enough to meet customer demand and having too much, which is costly in terms of finished goods, storage space, and warehouse staff. Stock may also lose value if it perishes or become unsaleable because of changes in fashion or obsolete technology.

Effective inventory management involves systems and programmes for sales forecasts, production targets, and actual inventory status – plus the physical tracking and handling of the different items. Barcodes and radio-frequency identification (RFID) tags have revolutionized inventory management, making it much easier to monitor stock levels.

Inventory management

Successful inventory management is a fine balance between satisfied customers and minimizing the risk of holding too much stock. In this example, the clothing company is managing the supply of blue T-shirts for a range of sites and for direct delivery to customers.

Make sales forecasts

Company sets production targets based on prediction of demand.

Order from suppliers

Decisions on the level of raw materials to hold are based on lead times and reliability of suppliers.

Production

The quality of raw materials and finished goods is checked at every stage of production.

Smaller storage

Firm may use smaller facilities to hold buffer stock, for example, to meet seasonal demand.

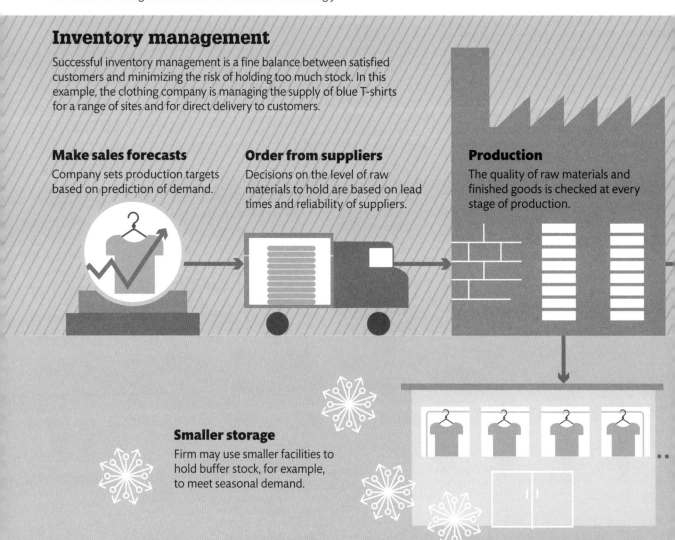

US$**1.8** trillion

lost globally in **2020** as a result of retailers' inventory mismanagement

Main warehouse

Company may have one main warehouse or a number of warehouses as hubs for smaller storage facilities.

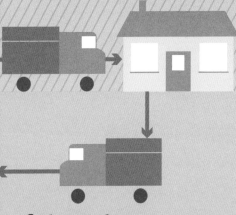

Delivery to customers

Efficient and timely delivery is part of the overall customer experience, especially as online shopping grows. Stock is checked in by scanning barcodes or RFID tags.

Customer returns

Returns are checked out by scanning barcodes or RFID tags. Batch number and other data can be monitored.

Quality control

There is a series of processes to ensure that a business maintains a prescribed level of quality in its products or services. Quality control is particularly important in industries where safety is an issue.

How it works

Businesses measure and manage the quality of their output against national legal standards and/or internal standards. For example, the manufacturing industry sets its own standards. Checking takes place against these and any national standards at various points along the production process, such as when raw materials arrive in the factory, during production, and before despatch of the finished goods to the customer.

Quality control relies on a predetermined percentage of products for inspection, agreed corrective action, and remedial efforts to minimize future defects. Industries in which safety is paramount, including food, clothing, pharmaceuticals, car, train, and aircraft manufacture, and construction, are subject to extremely strict standards of quality control. Some are there to protect workers, for instance, if they are handling chemicals, while others safeguard the consumer.

The bread and butter of quality control

Hygiene and safety are essential in the food industry, as in this example of quality control in a factory making prepacked sandwiches. Samples are tested all along the line. Any lapses in quality are not only a dangerous health hazard but would also be extremely damaging to the company's reputation.

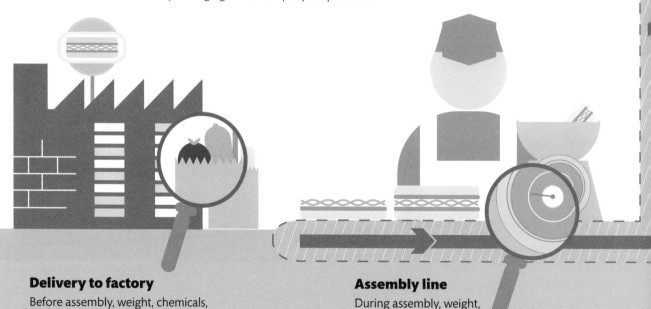

Delivery to factory
Before assembly, weight, chemicals, bacteria, taste, and interaction of individual ingredients are tested.

Assembly line
During assembly, weight, temperature, hygiene, and visual appearance are assessed.

GLOBAL FOOD STANDARDS

Ensuring the quality of food products as they cross the globe is vital for health and economies worldwide. Founded by the United Nations in 1963, the Codex Alimentarius is an internationally recognized set of food standards, guidelines, and codes of practice that helps do just that. Its voluntary, science-based provisions cover all aspects of food safety and quality, including hygiene, contaminants, and labelling.

US$18 billion

the projected size of the global prepacked sandwich market by 2025

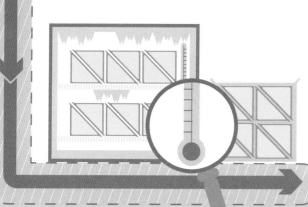

Packaging station
Samples are tested to check that sealing is accurate, labels are correctly applied, and overall presentation is good.

Storage
The temperature is checked for accuracy and safety, and samples are tested for taste, texture, and contamination by foreign objects.

Transport
The temperature in the vehicles and their delivery times are checked to ensure product freshness.

Six Sigma

Used in organizations to strive for near-perfect products and services, Six Sigma is a disciplined, data-driven approach for eliminating defects in any process.

How it works

The idea is that measuring the number of defects in any process makes it possible to systematically work out how to eliminate them and get as close to zero defects as possible. Individuals are trained to become experts in the different methods, creating a cadre of black belts, green belts, and champions.

Every Six Sigma project is carefully documented, follows a defined sequence of steps, and has quantified value targets, such as increasing customer satisfaction or reducing costs. To achieve Six Sigma quality, a manufacturing process must have 99.99966 per cent of output free of defects (3.4 defective parts per million).

SIX SIGMA ROLES

Six Sigma professionals are experts at improving processes. They drive the implementation of change.

 Master black belt Trains and coaches black belts and green belts; works at highest level, developing key measures and the strategic direction

 Black belt Leads problem-solving projects; coaches project teams, assigning roles and responsibilities; trains green belts

 Green belt Leads green-belt projects; helps with data collection and analysis for black-belt projects

 Champions Translate the company's vision, mission, and goals to create an organizational deployment (OD) plan and identify individual projects

 Executives Provide overall alignment by establishing strategic focus of the Six Sigma programme within the context of the organization's culture and its vision of what the customer sees and feels

5 Control

Perform before-and-after analysis; monitor systems; document results; work out recommendations for next steps.

4 Improve

Implement improvements and so address the root causes of major problems.

"**The** most dangerous **kind of waste is the** waste we don't recognize."

Shigeo Shingo, *industrial engineer and Six Sigma expert*

1

Define

Define the project's purpose and scope; identify processes that need improvement; determine customer needs and benefits.

Striving for perfection

The DMAIC methodology (standing for Define, Measure, Analyse, Improve, Control) is an integral part of Six Sigma. It is used for improving existing business processes that are falling below targets and where step-by-step improvements can be made.

2

Measure

Use data on current processes as a baseline; pinpoint problem locations and occurrences; identify potential areas for improvement.

3

Analyse

Identify root causes of problems and check them against data; determine precise improvements that need to be made.

CHAMPIONS

Mobile phone maker Motorola pioneered Six Sigma quality in the mid-1980s, using it as a goal for its manufacturing operations; under CEO Jack Welch, General Electric was another early adopter. Since then, firms as diverse as the Credit Suisse bank, shipping company Maersk, and electronics manufacturer Samsung have taken it up.

✔ **NEED TO KNOW**

❯ **Lean Six Sigma** A combination of Lean production (*see pp.288–289*) and Six Sigma. The Lean part focuses on removal of waste from all activities, whereas Six Sigma focuses on reducing the number of defects

❯ **DMAIC** Define, measure, analyse, improve, control – the cycle for improving existing processes to Six Sigma level

❯ **DMADV** Define, measure, analyse, design, verify – the cycle for designing new processes or products at Six Sigma level. Also known as Design for Six Sigma (DFSS)

Supply chain

Along the journey from raw material to finished item in the hands of a consumer, every business needs an efficient supply chain. Supply chain management involves different organizations, people, activities, and resources to take, for example, grains of corn from a field to a finished packet of cornflakes on the table of the consumer. The company may outsource parts of the chain to other firms. It may also send some activities, typically administrative functions, offshore.

Supply chain management

The traditional supply chain takes raw materials and resources through to a finished product for the consumer. The company has to manage costs and ensure standards, being particularly careful that it does not harm people or the environment along the way, from fair wages for labour at source to recyclable packaging after consumption. Supply chain is big business – 5.75 million people are employed in warehousing and transport alone in the US.

Raw materials and resources
Whether from a field or plantation, raw materials start somewhere.

Supplier and processor
The raw materials are processed, often near their source.

Manufacturer
Organizations bring resources together to manufacture goods, often near the customer.

64%

of retailers say they had to adapt their supply chain for e-commerce during the COVID-19 pandemic

EXTENDING THE CHAIN

› **Adding value** Companies may try to add value along the chain, rather than just seeing it as a way to transport a product from A to B. *See pp.324–325.*

› **Delegating functions** To save money and use specialist expertise, the business can outsource activities and/or have them done by local companies or a branch of its own company offshore. *See pp.326–329.*

› **Returning goods** Part of the supply chain involves an efficient system for dealing with goods returned by the consumer. *See pp.330–331.*

› **Competitive edge** At every stage, the company compares its performance with its competitors to see how it can improve. *See pp.332–333.*

› **Ethics and the environment** Taking responsibility for avoiding pollution and protecting workers' rights is part of the package. *See pp.334–335.*

Distribution

Finished goods are transported to storage depots or retailers.

Retailer

The shop displays the products for maximum appeal to the consumer.

Consumer

The consumer enjoys the finished product, and ideally recycles the packaging.

Value chain

Rather than looking at the supply chain as merely a series of activities, organizations are increasingly paying attention to how value is created by each stage of the process. Lowering costs or raising performance are key.

How it works

Harvard Business School professor Michael Porter first introduced the concept of a value chain in his book *Competitive Advantage*. Most organizations have numerous – possibly hundreds – of activities along the supply chain in the process of converting raw materials (inputs) to products or services (outputs). These can be classified generally as either primary or support activities that all businesses must undertake. The idea of the value chain is that how activities are organized and carried out determines a firm's costs and thus its margin (profit). Each link of the chain must communicate to other departments clearly and promptly. For example, marketing and sales must make accurate sales forecasts and pass them on in enough time for procurement to buy the correct type and quantity of raw materials, who in turn must liaise with inbound logistics so they can organize receipt of goods.

Porter's value chain

Primary activities work directly to create or deliver a product or service, while support activities help to improve their efficiency. To apply the value chain, a company has to identify each activity and either lower its cost or differentiate it from its competitors to add value in the customer's eye.

PRIMARY ACTIVITIES
Each department must cooperate and provide necessary information between value-chain activities to make a profit.

Inbound logistics
Involves relationships with suppliers, including all activities to receive, store, and allocate inputs

Operations
Activities required to transform inputs into outputs

SUPPORT ACTIVITIES
Although not directly involved in outputs, these support primary activities, improving their efficiency and successful function.

 Firm infrastructure

 Human resource management

 Technology development

 Procurement

CASE STUDY

Zara's value chain

The Spanish clothing brand is famous for rapidly responding to customers' needs along the value chain.

> **Inbound logistics** Bulk fabric orders, quick deliveries

> **Operations** Just-in-time manufacturing, near Spanish HQ

> **Outbound logistics** Twice-weekly store deliveries, low inventory, fast online fulfilment

> **Marketing** Few ads, strategic store locations, store data ensures products match customers' wants

> **Support activities** Tech to supply feedback, customer service training

ONLINE VALUE CHAIN

More than half of the world's population use the internet, doing everything from shopping to sharing photos, watching TV, working, and checking social media. To handle this volume, a complex value chain delivers internet services, made up of global and local firms with assets as diverse as content rights, communications and IT infrastructure, proprietary software, and global brands.

6,384

the number of **local Spanish firms supplying Zara's parent company Inditex** in 2020

Outbound logistics

Activities required to collect, store, and distribute the output

Marketing and sales

Activities that inform buyers, persuade them to purchase, and facilitate transaction

Service

Activities to keep product working effectively for buyer after it is received

PROFIT MARGIN
Profit equals the customer's willingness to pay more than the sum of all the activities in the value chain.

Functions such as accounting, legal, finance, planning, public affairs, and quality assurance

People activities: recruiting, hiring, training, developing, compensating, and terminating

Equipment, hardware, software, procedures, and technical knowledge used in transformation of inputs into outputs

Acquisition of inputs (raw materials) for the firm

Outsourcing

Firms may choose to pay outside suppliers to do work rather than complete the tasks internally. Handing over part or all of production or a service to a third party increases flexibility.

How it works

Outsourcing grew in the 1980s because firms looked to save costs by contracting peripheral business activities to third parties. But outsourcing today is no longer just about cost savings. It is a strategic tool that is increasingly important in the global economy in the 21st century. Firms may choose outsourcing for elements of the production process, for enabling functions such as accounting, or because they do not have the specialist knowledge or skills within the organization. Outsourcing may be to a firm in the same country or it may be to an organization in another country. Rapid expansion of logistics networks and information technology has made it easier to outsource, so accelerating the growth of outsourcing over the last decade.

What services are outsourced?

Growth and success for many businesses is underpinned by outsourcing, as a number of firms ask: why do it ourselves, if another firm can do it faster, better, or cheaper? Organizations recognize that using external capabilities, capacities, knowledge, and skills opens opportunities. Some firms now focus only on their core business; in a 2021 global survey by Deloitte, these were the main services that organizations outsourced to third-party providers.

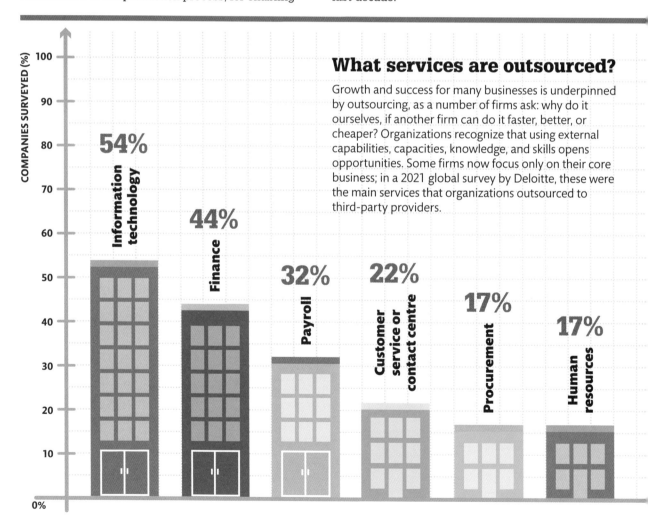

COMPANIES SURVEYED (%)

- **54%** Information technology
- **44%** Finance
- **32%** Payroll
- **22%** Customer service or contact centre
- **17%** Procurement
- **17%** Human resources

✓ NEED TO KNOW

- **Offshoring** Practice of moving a company's operating base to a foreign country where labour costs are cheaper
- **Network structure** Task or operation is performed by another firm – which may be in same country, an adjacent country, or overseas – within a network structure of organizations
- **Shared services** Practice of moving specific services that were formerly carried out in many parts of an organization (such as HR, finance, and IT) into a single unit. Differs from outsourcing in that no third parties are involved.

80%
of firms say they have no plans to move offshore services back in the short term

EXAMPLES OF BUSINESS TASKS THAT CAN BE OUTSOURCED

Outsourcing certain tasks within a business enables focus to remain on core business activities, which helps generate growth as well as income. Some tasks are better suited to outsourcing than others due to factors including expertise, how time consuming a task is, and how much face-to-face time it requires. IT operations, for example, can be highly expensive, requiring expert knowledge and can easily be managed remotely. Human resources, however, is more employee focused, so better suited to in-house.

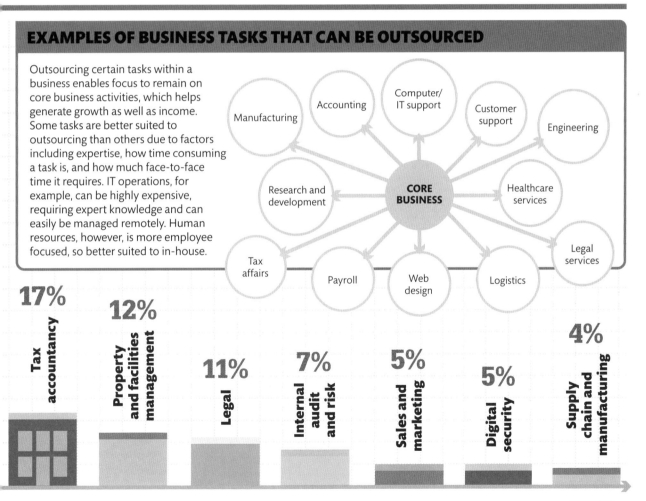

CORE BUSINESS

Manufacturing · Accounting · Computer/IT support · Customer support · Engineering · Research and development · Healthcare services · Tax affairs · Payroll · Web design · Logistics · Legal services

17% Tax accountancy

12% Property and facilities management

11% Legal

7% Internal audit and risk

5% Sales and marketing

5% Digital security

4% Supply chain and manufacturing

SERVICES

Offshoring

Moving jobs outside the country where a company is based is called offshoring. A company will set up operations overseas, and recruit local people to do the work, usually with the support of employees from the parent company.

How it works

Offshoring grew in the 1980s as Western companies with high labour costs realized they could make significant savings by manufacturing in countries with lower overheads. Information technology (IT) services followed, enabled by the internet and global communications. Some firms offshore manufacturing by setting up a factory in another country – perhaps to be close to a source of raw materials. They can also offshore services, such as call centres, in locations where there is a ready supply of skilled staff. In addition, companies can undertake offshore outsourcing, where work is handled by a third party. Firms that offshore must follow good ethical practice, such as paying local people a fair wage, and upholding health and safety standards in the workplace.

Global expertise

Offshoring started in India and today it still leads the way. The country's IT and business processing outsourcing export industries employ more than four million people and are worth US$147 billion. Other regions have different areas of expertise; for instance, Eastern Europe also specializes in IT services. This map shows examples of the areas of expertise available in different countries, and companies that offshore their operations.

Samsung

South Korean company Samsung runs manufacturing facilities in the **US**, which is a big market for its products.

Ford

Ford has manufacturing plants and facilities in **Mexico**.

Brazil

Offshoring benefits

❯ Attractive hiring costs
❯ Skilled labour pool
❯ Good IT infrastructure

Levi Strauss & Co

In 2019, Levi Strauss & Co acquired operating assets related to the Levi's and Dockers's brands from The Jeans Company (TJC), its distributor in **Chile, Peru, and Bolivia**, to enable it to increase growth across the region.

55%
India's share of the global outsourcing market

THE PROS OF OFFSHORING

> Cheaper labour costs
> Proximity to raw materials
> Access to specialized staff
> Tax benefits

THE CONS OF OFFSHORING

> Communication problems
> Working in different time zones
> Different working cultures can cause difficulties
> Can be vulnerable to geopolitical unrest

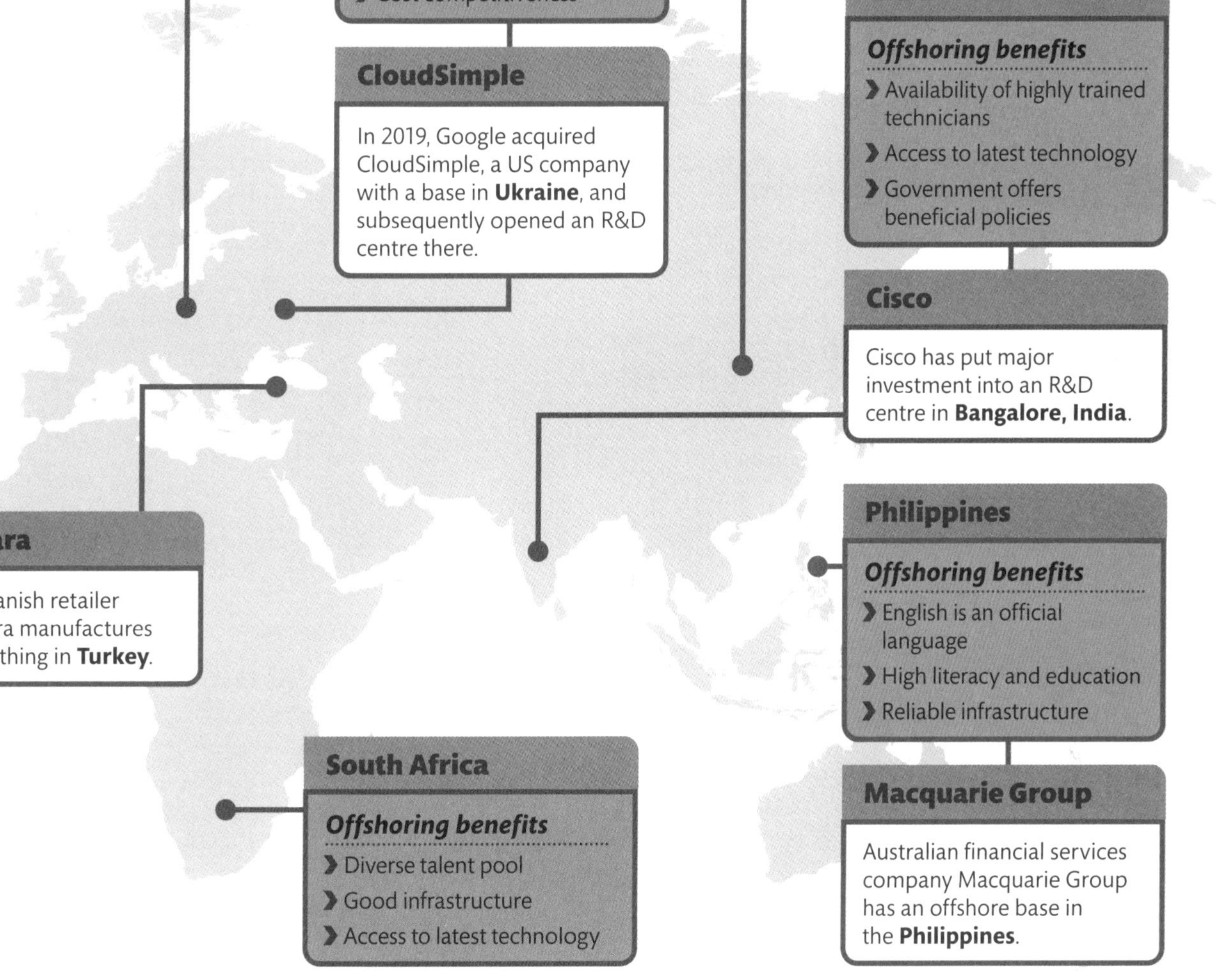

Jaguar Landrover

Jaguar Landrover has a cutting-edge manufacturing plant in **Slovakia**.

Ukraine

Offshoring benefits

> Engineering capability
> Access to people with software development skills
> Cost competitiveness

CloudSimple

In 2019, Google acquired CloudSimple, a US company with a base in **Ukraine**, and subsequently opened an R&D centre there.

Apple

Apple has had substantial operations in **China** for many years.

India

Offshoring benefits

> Availability of highly trained technicians
> Access to latest technology
> Government offers beneficial policies

Cisco

Cisco has put major investment into an R&D centre in **Bangalore, India**.

Zara

Spanish retailer Zara manufactures clothing in **Turkey**.

Philippines

Offshoring benefits

> English is an official language
> High literacy and education
> Reliable infrastructure

South Africa

Offshoring benefits

> Diverse talent pool
> Good infrastructure
> Access to latest technology

Macquarie Group

Australian financial services company Macquarie Group has an offshore base in the **Philippines**.

Reverse supply chain

Supply chain takes a product to a customer. Reverse supply chain is the series of activities it takes to retrieve an unwanted or used product from a customer and dispose of it, recycle, or resell it.

How it works

Companies have to focus on more than bringing a product to a customer. Now an efficient reverse supply chain is also essential, especially for the large number of online retailers. Manufacturers, too, in industries from carpets to computers, may need reverse supply to recycle products to meet environmental regulations.

For instance, companies have to manage products that are returned for a refund; products that do not sell and are returned to producers from retailers; or products near the end of their life. In a drive to improve sustainability, Swedish chain Ikea, offers to buy back old items of its furniture from customers.

Reverse logistics

The cost to companies of reverse supply is enormous. For example, in the US, statistics from the National Retail Federation show that consumers returned US$428 billion of goods in 2020 – with online returns almost doubling as consumers switched to internet shopping during the COVID-19 pandemic. This represents about 10 per cent of the US's total retail sales of US$4 trillion for the year.

Retrieve

Companies may have processes in place to collect used or unwanted items, whether from the customer or retailer.

CUSTOMER RETURNS

US retailers Sears and JCPenney were the first shops to allow consumers to return goods with no penalty. This pioneering move in the late 19th century encouraged people to shop with them and helped build a loyal following. These days, most high-street and online retailers allow customers to return unwanted items within a set time period and receive an exchange or refund. Consumers have the right to return faulty goods, which also forms part of the reverse supply chain.

Please return within 28 days

Eventual recycling or reconditioning may be considered at the start of design and manufacturing decisions.

Disposal management

NEED TO KNOW

> **Electronic waste (e-waste)** Electrical or electronic devices that are unwanted, do not work, or are obsolete

> **Warehousing** Administrative and physical functions necessary for storage of goods, either for selling or retrieval

84%
of Brazilian online shoppers are likely to make an extra purchase when returning an item to a physical store

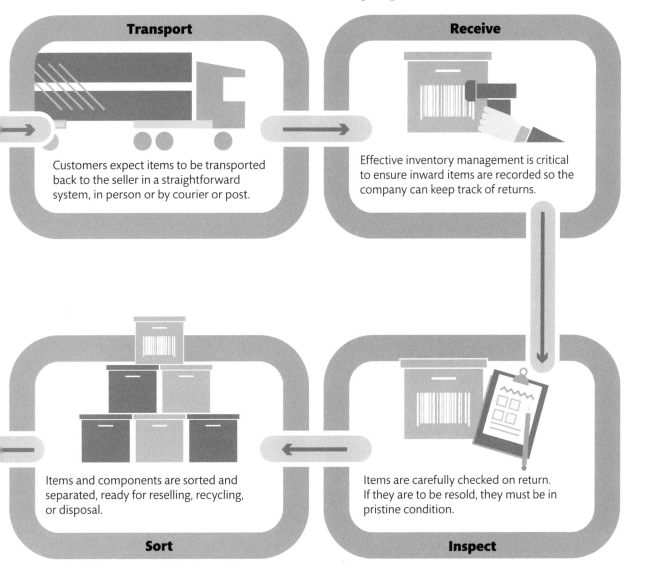

Transport

Customers expect items to be transported back to the seller in a straightforward system, in person or by courier or post.

Receive

Effective inventory management is critical to ensure inward items are recorded so the company can keep track of returns.

Sort

Items and components are sorted and separated, ready for reselling, recycling, or disposal.

Inspect

Items are carefully checked on return. If they are to be resold, they must be in pristine condition.

Benchmarking

Businesses use benchmarking to improve efficiency by comparing their performance with that of other organizations. The goal is to identify and learn from best practice within or outside the industry.

How it works

To improve results, a business may look outside the organization, industry, or country to explore others' levels of performance and identify how they achieve it. Benchmark areas include unit cost, customer ratings, and pay and benefits. The evaluation takes into account a range of factors, including training, technology platforms, and manufacturing equipment. For example, Formula 1 is often used as a benchmark for teamwork as pit-stop crews have perfected the changing of four tyres in less than seven seconds.

The process of benchmarking

There are several stages to benchmarking performance before a company can start to see costs saved and efficiency increased.

Company owns a commercial building

Identify need to benchmark

In this example, a company wants to improve its energy efficiency.

Compare to competition

The company gathers information on others' energy systems and costs.

Company replaces lighting

Monitor value

It measures how much its energy costs have gone down and how well the new lighting system works.

Company monitors energy and money saved

SOCIAL MEDIA MAKES IT EASY

It is now easier than ever before for organizations to gather data about their competitors. Social media can provide data on customer preferences, brands and campaigns of other organizations. Analytical tools are available to simplify benchmarking across many different channels.

"**Benchmarking** is the search for industry best practices that lead to superior performance."

Robert C. Camp, *benchmarking pioneer*

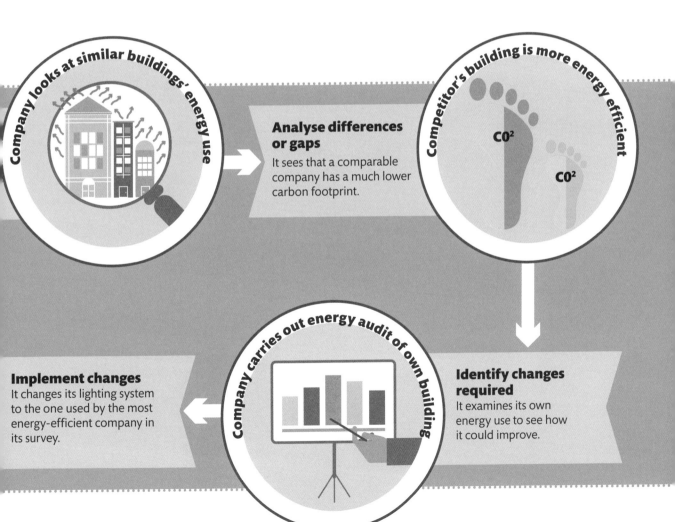

Company looks at similar buildings' energy use

Analyse differences or gaps
It sees that a comparable company has a much lower carbon footprint.

Competitor's building is more energy efficient

CO_2

CO_2

Company carries out energy audit of own building

Identify changes required
It examines its own energy use to see how it could improve.

Implement changes
It changes its lighting system to the one used by the most energy-efficient company in its survey.

Corporate social responsibility

Businesses today must aim not only to do no harm to the environment, people, or communities, but to show commitment to building a better society. This is termed corporate social responsibility (CSR).

How it works

For a business, CSR goes further than aiming to be compliant with national or international regulations, managing risks, or corporate philanthropy – it has to be an integral part of every aspect of operations, helping to create a sustainable business. A company still has to be competitive and profitable, but must avoid taking decisions merely for short-term gain. Instead, it has to consider the future impact on society, the environment, and a wide range of stakeholders. Companies now report annually on how they have met their CSR and are benchmarked and ranked against competitors.

Community
Housing; healthcare; infrastructure; partnering with local institutions; local supplier initiatives; education; training; local employment

100%
of the **top 100** companies in **Japan and Mexico** report on sustainability

Environment
Company's carbon footprint including recycling; water and waste management; energy usage; transport

Workforce
Workplace safety, health, and wellbeing; diversity; equal opportunities; learning and development; ethical policies and practices

Suppliers
Fairtrade, supply-chain ethics, and sustainability (including use of child labour); code of conduct; transport policies

CSR stakeholders

A number of different business areas have to be considered when assessing a company's CSR, from how it affects people working in and for the company to wider environmental and community implications.

Operations
Ethical trading including marketing practices and pricing; managing customers; financial reporting; policies; values

---

 CASE STUDY

AstraZeneca's biogas stoves

The pharmaceutical firm's CSR initiatives include funding a project to test biogas stoves in rural Kenya. The wood and charcoal-fuelled stoves traditionally used by many Kenyans release harmful smoke, contributing to climate change and causing respiratory problems in those using them (mostly women and girls). So, the firm partnered with Kenyan company Biogas International and the University of Cambridge's Institute for Sustainability to install smokeless stoves that run on biogas made from organic waste. AstraZeneca also runs other projects targeting ill health in developing countries, as well as a health and wellbeing strategy for its staff.

How companies work

The legal system of England and Wales, Scotland, and Northern Ireland allows for five business ownership structures: sole trader; three types of partnership; and limited company.

Sole trader

An individual carrying out business as a sole trader can take on staff but is personally responsible for losses made by the business, payment of debts, and maintaining records of earnings and expenditure. Sole traders are taxed on business profits as a single entity after submitting an annual online self-assessment form.

Partnerships

Under the law governing partnerships (the Partnership Act of 1890), every partner is equally liable for any debts even if they own just a small percentage of the business. An alternative form of partnership is a Limited Partnership, which consists of general partners who actively run the business and are fully liable for debts, and one or more limited partners – sometimes referred to as "sleeping partners" – who are not involved in managing the business and have only limited liability for debts.

One additional type of partnership is the Limited Liability Partnership, which has members rather than directors or shareholders. These members are protected from business debt and are only liable for personal income tax, rather than corporate taxes. Unlike a company, a Limited Liability Partnership can trade in any category of business and is not restricted by a Memorandum of Association that specifies the type of business being carried out.

Limited company

In terms of its legal status, a limited company is different from a partnership or sole-trader business in two fundamental ways. First, a company's assets belong to the company and not to its directors or shareholders. Second, a company's debts belong to the company, and directors are not held personally responsible for paying them. Several types of limited company are recognized under the UK legal system. Most companies are limited by shares, which means the company is owned by shareholders who are only liable for the capital they invest in their shares. There are a few other variations on the limited company:

Private company limited by guarantee, in which the directors or shareholders agree to back the organization up to a specified amount.

Private unlimited company, which is set up in the same way as a limited company, but the company members (usually shareholders) accept full responsibility for the company's debts. The advantage is that annual accounts do not have to be registered. This structure is rare in the UK and not encouraged.

Public limited company (PLC), which, unlike a private limited company, can offer shares to the public in order to raise capital. Before it can begin trading on the stock exchange, a PLC needs to have issued at least £50,000 worth of shares, and received at least a quarter of that value from shareholders. This structure is commonly used by larger companies.

Reporting requirements

Each financial year, a company must generate statutory accounts reflecting the year's business activity, send an annual return to Companies House, and submit a company tax return to Her Majesty's Revenue & Customs (HMRC). If the company is registered for Value Added Tax (VAT), it must also submit VAT returns and pay any VAT owing – this may be done annually, monthly, or quarterly depending on the accounting scheme being used by the company.

Company law

The UK's system of company registration was set up in 1844, and the law governing registration is the Companies Act of 2006. All companies must be registered at Companies House, which holds records of all companies in the UK. Within Companies House, there are three separate registers: one for England and Wales, which are treated as a single entity; one for Scotland; and one for Northern Ireland. Companies registered in England and Wales are subject to English law; companies registered in Scotland are subject to Scottish law; and companies registered in Northern Ireland are subject to the law of Northern Ireland.

Taxation and VAT

HMRC is the body responsible for collecting taxes from individuals and businesses. Any business with an annual turnover of more than £85,000, or expected to soon go over that amount, must register for Value Added Tax (VAT). VAT-registered companies add the 20 per cent tax on sales to customers, called output tax, and must pay the tax on purchases from other VAT-registered companies, called input tax. If the input tax is more than the output tax the business can claim the difference back from HMRC.

Some goods and services attract a reduced rate of VAT, such as children's car seats and household power, which are charged at 5 per cent. Other goods and services are zero-rated, meaning they attract 0 per cent VAT but are still considered taxable supplies, including food (excluding restaurant meals and hot takeaways), books and newspapers, children's clothing and shoes, and public transport. Certain items are exempt from VAT, including insurance, some education and training, charity fundraising events, most medical and dental services, and selling or leasing commercial property.

ORGANIZATIONS AND RESOURCES

The UK public sector information website, gov.uk, provides simplified information and instructions on the business structures permitted under UK law.
www.gov.uk/business-legal-structures/overview

Companies House sets out corporate policy and guidance as stipulated by law.
www.gov.uk/government/organisations/companies-house

VAT

HMRC offers information about VAT, how and when to register, and an explanation of accounting schemes. Simple interactive tutorials on how VAT works and VAT rates are available.
www.gov.uk/vat-businesses

Start-ups

England The National Enterprise Network offers independent advice and support to anyone thinking of starting a business or already running one.
www.nationalenterprisenetwork.org

Scotland Business Gateway provides research reports, company lists, commercial property searches, and professional advice across business activities.
www.bgateway.com

Northern Ireland NIBusinessInfo is a free online service with videos, tools, tutorials, and case studies on start-ups and managing established businesses.
www.nibusinessinfo.co.uk/start

Wales Business Wales has a helpline, step-by-step advice online, and face-to-face workshops on starting and running a business, growth, finance, and funding.
www.businesswales.gov.wales/starting-up

How finance works

The Companies Act 2006 is the main legislation governing financial reporting and accounting standards in the UK. It sets out how limited companies should prepare and submit their accounts.

Limited companies must fulfil a number of duties in order to lawfully meet their financial reporting obligations:

❯ Keep accounting records and make them available at all times for inspection – three years for private companies, and six years for public companies;

❯ Circulate copies of annual accounts and reports;

❯ Submit the company's accounts for tax purposes to HMRC at the end of the financial year;

❯ Submit the company's financial accounts, also called statutory accounts or audited accounts, to Companies House at the end of the financial year.

Other aspects of financial reporting covered by the law include auditing requirements and procedures for companies, and exemptions and specific rulings for small companies, which are generally not required to report to the same level of complexity and detail as larger companies.

Before Brexit, the UK law on financial reporting integrated the reporting requirements of European law, which meant that all listed European companies had to adhere to International Financial Reporting Standards (IFRSs). Now those companies must report under IFRSs approved for use in the UK, rather than the European Union (EU). Although practically identical at present, things may change. Other UK companies can choose to report either under UK-endorsed IFRSs or the UK's own reporting code, UK GAAP, an abbreviation of Generally Accepted Accounting Practice. This code sets out how a company's accounts should be prepared, including accounting standards and UK company law.

There are six financial reporting standards for the UK and Republic of Ireland, which come under the umbrella of UK GAAP. These are issued by the Financial Reporting Council (FRC), an independent body answerable to parliament and funded by fees from listed companies.

FRS 100 sets out a framework on how to prepare financial statements to ensure they meet legislation and accounting standards for the UK and Ireland.

FRS 101 applies to companies reporting under IFRS.

FRS 102 elaborates on the requirements for financial statements so that they accurately reflect the financial position of a business. It defines each component of the financial statement and explains how the value of each one should be measured.

FRS 103 specifically deals with insurance contracts, setting out accounting policies and measurement regulations for entities with insurance business.

FRS 104 deals with preparing interim financial reports.

FRS 105 lays out the accounting standards for small organizations applying a micro-entities regime.

Accounting periods

For UK companies, the accounting period for tax purposes is 12 months long and runs from 1 April to 31 March the following year. (For individuals, it runs from 6 April to 5 April the following year.)

A company's accounting period usually matches the financial year but if, for example, a company has been dormant and starts trading again, the accounting period may differ from the financial year.

Corporate fraud

The Serious Fraud Office (SFO) is an independent government department charged with investigating company fraud in England, Wales, and Northern Ireland. It identifies four main types of corporate fraud:

Asset stripping, where directors transfer the assets, but not the debts, of one company to another.

Fraudulent trading, according to the SFO, is where a company carries out business in order to defraud creditors or for any other fraudulent purpose.

Share ramping, where the price of shares is artificially manipulated by criminals with the intention of making profit on the value of shares.

Publishing false information, where a company's financial position is presented in a misleading way.

Company flotation and share issues

The London Stock Exchange hosts the Main Market for listed companies issuing shares. It is governed by UK Acts, regulations of the Financial Services Authority (FSA), and the Exchange's own rules. The FSA has statutory powers to control the admission of companies to the Exchange. Before any company can be listed, it must first approach the FSA, which also acts as the UK Listing Authority (UKLA), to request that the company's shares be admitted to the FSA's Official List. Second, the London Stock Exchange must admit the shares for trading. The Exchange also operates the Alternative Investment Market (AIM), which has less stringent entry requirements and is suited to smaller companies, such as start-ups.

To gain admission to the Official List, a company must satisfy the UK Listing Rules, which set out the minimum requirements for an IPO, including:

> Meeting basic legal rules governing the constitution and operation of the company;

> The market value of the securities being listed must be at least £700,000;

> At least 25 per cent of the shares should be sold to the public (not held by directors or persons connected with directors, or by anyone holding a 5 per cent or more interest in the share capital);

> For Premium Listings, which are harder to achieve but give investors greater confidence, companies must provide three years of accounts, and must show that there is enough working capital for the next 12 months.

ORGANIZATIONS AND RESOURCES

Financial reporting

The Financial Reporting Council is the source for UK accounting standards and code of corporate governance.
www.frc.org.uk

The Institute of Chartered Accountants in England and Wales (ICAEW) advises on regulations, and financial management and reporting.
www.icaew.com

ICAS is the professional body of chartered accountants worldwide. It compiles news and technical knowledge on specialist areas such as taxation and insolvency.
www.icas.com

The International Financial Reporting Standards (IFRS) Foundation is an independent, not-for-profit organization focused on developing uniform standards.
www.ifrs.org

HMRC has a detailed guide to managing corporation tax.
www.gov.uk/topic/business-tax/corporation-tax

Corporate fraud

The Serious Fraud Office provides information on how to recognize fraud and offers a confidential reporting scheme for witnesses. It explains the Public Interest Disclosure Act 1998, which protects employees who disclose evidence of fraud in the public interest.
www.sfo.gov.uk

Protect is a non-profit body that calls itself the "whistleblowing charity" and provides a helpline for individuals and businesses.
protect-advice.org.uk

The Financial Conduct Authority investigates allegations of corporate asset stripping and other fraud.
www.fca.org.uk

IPO and London Stock Exchange listing

Guides on the different types of share issues, specialist markets for share trading, and minimum regulations.
www.londonstockexchange.com

How sales and marketing work

Under UK law, all advertising and marketing must comply with advertising regulations and codes of practice, enforced by the Trading Standards office and the Competition & Markets Authority.

There are two legal regulations for advertising: one covers advertising to consumers and the other deals with advertising to businesses.

The Consumer Protection from Unfair Trading Regulations set out the legal rules for advertising to consumers. The key points of the regulations forbid businesses from misleading or harassing consumers by including false or deceptive messages, leaving out vital information, or using aggressive sale techniques.

For business-to-business advertising, the Business Protection from Misleading Marketing Regulations covers rulings on ad content, especially to do with competitors. Businesses should take care not to use a competitor's logo or trademark, or anything that looks similar. Nor should they compare their products with competitors where there is no genuine similarity.

As well as the regulations, there are two codes of practice enforced by the Advertising Standards Authority (ASA). The Committee of Advertising Practice's Codes cover non-broadcast advertising, sales promotion, and direct marketing. It specifies standards for advertising to children, anything that causes offence, and political advertising. The UK Code of Broadcast Advertising covers TV and radio. It sets standards to do with taste, decency, and product placements, including scheduling and timing for certain content. Further regulations apply to food, alcohol, cosmetics, environmentally friendly products, pharmaceutical products, and tobacco.

Data protection

The Data Protection Act incorporates a comprehensive list of principles. The key concerns are making sure the information is accurate, up-to-date, and secure. When collecting an individual's personal data, the business must reveal its identity and how the information will be used. Consumers have the right to see any information about them that an organization may hold, and to correct it if it is wrong.

Direct marketing

Much of the direct-marketing industry is self-regulated by the mandatory Code of Conduct written by the Direct Marketing Association (DMA) and adhered to by its members. The DMA also sets out additional voluntary guidelines. The Direct Marketing Commission (DMC) oversees the Code and investigates complaints, if the complaint is covered in the Code.

Legislation of direct marketing specifically concerns data protection and unsolicited contact, and businesses must comply with a number of regulations. They must:
> Check if customers want to be contacted by fax, phone, post, or email, and allow them to object;
> Ask customers' permission to send them offers;
> Ask customers' permission to share their details;
> Allow customers to opt out of contact – e.g., marketing emails must offer recipients the option of opting out;
> Check with the Telephone and Fax Preference Services to identify individuals who have asked not to be contacted. Companies that break the law by making unsolicited calls can be fined up to £500,000;
> Check with the Mail Preference Service to make sure that mailing lists do not include individuals who have asked not to receive direct mail;
> Only send emails or text messages to individuals who have given their permission. These emails or texts must clearly state who is sending them, what is being sold, and any promotions or conditions;
> Inform website visitors how cookies are used and ask if they will accept them.

E-commerce

In 2000, the UK government brought in the Consumer Protection (Distance Selling) Regulations, which are designed to protect consumers who are buying goods and services from businesses who sell online or by mail order, where there is no face-to-face contact with the seller. Distance Selling Regulations (DSR) are enforced by the Office of Fair Trading in England, Scotland, and Wales, and by the Department of Enterprise, Trade and Investment in Northern Ireland. The basic DSR requirements include the following key points.

❯ Consumers must have access to clear "prior information": any vital information in writing about the product and seller, such as the business name and location of the seller (a PO box is not enough); the price of the product, including any additional costs such as VAT and delivery; a satisfactory description of the product; cancellation and returns policies; and protection from payment-card fraud.

❯ Shoppers have the right to a seven-day cooling-off period, and if no cooling-off period is stated in the terms and conditions, consumers are automatically entitled to 90 days, during which they can change their mind. If consumers change their mind after examining the product during the cooling-off period, they are entitled to cancel the purchase, return the product, and receive a refund within 30 days.

E-commerce businesses must also adhere to the 2002 E-Commerce Regulations. All commercial websites must state the name, registered address, postal address, and email address of the business, along with the company registration and VAT numbers, and details of any trade or professional association memberships. One further compliance under the Disability Discrimination Act 1995 is that websites are accessible to users with disabilities such as impaired vision and dyslexia.

ORGANIZATIONS AND RESOURCES

Advertising

The ASA provides details of the UK Advertising Codes, how to comply with them, and how to make a complaint. *www.asa.org.uk*

Consumer Protection from Unfair Trading Regulations is a guide for businesses on consumer protection from misleading advertising and marketing. *www.gov.uk/government/publications/consumer-protection-from-unfair-trading-regulations-businesses*

Data protection

The Information Commissioner's Office is an independent authority responsible for upholding information rights in the public interest. It offers guidance on adhering to the data protection principles in the Data Protection Act. *ico.org.uk/for-organisations/guide-to-data-protection*

Direct marketing

Gov.uk gives the main stipulations for companies engaging in direct marketing, including telesales, email marketing, text messaging, and direct mail. *www.gov.uk/marketing-advertising-law/direct-marketing*

The DMA sets out its Code and provides guides to telemarketing, mobile marketing, and data usage. *dma.org.uk*

E-commerce and online shopping

This government website has the text of the Consumer Protection (Distance Selling) Regulations 2000. *www.legislation.gov.uk/uksi/2000/2334/contents/made*

This website summarizes the key points of the DSR, as well as articles on e-commerce regulations, returns policies, and protection from unfair trading. *www.onlineshoppingrights.co.uk/ConsumerRightsCategory.html*

How operations and production work

The UK Corporate Governance Code spells out the standards of good practice on board effectiveness, pay, accountability, and shareholder relations for public companies.

Any public company with a premium listing of shares on the London Stock Exchange is required to state how it has adhered to the Code in its annual reports and financial accounts. Although the Code does not specifically address corporate social responsibility (CSR), it does advise that "the board should set the company's values and standards and ensure that its obligations to shareholders and others are understood and met". An addition called the Turnbull Guidance, which covers risk assessment, notes the importance of managing financial risk responsibly as well as health, safety, and environmental issues.

The Companies Act 2006 also requires directors to attend to community and environmental matters, and CSR is generally seen as a matter of commercial survival, especially when it comes to the environment. The growing number of investors seeking to place their money in green and ethical investment funds has also spurred UK companies to implement proactive environmental policies, especially in manufacturing.

Manufacturing regulations

Comprehensive legislation is in place for producing materials, equipment, goods, or appliances for industry or households. Some of the key regulations are:

> Compliance with safety, health, and environmental requirements, and the placing of a UKCA marking, which indicates that the product meets UK safety regulations, is mandatory for certain products with safety concerns, such as toys, electrical goods, medical devices, and machinery. The UKCA marking was introduced in England, Scotland, and Wales after Brexit to replace the EU's CE marking, but the latter remains in use in Northern Ireland. Manufacturers whose products must carry the UKCA or CE marking

are responsible for testing the products for conformity, drawing up the necessary documentation, and marking the product with the appropriate initials.

> Food standards legislation is in place for labelling, composition, and safety parameters for specific foodstuffs that could potentially be replaced with lower-quality alternatives, including bottled water, bread and flour, fats and oils, fish, meat, and milk. These regulations are set and enforced by the Department for Environment, Food & Rural Affairs (DEFRA), the Foods Standards Agency (FSA), and the Department of Health. In addition, there are standards called Codex Alimentarius, which are being developed internationally with the World Health Organization, providing detailed codes of practice for the food and agricultural industries.

> Preventing pollution from paper and cardboard production is also governed by law. Adherence is required to a number of guides and regulations on noise and vibration, cooling towers, and the types and volumes of emissions during manufacture.

Liability, warranties, and guarantees

The Consumer Rights Act 2015 gives customers legal rights when buying products. Customers have a right to a refund, repair, or replacement if an item does not match the description given by the manufacturer or retailer, is not of satisfactory quality, and is not fit for purpose. If they make a claim within 30 days, they are entitled to a full refund. After that time but before six months is up, they are entitled to ask for a replacement or repair at the expense of the seller. Beyond that, customers need to prove beyond a reasonable doubt that any fault lies with the manufacturer. For goods or services bought online, customers are entitled to a full refund up to 14 days after purchase, regardless of whether there is a problem or not. Aside from these legal protections, a manufacturer may also provide a warranty, which is an additional insurance paid for by the consumer, or guarantee, provided free but often requiring registration of the product with the maker.

Intellectual property law

Protecting inventions, designs, creative works, and trademarks does not prevent copying but does make it easier to take legal action. There are separate channels for registering intellectual property (IP) in the UK, Europe, and internationally.

There are four main types of protection:

Copyright, which is an automatic right, covering literary works, art, photography, films, TV, music, web content, sound recordings, and other types of creative output. In the UK and many other countries, protection begins as soon as a work is created. For written, dramatic, musical, and artistic works, copyright lasts for 70 years after the author's death; for sound and music recording, 70 years from first publication; for broadcasts, 50 years from the first broadcast.

Trademarks must be a word, sound, logo, picture, or combination of any of these, and can be registered with the UK Intellectual Property Office in South Wales. Applicants must specify which class of goods and services the trademark is to be used for.

Patent protection is given in the UK through the Intellectual Property Office. Patents are granted for an invention that is new and inventive, not an obvious modification to an existing product. It is not possible to patent methods; ideas such as scientific discoveries; new types of plant, seed, or animal; literary, dramatic, musical, or artistic works; or some computer programs.

Registered designs can be protected against theft or copying and cover the unique appearance of a product, including its shape, packaging, patterns, colour, and decoration. Registering the design gives the owner 25 years of exclusive rights to use it.

ORGANIZATIONS AND RESOURCES

Corporate social responsibility

The Financial Reporting Council explains the UK Corporate Governance Code and includes links to download the latest version.
www.frc.org.uk/corporate/ukcgcode.cfm

Manufacturing regulations

Gov.uk lists guidance on legislation and manufacturing regulations for workshops and factories.
www.gov.uk/topic/business-enterprise/manufacturing

The Food Standards Agency gives comprehensive guidance on food law, policy, enforcement, and current topics covering food production across various types of businesses and industries.
www.food.gov.uk

Registering intellectual property

The UK Intellectual Property Office provides an online service for filing a patent application and conducting searches on any similar patent.
www.gov.uk/apply-for-a-patent

The European Patent Office offers a free online search facility, outline of the legal text and past case law on patents, and a guide to applying for a European patent.
www.epo.org

The World Intellectual Property Organization explains how to register a trademark in multiple countries with "Madrid" (the International Trademark System).
www.wipo.int/madrid/en

Index

Acknowledgments

Dorling Kindersley would like to thank Douglas Bell and Debra Wolter for editorial assistance; Margaret McCormack for the index; and Nicola Gary, Vaibhav Rastogi, and Riti Sodhi for design assistance.

Credits

Sources of statistics, facts, and quotes:
p.13: "Corporate Power in a Global Economy", Brian Roach, Global Development and Environment Institute, Tufts University, 2007; **p.15:** "Fact Sheets on the European Union: Small and medium-sized enterprises", European Parliament, April 2021; **p.16:** "Business population estimates for the UK and regions 2020: detailed tables" (Table 3), Department for Business, Energy & Industrial Strategy, 2020; **p.18:** "4 Things You Don't Know About Private Companies", forbes.com, 26 May 2013; **p.19:** "Number of Listed Companies/Shares", JPX.co.jp; **p.24:** *The Nonprofit Almanac*, 2016; **p.26:** "Business Formation Statistics", Census.gov, 2020; **p.27:** *2020/2021 Global Report*, Global Entrepreneurship Monitor (GEM); **p.29:** *Global Startup Ecosystem Report 2019*, Startup Genome; **p.30:** "Number of Fintech startups worldwide from 2018 to February 2021, by region", Statista; **p.32, p.35:** "What's next for the small business economy?", Quickbooks, September 2020; **p.37: start-up finance bar chart:** *2019 Business Finance Survey: SMEs*, British Business Bank; **p.39:** "The Road to Start-Up Acceleration", MassChallenge, February 2020; **p.41:** "Number & Value of M&A Worldwide", Institute for Mergers, Acquisitions and Alliances (IMAA); **p.43:** "Number & Value of M&A Asia-Pacific", Institute for Mergers, Acquisitions and Alliances (IMAA); **p.45:** "Corporate Restructuring", B. Espen Eckbo and Karin S. Thorburn, *Foundations and Trends in Finance*, 8 May 2013; **p.47:** *Defining what is vital for deal success: Value curve study validates holistic approach to M&A*, Grant Thornton, May 2018; **p.49:** "Leveraged Buyout (LBO)", Investopedia.com, 25 February 2021; **p.51:** "Why Some Leaders Have Their Employees' Trust, and Some Don't", Gallup, 13 June 2019; **p.53, p.55:** "Boards Around the World", SpencerStuart, 2020; **p.56:** "Born to be digital: How leading CIOs are preparing for a digital transformation", EY, 2014; **p.57:** "CEO compensation surged 14% in 2019 to $21.3 million", Economic Policy Institute, 18 August 2020; **p.59:** "The organization of the future: Arriving now", Deloitte, 28 February 2017; **p.60:** "Human rights abuse and corporate stock performance – an event study analysis", V. Kappel, P. Schmidt, and A. Ziegler, white paper, 21 December 2009; **p.63:** "European ESG Funds Pulled in Record $132 Billion in 2019", Bloomberg.com, 30 January 2020; **p.65:** *Culture's role in enabling organizational change*, Strategy&, 2013; **p.67 left and right:** "Communication networks", M. Shaw, in L. Berkowitz (ed.), *Advances in Experimental Social Psychology*, Academic Press, 1964; **p.69:** *Multichannel Customer Experience Report*, Econsultancy/Foviance, 2012; **p.71:** PepsiCo Annual Report 2020, p.66; **p.73:** "So the matrix is dead, is it?", Global Integration; **p.74:** "The Rise of the Networked Enterprise: Web 2.0 finds its payday", *McKinsey Quarterly*, 2010; **p.77:** *Global Human Capital Trends*, Deloitte, 2019; **p.79:** *Diversity wins: How inclusion matters*, McKinsey & Company, May 2020; **p.82:** "Statistics", LinkedIn.com; **p.87:** "What Is Employee Engagement and How Do You Improve It?", Gallup, 21 February 2020; **p.93:** Governance Report, John Lewis, 2021; **p.95:** "Insights and Trends: Current Portfolio, Programme, and Project Management Practices: The third global survey on the current state of project management", PwC, 2012; **p.97:** *The Definitive Book of Body Language*, Barbara and Allan Pease, 2006; **p.98:** *Most Professionals Excelled While Working from Home*, Harvard Business School Online, March 2021; **p.102:** *Key Facts and Trends in the Accountancy Profession*, Financial Reporting Council, October 2020; **p.105:** "Accounting for Time: Survey Results", SJD Accountancy, 2017; **p.109:** *The numbers that are changing the world: Revealing the growing appetite for responsible investing*, KPMG, 2019; **p.113:** "The 10 Worst Corporate Accounting Scandals of All Time", Accounting Degree Review; **p.125: life of fixed assets chart:** IRS, via "Modified Accelerated Cost Recovery System (MACRS)", Investopedia.com, 12 May 2021; **p.125:** The AA; **p.131:** "Big Four accounting firms", Wikipedia.com; **p.135:** *State of Cash Flow Report*, QuickBooks, 2019; **p.136:** *Integrated Performance Management: Plan. Budget. Forecast.*, Deloitte, 2014; **p.141:** "Wages and labour costs", Eurostat, March 2021; **p.142:** "Price and Value to Sales Ratios and Margins by Industry Sector – Global", pages.stern.nyu.edu/~adamodar, January 2021; **p.145:** *Guide to key performance indicators: Communicating the measures that matter*, PwC, 2007; **p.147:** *Balanced Scorecard Usage Survey 2020*, 2GC; **p.149:** "Financial Ratios", Inc.com; **p.151:** *Global State of Enterprise Analytics: Minding the Data-Driven Gap*, MicroStrategy, 2020; **p.152:** *Global Economic Crime and Fraud Survey*, PwC, 2020; **p.154:** "The Theory and Practice of Corporate Finance: Evidence from the Field", J. Graham and C. Harvey, *Journal of Financial Economics*, Vol. 60, 2001, pp.187–243; **p.157:** "Reporting on Payment Practices", Small Business Commissioner & Lloyds Bank, 2018; **p.158:** *Small Business Credit Survey*, Federal Reserve Banks, 2020; **p.161:** "Global IPO Watch: Q1 2021 in review", PwC, 2021; **p.163:** "Market Statistics", *Focus*, World Federation of Exchanges, July 2021; **p.165:** "If You Invested $100 in Apple's IPO, This Is How Much Money You'd Have Now", Fool.com, 24 November 2019; **p.167:** "Stock Market Crash of 1929 Facts, Causes, and Impact", www.thebalance.com, September 2020 **p.171:** "SIFMA Research Quarterly – 1Q21: US Fixed Income Markets – Issuance & Trading", SIFMA, April 2021; **p.181:** "Are you a 'harbinger of failure'?", MIT, 23 December 2015; **p.185:** "Advertising FAQ's: A Guide for Small Business", Federal Trade Commission; **p.187 graph:** "Liquor Cost Guide", www.getbackbar.com; **p.188:** "Amazon.com announces financial results and CEO transition", Amazon.com, February 2021; **p.190:** *State of Social*, Buffer.com, 2019; **p.193:** "Market research industry – Statistics & Facts", Statista, 27 January

ACKNOWLEDGMENTS

2021; **p.197:** "Women: Primed and Ready for Progress", Nielsen, 14 October 2019; **p.198:** The Pareto principle, suggested by management expert Joseph M. Juran and part of long-tail marketing theory; **p.201:** *A bias for action: The neuroscience behind the response-driving power of direct mail*, Canada Post, 31 July 2015; **p.203 doughnut charts:** *Global Ad Spend Forecasts*, Dentsu, June 2021; **p.203:** *Global Ad Spend Forecasts*, Dentsu, June 2021; **p.205:** "4 ways to make your app successful", Google, May 2021; **p.206:** *Millennials: Fueling the Experience Economy*, Eventbrite/Harris, 2014; **p.211:** *The State of Video Marketing 2021*, Wyzowl; **p.212:** *Global Ad Spend Forecasts*, Dentsu, June 2021; **p.212 bar chart:** *Profit Ability: the Business Case for Advertising: Special Report 2018*, Ebiquity and Gain Theory; **p.213:** "The Global TV Deck 2020", The Global TV Group; **p.214:** "Share of Facebook's mobile advertising revenue as of 3rd quarter 2019", Statista, October 2019; **p.214 doughnut chart:** *2021 Digital Marketing Report for Entrepreneurs & Small Business*, AWeber; **p.215:** "Ultimate Email Marketing Benchmarks for 2021: By Industry and Day", Campaign Monitor; **p.216:** "What is The Response Rate From Direct Mail Campaigns?", Data & Marketing Association, 21 May 2021; **p.221:** *Not Another State of Marketing Report*, HubSpot, 2021; **p.223: chart and stat:** *State of Inbound 2018*, HubSpot; **p.225:** "40% of the web uses WordPress", W3Techs, 10 February 2021; **p.226:** "1 Billion People Listen to Podcasts Every Week", Pikkal, 2021; **p.229:** *Index XVII: Accelerate*, sproutsocial.com, 2021; **p.230:** "We Analyzed 5 million Google Search Results: Here's What We Learned About Organic Click Through Rate", Backlinko.com, 27 August 2019; **p.233:** *Optimization Report*, Econsultancy/RedEye Optimisation, November 2018; **p.237 bar chart:** "Five Insights From the 2020 Chief Marketer B2B Marketing Outlook Survey", Chief Marketer; **p.238:** "12 Ecommerce Conversion Rate Statistics", Growcode, 21 January 2021; **p.241:** "15 fascinating insights from Econsultancy's 2014 reports", Econsultancy, 8 December 2014; **p.243:** *State of Email Report*, Litmus, 2020; **p.247:** *Harvey Nash/ KPMG CIO Survey 2019* and *Harvey Nash CIO Survey 2014*; **p.249:** *The Human Impact of Data Literacy Report*, Qlik/Accenture/ Data Literacy Project, 2020; **p.250:** *Global State of Enterprise Analytics: Minding the Data-Driven Gap*, MicroStrategy, 2020; **p.253:** "Number of marketing technology solutions available worldwide from 2011 to 2020", Statista, April 2020; **p.255:** "The consumer-data opportunity and the privacy imperative", McKinsey & Company, 27 April 2020; **p.256:** "Data Warehousing Market Insights – 2028", Allied Market Research, May 2021; **p.259:** *Pulse Check 2018*, Accenture Interactive; **p.263:** "What is Big Data?", Oracle; **p.263: data volumes per second statistics**: Internet Live Stats; **p.265:** "CRM pays back $8.71 for every dollar spent", Nucleus Research, June 2014; **p.267:** "Spam and phishing in 2020", Securelist by Kaspersky, 15 February 2021; **p.271:** World Bank via "China Manufacturing Output 1960-2021", Macrotrends; **p.273:** "This Is the Average Cost of a Wedding Dress Today", The Knot, 26 May 2020; **p.275:** "About the bread industry", Federation of Bakers; **p.277:** "2020 Production Statistics", International Organization of Motor Vehicle Manufacturers; **p.279:** "CES 2020 Survey by CITE Research Dassault Systèmes: Consumers Want Personalized Products but Won't Wait for Them and Expect a Cost Benefit for Their Data", Dassault Systèmes, 6 January 2020; **p.281:** *State of the Global Paper Industry 2018*, Environmental Paper Network; **p.284:** *Global Innovation Index 2020*, INSEAD/Cornell University/World Intellectual Property Organization (WIPO); **p.287:** "Netflix's (NASDAQ:NFLX) Scale Is The Key To Its Profitability", Michael Paige, Simply Wall St, Nasdaq.com, 17 March 2021; **p.289:** "Detailed sales, production, and export results", Toyota Motor Corporation; **p.291:** "Custom T-shirt Printing Market Size, Share & Trends Analysis Report By Printing Technique (Screen Printing, Digital Printing, Plot Printing), By Design, By Region, And Segment Forecasts, 2021– 2028", Grand View Research, Jan 2021; **p.293:** "Walt Disney World Statistics", MagicGuides; **p.295:** *The State of Project Management 2021*, Wellingtone; **p.297:** *Pulse of the Profession 2017*, PMI; **p.298:** "Business GCSE / National 5: Kaizen – new ideas to improve productivity", BBC Teach; **p.301:** "Euro area international trade in goods surplus €6.3 bn", Eurostat, January 2021; **p.303:** "Samsung Note 7 recall to cost at least $5.3 billion", Associated Press, 14 October 2016; **p.307:** "The business value of design", *McKinsey Quarterly*, 25 October 2018; **p.309:** *Global State of Quality 2 Research*, ASQ, 2016; **p.310:** United Nations Statistics Division via "China Is the World's Manufacturing Superpower", Statista, 4 May 2021; **p.313:** *FTSE 100 CEO pay in 2019 and during the pandemic*, CIPD/High Pay Centre, August 2020; **p.315:** "Q4 and FY2020 Update", Tesla, 27 January 2021; **p.317:** "Anyone See Canada? Retail's $1.8t Inventory Distortion Issue", IHL Group, August 2020; **p.319:** "Pre-packaged Sandwiches Market Size, Share & Trends Analysis Report By Product (Non-vegetarian, Vegetarian), By Application (Household, HoReCa), By Region, And Segment Forecasts, 2019– 2025", Grand View Research, August 2019; **p.323:** *CEO Retailer Pulse #2*, RetailNext, April 2020; **p.325:** *The Internet Value Chain*, GSMA/AT Kearney, May 2016; **p.326: bar chart:** *Global Shared Services and Outsourcing Survey Report*, Deloitte, 2021; **p.327:** *Global Shared Services and Outsourcing Survey Report*, Deloitte, 2021; **p.328:** "Sector – IT & BPM", Invest India; **p.331:** *UPS Pulse of the Online Shopper™ Study*, April 2018; **p.334:** *The KPMG Survey of Sustainability Reporting 2020*.

Second edition

Senior Editor Chauney Dunford
Project Art Editor Katie Cavanagh
Jacket Design Development Manager Sophia MTT
Jacket Designer Tanya Mehrotra
Senior DTP Designer Harish Aggarwal
Production Controller Rachel Ng
Production Editor Kavita Varma
Senior Mangaging Art Editor Lee Griffiths
Managing Editor Gareth Jones
Associate Publishing Director Liz Wheeler
Art Director Karen Self
Design Director Phil Ormerod
Publishing Director Jonathan Metcalf

Delhi team
Senior Jackets Editorial Coordinator Priyanka Sharma
Senior Jacket Designer Suhita Dharamjit